MW00564737

Organization and Management Innovation

Series Editor: M. Sulzberger

Springer
Berlin
Heidelberg
New York
Barcelona
Hong Kong
London
Milan
Paris
Tokyo

Bruno S. Frey · Margit Osterloh
(Editors)

Successful Management by Motivation

Balancing Intrinsic and Extrinsic Incentives

With 24 Figures and 11 Tables

Professor Bruno S. Frey
University of Zurich
Institute for Empirical Research in Economics
Blümlisalpstrasse 10
CH-8006 Zurich
Switzerland
bsfrey@iew.unizh.ch

Professor Margit Osterloh
University of Zurich
Institute for Research in Business Administration
Plattenstrasse 14
CH-8032 Zurich
Switzerland
osterloh@ifbf.unizh.ch

and
Swiss Association for Organization and Management
Flughofstrasse 50
CH-8032 Zurich
Switzerland

Translated from the German by CLS Corporate Language Services AG
www.cls.ch

ISBN 3-540-42401-6 Springer-Verlag Berlin Heidelberg New York

Library of Congress Cataloging-in-Publication Data applied for
Die Deutsche Bibliothek – CIP-Einheitsaufnahme
Successful management by motivation: balancing intrinsic and extrinsic incentives; with 11 tables / Bruno S. Frey; Margit Osterloh (ed.). – Berlin; Heidelberg; New York; Barcelona; Hong Kong; London; Milan; Paris; Tokyo: Springer, 2002
(Organization and management innovation)
ISBN 3-540-42401-6

Springer-Verlag Berlin Heidelberg New York
a member of BertelsmannSpringer Science+Business Media GmbH

http://www.springer.de

Hardcover-Design: Erich Kirchner, Heidelberg

SPIN 10847828 43/2202-5 4 3 2 1 0 – Printed on acid-free paper

Foreword

There are few subjects considered in both the theory and practice of business management to be of such undisputed importance for entrepreneurial success as motivation. Numerous theoretical approaches and practical application models have been tried and tested, rejected and implemented over the years. The almost daunting selection of publications and wide array of seminars, conferences and workshops available on the subject would seem to offer us easy access to this extremely complex topic.

As a result, we might well ask whether everything has not already been said on the subject long ago. The Swiss Association for Organization and Management (SGO), for one, did not share this conviction when it launched a research project called "Motivation." The reasons for this project were the following:

- In the last few years the environment in which businesses and public institutions operate, and in which the people they employ work, has changed with a speed and intensity never experienced before. A reevaluation of the factor of motivation thus appears both necessary and appropriate.

- Scientific research into the business, economic and psychological aspects of motivation has produced numerous new findings on the subject. At the same time, these have placed increasing emphasis on a holistic approach encompassing all the above-mentioned disciplines.

- The onward march of globalization has in the last few years been both rapid and overwhelming, and has produced a varied and complex patchwork of values and cultural styles, all of which shape the corporate work environment as we know it today. This has brought many new opportunities and risks to the realm of motivation.

- Entrepreneurism, responsibility, equal rights and individualization are all central issues and concerns in modern society, science and practice. This has given rise to a multitude of changes in the motivational road map that is the navigational aid of both management techniques and the tools used to foster motivation.

Bruno S. Frey and Margit Osterloh, who led this project, offer a penetrating analysis of the subject matter using the aforementioned holistic overlay, combining specifically business management and economic aspects. In doing so they present a number of new findings along with critical questions, recommendations and practical examples, the results of which are described, explained and documented in the present book. Their examination provides convincing proof that motivation is a critical success factor in the workplace and for business as a whole.

Motivation lies at the center of a highly controversial debate on the factors that drive human activity, the use of tools to promote motivation and the role of simple person-to-person interaction in everyday life. As the old proverb "You can lead a horse to water but you can't make it drink" illustrates, motivation is not something that can be commanded.

The solution is thus to create favorable conditions that foster a consistently high level of motivation. Of central importance is the nurturing of motivation in subtle, finely balanced doses, applying a broad range of already familiar motivational tools with the necessary care and appropriateness. From the manager's perspective, the aim must be to find an optimal mix of intrinsic and extrinsic motivation. Beyond this – and just as important – is the need for all employees to actively cultivate motivation, treat their fellow colleagues with fairness and to approach critically any unthinking inclination to maximize monetary gains.

This book explores the "age-old" theme of motivation, in today's modern and rapidly changing context. New findings and an empirical review of the opportunities and risks involved give rise to new solutions or a different weighting of the motivational tools we use. The results thus fulfill the objectives of the research project in impressive measure. I hope that "Management by Motivation" will provide food for further discussion in this field and will make enjoyable reading for a wide spectrum of people.

Zurich, July 2001

Markus Sulzberger
President of the Foundation of the
Swiss Association for
Organization and Management

Preface

Successful companies need motivated employees. But motivating people is easier said than done. Employees cannot be programmed to embrace a company's objectives just like that. Today employers try to motivate their employees mainly, and sometimes exclusively, by means of monetary incentives. "Performance-related pay" is the new mantra which is adopted unquestioningly by many companies.

In this book, we demonstrate that this one-sided focus is misguided. Alongside monetary incentives, ways of fostering and sustaining intrinsic motivation – especially in the form of work morale – must be found. Typically, goals cannot be successfully met unless both types of motivation are present. However, there is often a direct trade-off between intrinsic and extrinsic (monetary) motivation. As a result, the task of managing motivation is an extremely difficult one. The purpose of this book is to identify the various aspects of motivation in companies and show how the right combination of intrinsic and extrinsic motivation can be achieved.

The editors and authors are both authorities in the field of business management and economics. The book is thus also an attempt to transcend the frontiers of both disciplines. To this end, various methodical approaches have been used, from surveys through case studies to econometric analyses (presented in a reader-friendly form).

In **Part I**, the basic theme of the book is set out with a discussion of motivation as a key management task.

Chapter one defines the constituent elements of employee motivation. The interaction between intrinsic and extrinsic motivation is described, and the chapter explains why strong employee morale, i.e. intrinsic motivation, is crucial for a company.

Chapter two illustrates why motivation and knowledge management are key strategic resources in a company's effort to achieve competitive advantage. In addition, it outlines the latest developments in strategy research and examines the relationship between the strategic resources knowledge and motivation.

Part II of the book shows how extrinsic incentives affect motivation. This section points up the problem of focusing too exclusively on extrinsic incentives and why this all too often produces undesirable side effects. Central to the discussion is the relationship between motivation and compensation.

In Chapter three, the concept of variable pay for performance is discussed in detail. It demonstrates that, instead of boosting employees' performance, variable performance-related remuneration more often tends to crowd out, or suppress, intrinsic motivation. This chapter also explains how different types of employees react to monetary compensation and other motivational tools such as praise, commands, participation and autonomy.

Stock options are an increasingly popular form of compensation at the management level today. They are designed to encourage managers to devote more of their time and energy to increasing corporate value. Chapter four demonstrates that stock options rarely achieve this effect. Instead they enable managers to accumulate very large incomes at the expense of the shareholders.

Chapter five researches an often neglected side effect of performance-related pay – its selection effect. In other words, monetary incentives may lead to inefficient activities because they entice less qualified employees into areas of activity that are rewarded by performance-related pay. This effect is analyzed in a comprehensive empirical study of employee suggestion plans in over 1,400 Swiss companies.

Part III of the book deals with ways of creating and nurturing intrinsic motivation in the corporate environment. This section focuses on the relationship between motivation and work organization.

Chapter six examines how motivation and a company's organizational structures are connected. It is shown how different forms of organization influence employees' motivation differently.

In *Chapter seven*, the importance of justice and fairness in the workplace is explained. The influence that perceived fairness has on the attitude and behavior of employees is demonstrated. This chapter also discusses the relationship between fairness and organizational citizenship behavior.

Chapter eight provides an in-depth examination of two work organization tools used to motivate employees – participation and communication. Using a large-scale survey, this chapter illustrates how management based on participation and communication can significantly improve the quality of work relationships.

Part IV of this book contains two case studies which illustrate in greater depth how motivation management works in practice.

Chapter nine discusses motivation management in the banking sector using ING Barings as an example. ING Barings has recognized that performance-based compensation alone is not sufficient to significantly enhance employee performance and increase the length of time an employee stays with a company. Instead, it has developed an extensive repertoire of motivational tools.

Chapter ten deals with motivation management in software development based on the case study of SAP AG. Employee motivation is a major contributing factor to productivity at software companies. The SAP case study describes the role played by employee motivation in the success of projects to improve software development.

Part V of the book summarizes the conclusions that can be drawn for the management of motivation.

The Swiss Association for Organization and Management (SGO) provided the editors with invaluable support during the preparation and documentation of the studies. We would especially like to thank the President of the SGO research foundation, Dr. Markus Sulzberger, for his motivating interest, never-failing encouragement and positive criticism. Heinrich Frost deserves our thanks for his apt wording of many passages in the text. We would also like to express our gratitude to Matthias Benz, who produced the book with the active support of Reto Jegen. Lastly, we are indebted to the authors for helping us in numerous rounds of revisions to transform their individual contributions into a coherent whole.

Zurich, July 2001 *Bruno S. Frey and Margit Osterloh*

Table of Contents

Part One

Motivation as a Function of Management

Chapter One

BRUNO S. FREY AND MARGIT OSTERLOH

Motivation – A Dual-Edged Factor of Production

Introduction

Employees may work hard for one of two reasons: because they are interested in the work itself (intrinsic motivation) or because they are being paid (extrinsic motivation). These two forms of motivation are interlinked and, as such, companies cannot opt for one or the other in isolation. Under certain circumstances, an extrinsic incentive in the form of variable performance-related pay will undermine intrinsic motivation. This "crowding-out effect" can be clearly illustrated by means of examples. It is also a well-documented phenomenon in economic research, proven in laboratory experiments, field studies and econometric analyses. The crowding out of intrinsic motivation in a work context can be explained by the reduction in self-determination that often accompanies variable performance-related pay and the breaking of a "psychological contract" based on mutual trust.

High employee morale, i.e. intrinsic motivation, is imperative in a company for a variety of reasons. It is needed so pooled resources can be used effectively because not all activities can be adequately remunerated (the problem of multi-tasking) and in many instances, the precise objective of a particular activity cannot be specified (the problem of fuzzy tasking). Only in this way can tacit, i.e. indefinable knowledge, be transferred within a company. And, finally, intrinsic motivation is a prerequisite of creativity and innovation.

However, extrinsic motivation, too, is of considerable significance within a company. Intrinsic motivation cannot easily be generated and may even be undesirable in certain circumstances. Extrinsic motivation, on the other hand, can be more accurately targeted and offers a means of maintaining discipline.

One of the key functions of a company is to generate and sustain the "right" form of motivation. "Management by motivation" means selecting the most appropriate combination of intrinsic and extrinsic motivation.

1. What Motivates People to Perform?

In management, the prevailing approach to motivation is ambivalent. On the one hand, more and more companies and organizations are introducing individual, variable, performance-related pay. This form of remuneration appeals to employees' self-interest, rewarding exceptional performance on an individual basis. As a result, managerial salaries in particular have risen dramatically in the last few years, due primarily to the introduction of stock option plans (see Chapters 3 and 4). On the other hand, the importance of employees identifying with their job and with the company for which they work is emphasized time and again. A common corporate culture in the sense of shared values and standards is one of the key factors of success. Semi-autonomous working arrangements in self-organized groups and decentralized decision-making procedures are the norm in almost every modern organizational structure, from process management to project and network organization. Consequently, performance-related piecework pay is disappearing from the corporate landscape. As knowledge becomes more important to the work done within a company, so the "mistrust-based organization" will increasingly give way to the "trust-based organization" (see Chapter 2).

These two approaches would appear to be in conflict with one another: are employees motivated by exogenous salaries and constraints (extrinsic motivation) or by internal factors such as job satisfaction and identification with common values (intrinsic motivation)? And must management choose between the two approaches?

This is an issue on which science, too, is unable to agree. Economic theory favors the notion of homo oeconomicus, i.e. a self-interested individual with a stable concept of his or her preferences, whose primary interest is financial gain. This view of the individual has also been applied to other areas – politics, law, sports, criminology, even the family and art – with great success.

Traditional sociology and psychology, on the other hand, assume that human conduct is shaped by standards and preferences that are by no means stable and often reap no financial reward. Values such as decency, honor and dignity, and emotions such as envy, love and hate are a case in point.

In the course of this chapter, we will develop a model that incorporates these conflicting views in practice and in theory. First, however, let us examine the concepts of intrinsic and extrinsic motivation in a little more detail.

2. Extrinsic and Intrinsic Motivation

Extrinsic motivation serves to satisfy indirect or instrumental needs. As such, money is almost always the means to an end – paying for a vacation or buying a car, for instance – and not an end in itself. In a career context, extrinsic motivation stems from the desire to satisfy directly one's non-work-related needs. In this instance, a job is simply a tool with which to satisfy one's actual needs by means of the salary it pays.

In the case of *intrinsic* motivation, on the other hand, the activity itself or the corresponding end goal satisfies a direct need in its own right. Three of the main forms of intrinsic motivation are illustrated in Figure 1-1.

In the first case, the activity itself is a source of satisfaction, providing an enjoyable experience. Examples might include skiing, playing music or reading a good novel. In each case, pleasure is derived from the activity itself, not simply its culmination, i.e. from reading the novel, not merely from reaching the last page. The end goal and the action itself are equally important. In the second example, it is a matter of meeting standards for their own sake. These may be ethical standards which one feels it right to respect, such as professional codes of practice or the renunciation of violence. In organizations, standards of fairness and group membership (team spirit) are also particularly important. Empirical research shows that where employees feel that standards of material or procedural fairness are not being met, productivity will fall, and they will even be willing to put personal advantage to one side in order to rectify the situation (see Chapter 7). The third form of intrinsic motivation comes from achieving a goal which one has set oneself, even if the process itself is anything but enjoyable, for instance writing an examination paper or climbing a mountain. Climbers will tell you that they by no means always relish the arduous ascent or the attendant risk. You could say they have a real love-hate relationship with the sport. Nevertheless, they gladly dedicate a large proportion of their income to their hobby in order to experience the thrill of reaching the top of the mountain.

It is not always possible to draw a clear empirical distinction between intrinsic and extrinsic motivation. When someone climbs a mountain for pleasure, there is almost always an extrinsic motive in play, such as physical training or peer-group recognition. As a rule, intrinsic and extrinsic motivation go hand in hand. What makes the difference is whether a goal is being pursued simply as a means of achieving another, in which case the first goal loses inherent value. In this case, the crowding-out effect, as discussed below, enters into the picture.

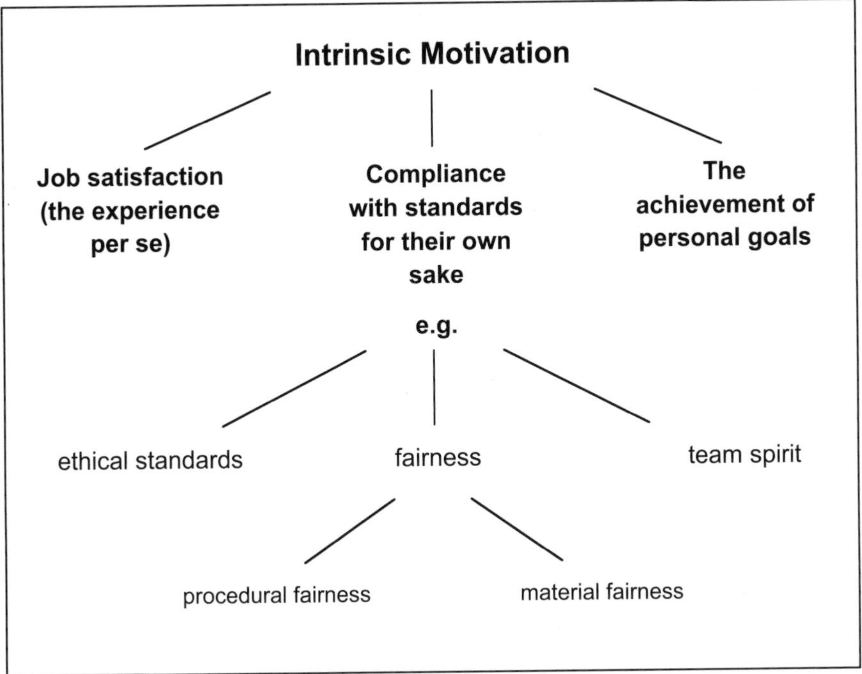

Figure 1-1

2.1 The Crowding-Out Effect

For a long time, it was assumed that extrinsic and intrinsic motivation were independent of one another. This being the case, one could, for instance, attempt to motivate a member of staff intrinsically by making his or her job as interesting as possible and extrinsically by promising a bonus. Equally, one could allow a manager to handle an exciting project independently whilst at the same time keeping an eye on events by means of strict project control. However, numerous socio-psychological experiments have shown that, under certain circumstances, there is a trade-off between intrinsic and extrinsic motivation.

Parents are familiar with this phenomenon. Children who are initially enthusiastic about their homework, for instance, lose some of that interest when promised a reward. This approach may work in the short run, but in the longer run the result is that the child will only do its homework in return for a monetary reward. In other words, the crowding out effect has set in. In the worst-case scenario, the child will eventually be unwilling even to take the garbage out without a reward. Box 1-1 recounts an old Jewish fable which illustrates the crowding-out effect.

The story begins with an angry mob hurling abuse at the main character, an elderly man, simply for the fun of it. But when the wise old man begins to pay them for their efforts – absurd though this may sound – the mob's motivation switches from the enjoyment they derive from their action to the financial rewards it brings. When payment is withdrawn, the incentive is gone and the old man's problems are solved. The moral of the story is that the motivation to do something can be eroded by turning it into a financial transaction.

Box 1-1 also tells of a true case in point concerning the punctuality of parents collecting their children from a daycare center.

Box 1-1

An Old Jewish Fable

It seem that bigots were eager to rid their town of a Jewish man who had opened a tailor shop on Main Street, so they sent a group of rowdies to harass the tailor.

Each day, the ruffians would show up to jeer. The situation was grim, but the tailor was ingenious. One day when the hoodlums arrived, he gave each of them a dime for their efforts. Delighted, they shouted their insults and moved on. The next day they returned to shout, expecting their dime. But the tailor said he could only afford a nickel and proceeded to hand a nickel to each of them. Well, they were a bit disappointed, but a nickel after all is a nickel, so they took it, did their jeering, and left.

The next day, they returned once again and the tailor said he had only a penny for them and held out his hand. Indignant, the young toughs sneered and proclaimed that they would certainly not spend their time jeering at him for a measly penny. So they didn't. And all was well for the tailor.

Source: Deci, E.L./Flaste, R. (1996): Why We Do What We Do. The Dynamics of Personal Autonomy, New York, p. 26.

The Collection of Children from Daycare Centers: A Case Study

Daycare centers frequently have problems with parents failing to collect their children on time, thereby forcing staff to work beyond the official end of the day.

A daycare center in Israel decided to keep an accurate record of how often the problem occurred. As a result of its findings, a hefty fine was imposed on parents who failed to collect their children on time. The expectation was that this financial penalty would induce parents to respect the center's closing times.

A follow-up survey was then conducted to see how many parents were still arriving late. Contrary to expectations, the number of parents failing to collect their children on time *rose dramatically.*

Source: Gneezy, U./Rustichini, A. (2000): A Fine is a Price, in: Journal of Legal Studies, pp. 1-18.

In a case like this, parents will generally endeavor to collect their children at the agreed time out of fairness to the staff of the daycare center. This may not always be possible, but the parents feel guilty if they are late and will therefore do their best to be punctual. However, the introduction of a substantial fine for late arrival puts an entirely new complexion on things. The parents now feel that they are paying to leave their children at the center longer: it has become a commercial transaction and the parents no longer feel any guilt if they arrive late. Actually, the Israeli daycare center on which the case study was based discovered that parents subsequently felt it was worth leaving their children at the center longer. As a result, the number of children collected "late" – i.e. as understood by the center management – went up. In this case, the introduction of a monetary charge had the opposite of the desired effect.

As such, the crowding-out effect can be said to create a relationship between extrinsic and intrinsic motivation. An activity that is carried out for its own sake (intrinsic) can be undermined or even corrupted by external (extrinsic) intervention. The social and economic importance of the crowding-out effect has been widely observed. The phenomenon is also well-founded in empirical research.

1. Meticulous *laboratory experiments* have confirmed the crowding-out effect. In fact, so many of these experiments have now been conducted that it is difficult to see the forest for the trees. For this reason, a number of meta-analyses have been carried out, using a special method to summarize the findings of the various individual experiments. The latest and most comprehensive meta-study (Deci/Koestner/Ryan 1999) comes to a clear conclusion: the available experimental evidence overwhelmingly supports the crowding-out effect.

2. *Field studies* reveal the same picture: external intervention will undermine intrinsic motivation under certain circumstances, i.e. when a relationship that was previously based on mutual consideration assumes a financial dimension, making it a commercial relationship. The field study in Box 1-1 involving the late collection of children from a daycare center is a case in point.

3. The crowding-out effect has also been analyzed on an *econometric* basis, for instance in the context of the so-called "NIMBY" – Not In My Back Yard – syndrome. This is the phenomenon whereby people are in favor of a particular product or service necessary to society but, as the name suggests, would rather it were manufactured or located elsewhere. Box 1-2 examines a prime example.

Box 1-2

The Storage of Nuclear Waste
The mountain village of Wolfenschiessen in central Switzerland was selected as the site of a treatment plant for low- and intermediate-level nuclear waste.

In preparation, a survey and econometric study were conducted in the spring of 1993.

Those questioned were asked about their willingness to accept the plant in their region. 50.8% of respondents were willing to accept the proposed plant without financial compensation. When, under otherwise identical conditions, substantial financial compensation was offered, the acceptance rate dropped to 24.6%.

Varying the level of compensation had no impact on the acceptance rate. In other words, the low acceptance rate cannot be attributed to the fact that the level of compensation on offer was perceived as inadequate.

Source: Frey, B. S./Oberholzer-Gee, F. (1997): The Cost of Price Incentives: An Empirical Analysis of Motivation Crowding-Out, in: American Economic Review 87, pp. 746-755.

As any reasonable person would agree, every care must be taken when it comes to storing nuclear waste. Time and again, however, the residents of communities destined to accommodate facilities of this kind fight the proposals tooth and nail, preferring that they be located on someone else's doorstep. This phenomenon has come to be known as the NIMBY syndrome – Not In My Back Yard. In the case examined here, the offer of monetary compensation in return for acceptance of a waste treatment plant led to a pronounced crowding-out effect. As a survey revealed, the residents of the community in question felt that a financial compensation package would compromise their self-determination and self-esteem. As a result, they responded by protesting against the proposal.

Thus it is clear that, under certain circumstances, a reward will undermine intrinsic motivation. In social psychology, this phenomenon has been referred to as "the hidden costs of reward" or "the corruption effect of extrinsic motivation." In economics, the concept was introduced by Bruno Frey, who coined the phrase "crowding out." A material reward will have a stronger crowding-out effect than a symbolic one. Likewise, an expected reward will have more of an effect than an unexpected one. The trade-off between reward and performance is greater in the case of complex problems than those of a simpler nature. A bonus system will therefore usually – though not always – cause staff to lose interest in the immediate objective (e.g. increased customer satisfaction). The two complementary views below provide insight into this phenomenon.

Diminished Self-Determination

One's response to an event depends upon whether one attributes the outcome to one's own actions (perceived internal control) or exogenous factors (perceived external control). This can be affected by the way in which one perceives rewards. There are two aspects to every reward, a controlling and an informing aspect. The controlling aspect strengthens perceived external control and the feeling of being directed from the outside. The informing aspect influences one's perceived competence and strengthens the feeling of internal control. Depending on which aspect is prominent, either intrinsic or extrinsic motivation will be fostered in a self-reinforcing process. If a dedicated salesperson or an enthusiastic athlete, scientist or artist, for instance, receives a material or symbolic reward, this will not automatically have a crowding-out effect. The recipient's intrinsic motivation will only be undermined if their perception is that the controlling outweighs the informing effect. Conversely, the reward will serve to increase motivation if the informing effect is dominant. In this case, the recipient's sense of competence and self-control will increase, and the effect of the reward is positive.

Here we have an example of the crowding-out effect in action:

Jacqueline is a dedicated saleswoman. She finds her job interesting and gets a tremendous sense of achievement from serving her customers. When a bonus system is introduced, however, she begins to feel that her employer attributes her good work not to her personal commitment but to the fact that her performance is being monitored. As a result, Jacqueline becomes more interested in the financial reward than customer satisfaction. What has happened is that Jacqueline's intrinsic motivation has been eroded. The following graphs illustrate the mechanics of this phenomenon.

Figure 1-2 shows the relationship between bonus and performance *before* the crowding-out effect has set in.

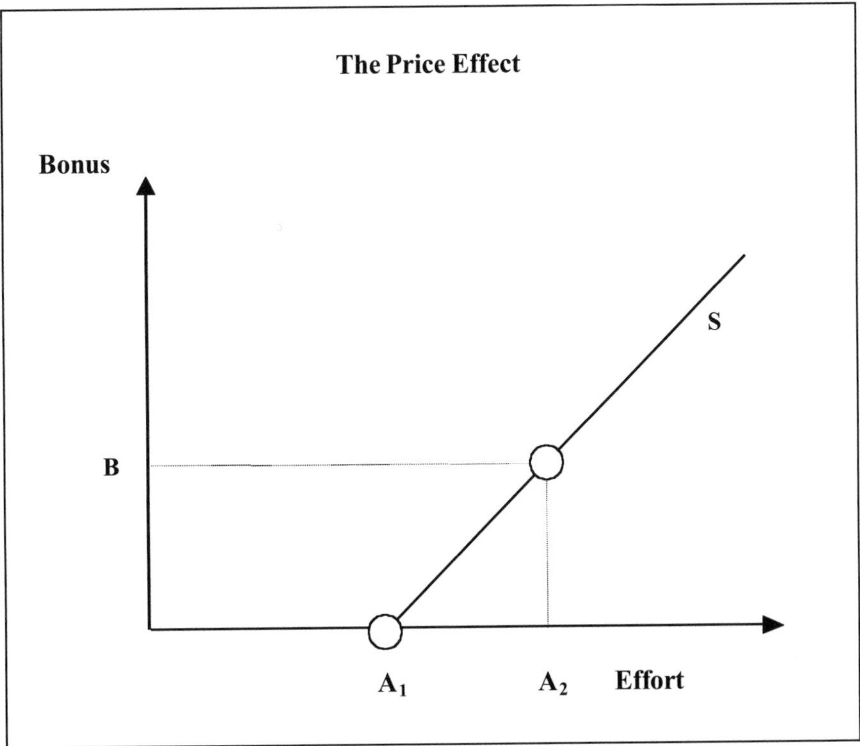

Figure 1-2

Without a bonus, Jacqueline puts in effort A1. Provided there is no crowding-out effect, a bonus with the value of B will increase her effort from A1 to A2. Here, we are talking about a pure price effect.

Let us now assume that Jacqueline begins to lose interest as a result of the bonus scheme and the associated control. The money becomes more important than customer satisfaction. In other words, her intrinsic motivation has diminished (see Figure 1-3). The supply curve for effort shifts to the left from S to S'. As a result, Jacqueline's effort falls to A3.

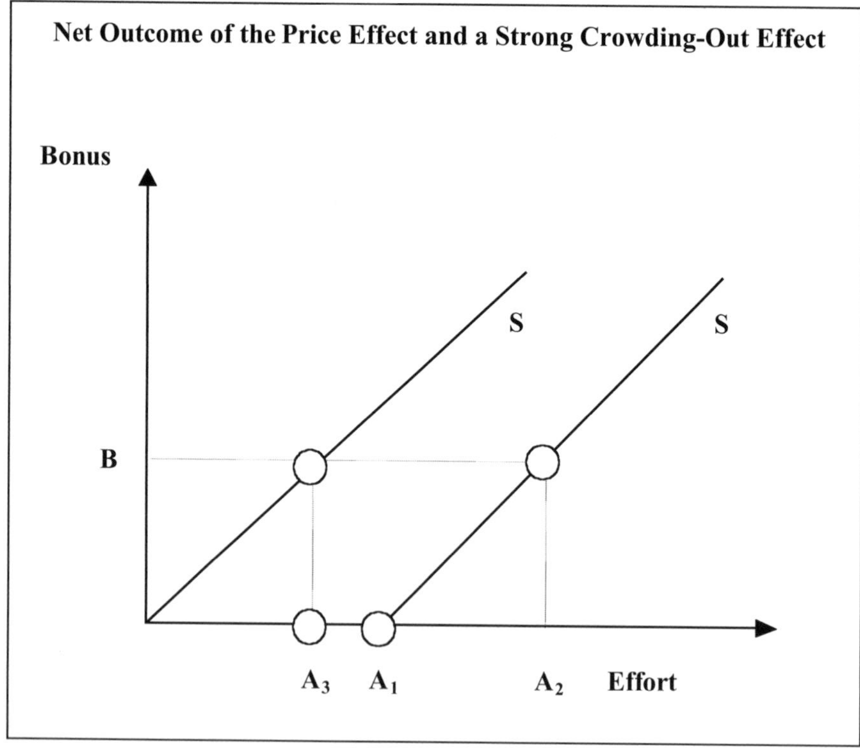

Figure 1-3

In this instance, the price effect from A1 to A2 is outweighed by the crowding-out effect from A2 to A3. However, this need not necessarily be the case. As illustrated in Figure 1-4, it very much depends on the intensity of the crowding-out effect. In Figure 1-4, the crowding-out effect shifts the supply curve for effort from S to S". The bonus increases effort from A1 to A4. However, it is still doubtful whether this will result in more innovative services or a higher level of customer satisfaction. In this particular scenario, greater effort is more likely to have the effect of increasing sales.

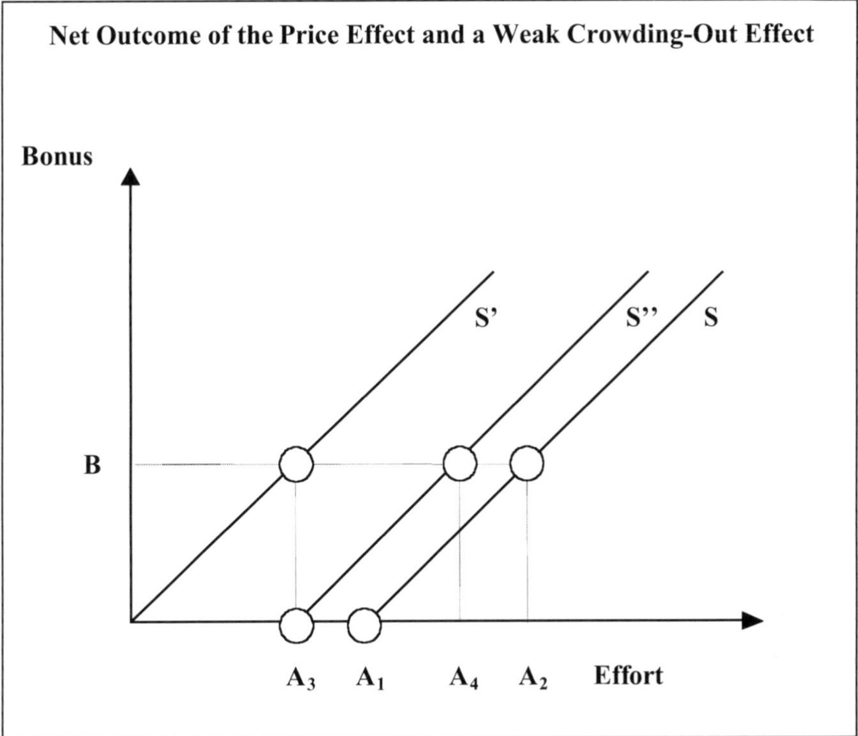

Figure 1-4

Thus, the crowding-out effect can be seen to counteract the price effect. It is difficult to forecast whether the price or crowding-out effect will predominate in any given case. What we do know is that personality traits (see Chapter 3) and the working environment (see Chapters 6 to 8) have a bearing on the outcome. Be that as it may, the price effect never has exactly the impact that was intended.

One prerequisite is essential: intrinsic motivation must have been present at the outset, otherwise there would be nothing to undermine. In the case of straightforward activities, for instance, where intrinsic motivation is often scarce, there will be no discernible crowding-out effect.

Psychological Contracts

The employee/employer relationship is based, in the first instance, on a mutual agreement (or transactional contract), whereby staff members exchange their labor for financial remuneration. In most cases, however, employees also enter into a psychological (relational) contract, the emphasis of which is the recognition of one another's motives. The main difference between a transactional and a relational contract lies in the reciprocal nature of the transactional contract, which operates on a *quid pro quo* basis. Mutual respect for one another's motivation has no place here. When you go to a restaurant, for example, it doesn't matter if the chef wants to cook for you or not, as long as the cost/benefit ratio is right. You simply pay the price on the menu (and leave a tip for the server). However, if you were to be invited to a social occasion and you offered the hostess money at the end of the evening as a token of your appreciation, this would undoubtedly cause offence. A symbolic gift such as a bouquet of flowers, on the other hand, would be gratefully received. A chef in a restaurant is unlikely to welcome a bouquet of flowers instead of money. So what is the difference between the relational contract between guest and host and the transactional contract in a restaurant? If you were to offer your hostess money, you would be failing to acknowledge the pleasure derived from issuing the invitation; her feelings would be hurt. Payment in a restaurant, on the other hand, evokes no such reaction. Here, the transactional nature of the contract serves to normalize the motives of those concerned, making it perfectly acceptable to pay for the provision of a service. In other words, the transactional contract is based on extrinsic motivation, the relational contract on intrinsic motivation. Relational contracts are always, to a certain extent, voluntary. This explains why commands crowd out intrinsic motivation more than the use of prices. Commands take no account of the subject's motives, whereas the price system allows those concerned to decide whether they wish to receive the reward or not.

Employment contracts generally have both a transactional *and* a relational component. The boss expects the secretary to deal with his or her correspondence efficiently. That is the transactional element of the contract. The social chit-chat and traditional bouquet of flowers on the employee's birthday are part of the relational contract, which is founded on mutual esteem. However, the relational contract will crumble if the secretary perceives the small-talk and birthday gift as instrumental actions. In this event, the relational contract assumes a transactional character and the crowding-out effect comes into play.

The psychological contract theory also explains why performance suffers when corporate practices are not perceived to be fair. Experimental studies show that where voluntary cooperation is the norm, productivity falls disproportionately when subjects are threatened with fines for shirking (Fehr/Gächter 1998). The threat of fines and the attendant controls are seen as incompatible with a fair relationship based on trust and the recognition of voluntary labor.

3. The Importance of Intrinsic Motivation

Companies are dependent on the motivation of their employees for at least five major reasons.

3.1 Firm-Specific Pool Resources

Companies are born when the market simply fails to perform a particular activity or cannot do so adequately. This type of activity includes all employee activities which have ramifications for other employees (so-called external effects), but cannot be precisely attributed to a single employee. Examples include a company's good name, its unique corporate culture, good relations with its customers and suppliers, and accumulated knowledge. These are firm-specific common goods or pool resources. Every employee benefits from these firm-specific pool resources even if he or she has not contributed to them. Self-centered employees, interested only in their personal gain, will contribute nothing of their own volition. Here we have the classic problem of "free-riding." Under these circumstances, the resource pool would only be created in the presence of a line manager acting in a command and control capacity. However, intangible resources of the kind outlined above can hardly be created effectively like this. Only intrinsically motivated employees will endeavor to contribute to the firm-specific resource pool (see also Chapter 2 and the discussion of organizational citizenship behavior in Chapter 7).

3.2 Multi-Tasking

The term "multi-tasking" refers to the following problem associated with firm-specific pool resources. If a company pays its employees on the basis of targets (e.g. sales and customer satisfaction) and the targets in question vary in terms of the ease with which they can be quantified (for instance, sales can be measured more easily and clearly than customer satisfaction), then extrinsically motivated employees will concentrate on those areas which can best be measured. Activities which are less easily quantifiable will be neglected. However, these include many key aspects of working life, such as respect for one's colleagues, discretion, initiative and team spirit. The more diverse and complex the job, therefore, the more imperative the intrinsic motivation of the workforce becomes.

3.3 Fuzzy Tasking

Line managers are often simply not in a position to set clear, quantifiable goals for their staff. They are dependent on employees' participation in the goal-setting process. If employees are paid according to clear, concrete targets, however, they will be less inclined to come up with inevitably less clearly quantifiable changes to the system. This is confirmed by the following empirical study. Given free choice, students will opt for problems which will challenge them. If a financial incentive is introduced, however, they will choose simple, easily quantifiable problems in order to improve their chance of getting a reward (Shapira 1976). The result is a second-rate system of targets, lacking in innovation. At the end of the day, new ideas cannot be measured by archaic standards. They have a saying at IBM that puts it in a nutshell: "If a senior executive hasn't screamed at you recently, you're probably not doing your job" (The Economist, February 20, 1999, p. 12).

3.4 The Transfer of Tacit Knowledge

Certain aspects of the knowledge at a firm's disposal – often the most important – cannot be written down or expressed in symbols. The distinction between *explicit and tacit knowledge* is crucial. Explicit knowledge is coded knowledge which can be conveyed in writing or symbols. The transfer of such knowledge is easily managed. However, only a small proportion of knowledge is explicit, since "we know more than we know how to say" (Polanyi 1985, p. 14). In terms of our total knowledge, explicit knowledge is merely the tip of the iceberg. A far greater proportion of knowledge is tacit. This knowledge cannot be coded because it is not made up of conscious routines or information. It is far more difficult to ensure the transfer of tacit than explicit knowledge by means of either the carrot or the stick. This is because tacit knowledge is not generally tradable and its bearing on commercial success is often unclear. To a large extent, therefore, the transfer of tacit knowledge is dependent on the intrinsic motivation of the employees in question. Only when implicit and tacit knowledge are combined, however, is new knowledge created. In today's market, the capacity to perpetually generate new knowledge is the single most important strategic competitive advantage. As such, the underlying intrinsic motivation of employees is a key strategic resource (see Chapter 2).

3.5 Creativity and Innovation

Activities of a creative, innovative nature depend heavily on intrinsic motivation. Extrinsic motivation, on the other hand, slows down and diminishes the learning process. Experimental studies show that conceptual understanding and the speed at which we learn are adversely affected by supervision. Under the pressure of a reward-based system, the preference is for a less rigorous learning effort. Work is more hurried, less meticulous. As a result, extrinsically motivated employees tend simply to follow the tried-and-tested route without question. Moreover, if external factors intervene to prevent employees carrying out a task perceived as more challenging, fatigue is likely to set in.

On balance, one can conclude that the more complex, diverse and demanding the activity, and the more difficult it is to specify the requirements in a hard-and-fast job description, the more crucial intrinsic motivation becomes. As such, it acquires the status of a strategic resource (see Chapter 2).

4. Why Extrinsic Motivation Is Nevertheless Indispensable

Intrinsic motivation is important; we cannot emphasize that enough. Unlike some other authors, however, we are of the opinion that, under certain circumstances, extrinsic motivation is also indispensable.

The "Right" Intrinsic Motivation is Difficult to Create

Motivation is not an end in itself, but should serve the objectives of the firm. The aim is not to engender intrinsic motivation per se, for instance the motivation to surf the Net extensively or take up mountaineering, but to ensure *a coordinated employee effort in keeping with corporate objectives.* If this is not achieved, even the crowding-out effect can do no harm. We have some idea as to how to foster intrinsic motivation in line with corporate objectives, namely by means of an interesting and challenging job, fairness, participation and communication in particular (see Chapters 6 to 8). However, there is far more theoretical and empirical data on the *crowding out* of intrinsic motivation than on its *creation.* The motivation of volunteers in non-profit organizations is a prime example. Here, fundamental disagreements over objectives are not uncommon, whereas private-sector companies need pay less heed to the personal convictions of their employees provided they pay them well and keep supervisory costs within reasonable limits. In fact, the company that refrains from attempting to "persuade its members how wonderful the marvelous fruit jam is that it produces" (Luhmann 1973, p. 142) will enjoy greater elasticity. The reason for this lies in the price effect (see Figure 1-2), which holds true for jobs of little inherent interest. Empirical research shows that, in the case of jobs perceived as monotonous, the offer of a reward does nothing to make the job itself more interesting but does improve employee satisfaction (Calder/Staw 1975). However, the passion that inspires the ardent climber to scale new heights, for instance, is notable by its absence.

Intrinsic Motivation Can Also Assume an Immoral Dimension

Intrinsic motivation can also assume an immoral or undesirable dimension. History has shown that the worst crimes against humanity are often intrinsically motivated. Fanatics such as Hitler and Stalin are prime examples. Envy, vengeance and the lust for power are no less intrinsically motivated than altruism, conscience and love. On the other hand, there are occasions when extrinsic motivation leads professional soldiers and mercenaries alike to show greater compassion towards prisoners of war, for instance (Frey 1999, Ch. 7).

Extrinsic Motivation Can Keep Unwelcome Emotions in Check

Extrinsic motivation can serve to discipline emotions. A lid can be kept on undesirable emotional conflict within a company if employees have a common vested financial interest. The emotional conflict can be harnessed as a means of satisfying employees' non-work-related aspirations such as taking up an expensive hobby. Of course, this does not resolve the underlying conflict, but it does put it into perspective.

This effect can be seen throughout history. As Hirschman (1987) notes, there have been many occasions when seething passions of one kind or another have been kept in check by economic interests. As far back as the sixteenth and seventeenth centuries, it was widely recognized that the price system has a positive disciplining effect on otherwise unbridled passions. For the French philosophical historian Montesquieu (1749, Volume XX) in his doctrine of "sweet commerce" (doux commerce), it was obvious that "commerce improves and mitigates our behavior, as we can see every day." The vagaries of human emotion are a law unto themselves, whereas the pursuit of material interests leads to reliability, order and cooperation.

Rewards Can Sometimes Serve to Create Intrinsic Motivation

If intrinsic motivation arises as a result of a combination of self-determination and a sense of competence, and this also gives rise to a "pleasant flow experience," then a reward can lead people to tackle tasks which are initially unfamiliar and perceived as excessively demanding. Over time, as the person concerned gains experience, new intrinsic motivation is fostered. These "hidden benefits of inadequate reward" are the flip side of the coin to the "hidden costs of reward." But they are not symmetrical. It is easier to destroy employees' morale than to create it. It is therefore difficult to know where to draw the line so as to avoid creating intrinsic motivation only to undermine it with misplaced rewards. This requires an "educational skill which is out of the ordinary" (Heckhausen 1989, p. 465).

Financial incentives can also foster intrinsic motivation if the activity itself – indulging in a game of chance or playing the stock markets, for instance – is, by its very nature, monetary. In this instance, money is no longer a means to an end, but serves to satisfy an immediate need.

5. The Art of Creating the "Right" Motivation

If firms are to come up with appropriate incentive measures, they must weigh the difficulties and imponderables of generating and undermining intrinsic motivation (the crowding-out effect) against the fairly predictable impact of sanctions (price effect). Chapter 2 will argue that this is worth doing and will explain why. The subsequent chapters will then present the current thinking on how management by motivation can work in theory and in practice.

6. Further Reading

Modern organizational structures which meet the requirements of knowledge-based activities and incorporate the interaction of tacit and explicit knowledge are examined in:

Nonaka, I./Takeuchi, H. (1995): The Knowledge-Creating Company, New York/Oxford.

Osterloh, M./Frost, J. (1998): Prozessmanagement als Kernkompetenz. Wie Sie Business Reengineering strategisch nutzen können, 2nd edn, Wiesbaden.
Osterloh, M./Wübker, S. (1999): Wettbewerbsfähiger durch Prozess- und Wissensmanagement. Mit Chancengleichheit auf Erfolgskurs, Wiesbaden.

The application of the economic model to areas other than the economy, i.e. politics, the law, criminology, family life and art, is discussed in:

Becker, G. (1976): The Economic Approach to Human Behavior, Chicago.
Frey, B. S. (1999): Economics as a Science of Human Behavior. Extended Second Edition, Boston.

For further information on intrinsic motivation in its various guises, see also:

Csikszentmihalyi, M. (1975): Beyond Boredom and Anxiety, San Francisco.
Heckhausen, H. (1989): Motivation und Handeln, 2nd edn, Berlin.
Kruglanski, A. W. (1975): The Endogenous-Exogenous Partition in Attribution Theory, in: Psychological Review 82, pp 387–406.

A vivid personal account of the climber's love-hate relationship with his hobby can be found in:

Loewenstein, G. (1999): Because It Is There: The Challenge of Mountaineering... for Utility Theory, in: Kyklos 52, pp 315–343.
Oelz, O. (1999): Mit Eispickel und Stethoskop, Zurich.

The relationship between self-imposed moral obligation and intrinsic motivation is discussed in:

Kliemt, H. (1993): Ökonomische Analyse der Moral, in: Ramb, B.-T./Tietzel, M. (eds): Ökonomische Verhaltenstheorie, Munich, pp 281–310.
Osterloh, M./Löhr, A. (1994): Ökonomik oder Ethik als Grundlage der sozialen Ordnung?, in: Wirtschaftswissenschaftliches Studium, p 406.
Baurmann, M. (1996): Der Markt der Tugend, Tübingen.

A popular socio-psychological analysis of "the hidden costs of reward" can be found in:

Deci, E. L./Flaste, R. (1995): Why We Do What We Do: The Dynamics of Personal Autonomy, New York.

Sprenger, R. K. (2000a): Mythos Motivation (anniversary edition). Wege aus einer Sackgasse, Frankfurt.
Sprenger, R. K. (2000b): Das Prinzip Selbstverantwortung (anniversary edition). Wege zur Motivation, Frankfurt.
Kohn, A. (1993): Punished by Reward: The Trouble With Gold Stars, Incentive Plans, A's, Praise, and Other Bribes, Boston.
Kohn, A. (1993): Why Incentive Plans Cannot Work, in: Harvard Business Review 5, pp 54-63.

The current scientific debate over "the hidden costs of reward" is chronicled in:

Deci, E. L./Koestner, R./Ryan, R. M. (1999): A Meta-Analytic Review of Experiments Examining the Effects of Extrinsic Rewards on Intrinsic Motivation, in: Psychological Bulletin 125 (3), pp 627-668.

Further articles on this topic can also be found in the above volume of the *Psychological Bulletin.*

The application of the crowding-out effect in the economy is examined in:

Frey, B. S. (1997a): Not Just for the Money. An Economic Theory of Personal Motivation. Cheltenham/Northampton.

Details of research into psychological contracts and the link between fairness and voluntary staff commitment can be found in Chapter 7 of this book and in the following publications:

Schein, E. (1965): Organization Psychology, Englewood Cliffs, NJ.
Rousseau, D. M. (1995): Psychological Contracts in Organizations: Understanding Written and Unwritten Agreements, Thousand Oaks/London/New Delhi.
Rousseau, D. M./McLean Parks, J. (1993): The Contracts of Individuals and Organizations, in: Research in Organizational Behavior 15, pp 1–43.
Fehr, E./Gächter, S. (1998): Reciprocity and Economics: The Economic Implications of "Homo Reciprocans," in: European Economic Review 42, pp. 845–859.
Bierhoff, H. W./Herner, M. J. (1999): Arbeitsengagement aus freien Stücken: Zur Rolle der Führung, in: Schreyögg, G./Sydow, J. (eds): Managementforschung 9. Führung – neu gesehen, Berlin/New York, pp 55–87.

For an examination of the problem of multi-tasking and the difficulties of evaluating performance in respect of complex activities from the point of view of organizational and microeconomic theory, see:

Pearce, J. L. (1987): Why Merit Pay Doesn't Work: Implications From Organizational Theory, in: Balkin, D. B./Gomez-Mejia, L. R. (eds): New Perspectives on Compensation, pp 169–178.

Holmström, B./Milgrom, P. (1991): Multi-Task Principal Agent Analyses: Incentive Contracts, Asset Ownership and Job Design, in: Journal of Law, Economics and Organizations 7, pp 24-52.

Prendergast, C. (1999): The Provision of Incentives in Firms, in: Journal of Economic Literature 37, pp 7-63.

The importance of intrinsic motivation for creativity and innovation is considered in:

Amabile, T. (1996): Creativity in Context: Update to the Social Psychology of Creativity, Boulder, CO.

Amabile, T. (1998): How to Kill Creativity, in: Harvard Business Review, September/October, pp 77–87.

Schwartz, B. (1990): The Creation and Destruction of Value, in: American Psychologist 45, pp 7-15.

Shapira, Z. (1976): Expectancy Determinants of Intrinsically Motivated Behavior, in: Journal of Personality and Social Psychology 34, pp 1235–1244.

Chapter Two

MARGIT OSTERLOH AND JETTA FROST

Motivation and Knowledge as Strategic Resources

Introduction

This chapter will explain why motivation and knowledge management are key strategic resources when it comes to the competitiveness of a company. In addition, it will outline the latest strategy research developments, define the characteristics of strategic resources and examine the relationship between knowledge and motivation.

More and more companies are coming to realize that the knowledge, motivation and service ethic of their employees are crucial to the success of their business. The extent to which knowledge and motivation are intertwined can be seen in the case of many of the companies listed on the stock market under the banner of the so-called "new economy." Despite enormous losses, the market value of shares in these companies is rising. This positive price trend is based on the potential that underpins these companies in the form of a highly motivated group of employees who will ensure success through innovative ideas and a proven capacity to develop new, revenue-generating products and services. On the other hand, the fact that they possess such specialized knowledge serves to keep the workforce motivated. As such, it is plain to see that both motivation management and knowledge management are key strategic resources when it comes to business competitiveness. This view is supported by the latest strategy research, which will be presented in the opening section of this chapter. The second section will look at the characteristics of strategic resources. The third and final section will deal with the relationship between knowledge and motivation, explaining why both are relevant resources when it comes to sustainable competitiveness.

1. The Latest Developments in Strategy Research: From a Market-Based to a Resource-Based View

A corporate strategy seeks to answer the following key question: how can a sustainable, above-average profit be achieved in a competitive market? Recognizing that they cannot afford to take a rest, companies will strive to emulate the success of their competitors in the pursuit of such profits. If successful, the above-average profit enjoyed by one company is gained at the expense of another. So how can a company prevent such an outcome? Modern strategic theory has developed two approaches that attempt to explain how companies can achieve a sustainable competitive advantage: the "market-based" and the "resource-based" views of strategy. The fundamental concepts behind the two views are illustrated in Figure 2-1.

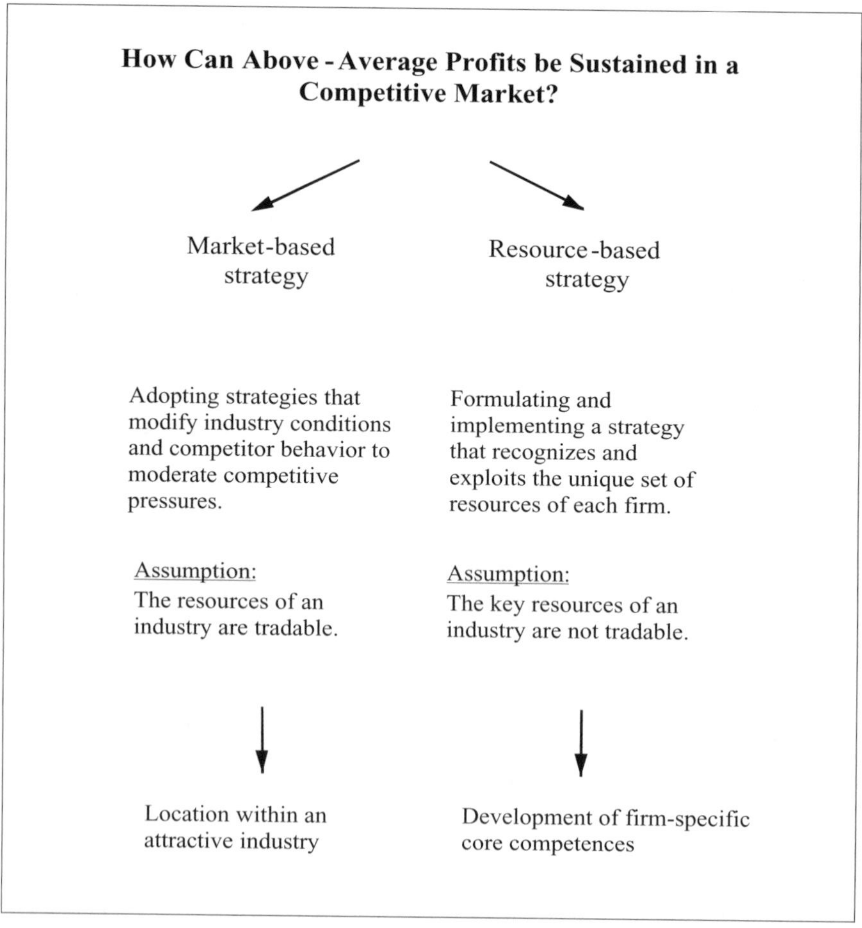
How Can Above - Average Profits be Sustained in a Competitive Market?
Market-based strategy
Resource-based strategy
Adopting strategies that modify industry conditions and competitor behavior to moderate competitive pressures.
Formulating and implementing a strategy that recognizes and exploits the unique set of resources of each firm.
Assumption:
The resources of an industry are tradable.
Assumption:
The key resources of an industry are not tradable.
Location within an attractive industry
Development of firm-specific core competences

Figure 2-1

From a *market-based* point of view, a sustainable competitive advantage results from strategic positioning within an attractive industry where market imperfections are particularly evident, and achieving a competitive advantage over rivals (Porter 1998). In this way, a company achieves monopolistic status. The profits associated with this limited competition are referred to as monopoly rents. It is assumed here that the structural conditions in the industry in question are conducive to business success. The purpose of a firm's strategy is to answer the questions "which industry should we be in?" and "how should we compete?". An attractive industry, based on this approach, is an industry with few competitors. This, however, further assumes that all companies have access to the same fundamental resources. In other words, that every company has the opportunity to procure the essential resources required to conquer a market. These may include raw materials, equipment, software, consultancy services, licenses and qualified employees.

In contrast, the *resource-based* view assumes that a monopolistic structure does not guarantee long-term protection against competitors (Grant 1998). If all companies had access to the same set of resources, such that they could, for example, purchase the same software or recruit equally qualified employees, then it would not be possible to maintain a monopoly of a given market in the long run. Establishing a sustainable competitive advantage is concerned with formulating and implementing a strategy that recognizes and exploits a unique bundle of highly firm-specific resources. These resources can then be developed as *core competencies* (Prahalad/Hamel 1990).

Core competencies are characterized as follows:

- They are *valuable,* i.e. customers are willing to pay more for the extra benefits derived from these resources as against comparable rival products and services.
- They are *scarce,* i.e. their availability is not unlimited.
- They are *not easily substituted,* i.e. there are no alternative resources that offer the very same extra utility that they provide.
- They are *difficult to imitate,* i.e. other companies cannot easily replicate them.
- They are *transferable,* i.e. they provide a basis for entering new markets. As a result, they can be used to meet future customer needs which are, as yet, unknown.

The most important of these characteristics as regards competitiveness are *transferability and inimitability.* Resources with these attributes cannot normally be bought, but must be generated by means of an extensive process within the company itself. The result of emphasizing these characteristics is that traditional material resources such as labor, land and real capital move down the agenda in favor of intangible resources such as human, organizational and social capital. Social capital corresponds to the sum of the relationships within an organization, thereby facilitating individuals' dealings with one another at the interpersonal level. It is the product of something akin to a leverage effect arising from the total human capital of a company, within which trust and fairness are the key tenets of management (see Chapter 7). As such, attempting to obtain social capital from the market is the most difficult endeavor that a company can possibly embark on. Individual human capital can be bought in by "poaching" employees from another company, but an existing social set-up can only be acquired en masse in the context of a corporate takeover, i.e. the acquisition of an entire company.

Core competencies cannot be purchased, but arise from the successful interplay of knowledge within a company. In-house technical expertise, for instance, is an important asset in terms of competitive advantage, but this alone is not enough to create core competencies. What counts is the ability to combine this expertise with the knowledge and skills of the workforce to develop such competencies. This is vividly illustrated by the case of Swatch as set out in Box 2-1.

The core competency model focuses not on the tradable or tangible aspects of resources, but on the non-tradable and likewise intangible attributes that underlie the inimitability and transferability of resources, as illustrated in Figure 2-2. Non-tradable and intangible resources include the unique relationship between customer and supplier, organizational knowledge and employee loyalty. These resources afford the greatest protection against imitation and can be developed as *core competencies* as the benefits that they bring are specific to a particular corporate structure and culture. Patents and licenses also qualify as intangible resources, though these may be traded or sold.

Box 2-1

The Core Competency of SWATCH

At the beginning of the 1980s, the traditional Swiss watch industry was in dire straits. Banks were no longer willing to grant credit to the prestigious brand names that had once been at the pinnacle of their business, and many workshops were forced to amalgamate or close down altogether. However, these difficult times were to pave the way for the development of a new type of watch, which was ultimately to revolutionize the industry: Swatch.

Nevertheless, a product like Swatch is not born overnight – and no one knows exactly how it was that Swatch became one of the most popular products in the world. With the *core competency "time in a designer package,"* Swatch successfully combines expertise in technology, design, pop art, marketing and distribution. Technically, the company was able to develop a highly accurate watch whose components were molded in pre-fabricated plastic. In this way, the number of components was reduced from 151 to just 51 standard parts. This represented a major breakthrough for the Swiss watch industry, which had traditionally relied heavily on expensive mechanical systems. As such, it was initially feared that the use of plastic would tarnish the industry's image, but the Swatch innovators worked hard to avoid being labeled as producers of down-market watches. Throughout the factory, the pioneering spirit prevailed. The debate as to how best to combine design, technology and marketing was heated. The aim was to change customer expectations: Swatch was about more than just the measurement of time, it was the successful embodiment of the spirit of its age. The slogans "Fashion that ticks" and "Swatch: you don't wear the same tie every day" illustrate the key to the brand's global success: Swatch owners change their watches as though they were ties – depending on the time of day and mood. As such, Swatch became a basic fashion accessory, unrivalled in terms of price, service and quality.

Translated from: Schulz, B. (1999): Swatch oder die Erfolgsgeschichte des Nicolas Hayek, Dusseldorf.

Properties of Resources		
	Tangible Resources	Intangible Resources
Tradable Resources	• Machines • Personnel • Standard software	• Licenses • Individual expert knowledge
Non-tradable Resources	• Assembled equipment • Internal software	• Corporate culture • Unique stakeholder relationships • Company-specific training • Unique customer and supplier relationships • Organizational knowledge • Trust

Figure 2-2

2. What Characterizes Corporate Resources That Are Relevant to Sustainable Competitive Advantage?

Corporate resources that can be developed into *core competencies* of a kind that are difficult to imitate have a role to play in achieving competitive advantage. But this requires that a company be more adept than its competitors and remain so in the long term. So when and why can this be said to be true of a particular company? To answer this question, let us start by considering those activities that are carried out by a single company and not between independent market players (see also Chapter 6).

2.1 Why Do Firms Exist?

Firm-Specific Pool Resources

In Chapter 1, we established that firms exist because – unlike markets – they provide a place where shared, complementary resources that are specific to the firm can be generated and used. Firm-specific pool resources are assembled in integrated clusters and cannot be reduced to individual skills. This is evident, for instance, when the activity of a given individual has a positive impact on the activities of other members of the organization in question. Firm-specific pool resources facilitate knowledge integration so that the firm's intellectual capacity exceeds the capacity of individuals and generates outcomes of which the participating firm members would not be individually capable. This applies to the majority of activities dedicated to cutting overheads, such as strategic personnel planning and controlling. Other, less easily discernible, examples include the external benefits of tried-and-tested software, functional routines and workflows, team spirit, trust-based relationships, accumulated organizational knowledge, or simply a positive corporate image and other reputational assets.

In such instances, it is nearly impossible to single out precisely how much a particular individual has contributed to the generation of these firm-specific pool resources and what percentage of these resources, in turn, go into the firm's products and services. The incalculable nature of the process also makes it impossible to specify the relevant services and reciprocal considerations (prices) on a clear contractual basis. If this were possible, there would be no reason for a firm not to go to the market to procure the requisite resources through an external service agreement or outsourcing. These days, many companies routinely contract out certain maintenance activities. The type of service to be provided and the corresponding fee is set out in a contract. This is a tradable activity that may also be purchased by a company's competitors and is easy to imitate.

Incomplete Contracts, Regulation and Control

What is the difference between an employment contract in a company and a purchase order or service agreement in the marketplace? Both are contracts that lay down the service to be provided and the payment due in return. The difference lies in the fact that market contracts are normally *complete.* A typical example is the contract between a restaurant owner and a produce supplier. Here, the applicable prices and services are clearly laid down. Once the product or service has been provided and the price paid, the agreement is deemed to have been honored and that is the end of the story. By contrast, an employment contract within a company is always *incomplete*. Take the employment contract of a chef in a restaurant, for instance. This is an incomplete contract as the full extent of the services that the chef must subsequently provide (apart from cooking) is not precisely specified at the time the contract is signed.

Incomplete contracts arise because, where resources are pooled, costs and revenues cannot be accurately ascribed to individual employees. Unfortunately, there is a resultant tendency for less scrupulous employees to attempt to benefit from the firm-specific pool resources without contributing anything in return. Ultimately, under this voluntary system, a given employee may produce too little or nothing at all. In response to this free-rider problem, firms have traditionally introduced systems of regulation and control.

To sum up, employment contracts differ from market contracts firstly in their incomplete nature. Secondly, they involve an obligation. The fulfillment of this obligation is characterized by an unspoken desire to avoid official regulation and control within a so-called "indifference zone" (Barnard 1938).

But how can employees be controlled when the firm is seeking to establish pool resources? Contrary to conventional wisdom, we would argue that, under such circumstances, control is only possible to a limited extent.

There are essentially two forms of control: workflow control and performance control. What follows is a discussion of these.

Workflow Control

In the traditional bureaucratic organization as per the Taylor model (see Chapter 6), workflow is continuously controlled. Checks are carried out to establish whether employees are correctly following the prescribed workflow procedures. A restaurant manager reputedly once said, "The aim of the checking process is to see if the kitchen has been properly cleaned, not what the food ultimately tastes like." However, this approach can prove rigid and costly. It can also discourage innovation and undermine employee motivation. The more dynamic the environment and the more complex the nature of the task, the less appropriate this form of control becomes.

Performance Control

In light of the particular nature of bureaucratic organizations, attempts were soon under way to achieve control by monitoring performance rather than workflow. Typical examples include management by objectives and the new value-based management.

Under management by objectives, the employer and employee agree to common, clearly defined goals to be reached within a given timeframe. Value-based management, on the other hand, seeks to link traditional profit measurement with the market value approach of capital theory. Concepts such as economic value added (EVA) are central to this model.

The basic principle is as follows. Companies are decentralized as much as possible. In other words, the company is divided into a number of autonomous divisions, each of which is given the clear task of maximizing the value that it contributes. The sum of all the individual divisional contributions equals the shareholder value. But if, as often proposed by practitioners, we link pay packages to these contributions, then we again encounter the free-rider problem. As a result,

- either the sum of the contributions remains below the maximum shareholder value, or
- insufficient contributions are made to the firm-specific pool resources.

The first scenario occurs if the contribution of each employee is based on the total corporate value. In the case of pay packages covering several people, the greater the number concerned, the lower the total contribution ascribed to each. Economists refer to this as the "1/n problem." The greater the value of "n," the lower the individual contribution to the total will be. The resultant performance-related pay package will therefore also be lower. This, in turn, might cause tension between the employees in question and ultimately undermine shareholder value.

The second scenario occurs if, given a high "n," for instance, an individual performance evaluation is carried out. In other words, if each employee is assigned a specific, quantifiable sub-target upon which bonuses are based, then multi-tasking and fuzzy tasking problems arise. Extrinsically motivated employees will focus on these quantifiable targets and neglect other, less tangible aspects such as team spirit, the voluntary transfer of knowledge and cooperation in the formulation of new and challenging goals. Employees will be particularly reluctant to contribute to firm-specific pool resources in areas which are difficult to quantify and ascribe. Yet herein, as we have already explained, lies the company's very *raison d'être.*

Thus, where complex tasks are concerned, a highly variable or performance-related remuneration policy does not generally serve well. As empirical research has shown time and again, there is only a very limited positive correlation, if any, between variable performance-related pay and corporate performance (see Chapters 3 and 4). A fixed salary, on the other hand, only leads to a situation fraught with tension when it comes to extrinsically motivated employees. One thing, however, is clear: in the absence of intrinsic motivation, control will always be a problem.

Long-Term Relationships

Many theorists, particularly those who are heavily influenced by game theory, believe that the solution to the problem of control lies in the establishment of long-term relationships. Here, the drawbacks of variable pay are avoided by fixing salary levels. The motivation to perform comes from competition for a possible promotion within the organization.

As we have already explained, under incomplete contracts there are no precise criteria governing the contribution of each employee. In the framework of long-term relationships, however, managers can carry out a subjective evaluation of employees' performance. This evaluation serves as the basis for promotion-related decisions. The resultant competitive spirit as employees endeavor to climb the corporate ladder is believed to negate the need to actively foster intrinsic motivation.

However, this argument disregards empirical research into so-called organizational citizenship behavior and extra-role behavior. According to this theory, there is such a thing as an organizational sense of citizenship, which causes the members of an organization to go beyond what is required in the applicable list of obligations or job description (see Chapter 7).

The willingness to make unquantifiable contributions is said to depend on the perceived fairness of management. Such fairness is based on standards of reciprocity: employees who are treated fairly will work industriously as a token of their gratitude, whilst those who are not will express their dissatisfaction by withholding their goodwill. However, standards of reciprocity are, for their part, intrinsic, serving a direct need arising from the prevailing conditions. Thus, in the context of organizational citizenship behavior, intrinsic motivation is an important factor.

Summary: Why Do Firms Exist?

The collective generation of non-tradable firm-specific pool resources is the reason why firms exist and why not all activities are carried out in the market. As the product of a collective effort, a company's pool resources cannot be created by a single individual. It is therefore important to establish conditions within a company that encourage employees to work together towards a common goal, namely ensuring that the company flourishes and grows. Regulation and control mechanisms are not the answer, as they encourage team members to focus on quantifiable, governable factors.

Let us take the case of an advertising agency team that devises a new media campaign for one of its clients. It is not possible to establish who did most of the critical work after the event. Assuming that the campaign is a success, who takes the credit? The copywriter? The artistic director? The press officer? Or maybe the graphic designer? The success of the campaign is rooted in teamwork, with each team member striving to come up with ideas, provide valuable input, shape the process and offer the benefit of his or her expertise.

The contribution of each team member is crucial if the project is to succeed, and this cannot be accomplished solely by means of extrinsic motivators such as financial inducements or sanctions of some kind. Instead, fair treatment and the creation of a working environment conducive to intrinsic motivation (see Chapters 7 and 8) would seem to be the way forward. In Chapter 1, we discussed the "crowding-out" effect, whereby control mechanisms often serve to undermine intrinsic motivation. For this reason, the management of firm-specific pool resources and motivation management must be inextricably linked.

2.2 Why Are the Resources of Some Companies Superior to Those of Their Competitors?

According to the resource-based view, the inimitability of resources and their transferability to new products are the key factors when it comes to generating sustainable competitive advantages. Our earlier examination of the reasons why firms exist established that firm-specific pool resources and incomplete contracts constitute the essence of a firm. Pooled resources are difficult to imitate in that they cannot be bought on the market or simply created on demand. Thus, the achievement of sustainable competitive advantage depends on the skills and knowledge at a company's disposal for the generation of such inimitable pool resources.

In the following section, we will show why organizational knowledge – together with the intrinsic motivation of the workforce – is the most important factor in the development of sustainable and defendable competitive advantages, thus fulfilling the criteria for firm-specific pool resources in a special way.

3. Knowledge and Motivation as Sources of Sustainable Resources Crucial to Competitive Advantage

3M is a highly innovative company. It encourages creativity on the part of its employees by granting them considerable autonomy. Those working in research and development, for instance, are free to spend 15% of the working week on projects of their own choosing. There are no checks on how or where employees spend this time. As a result, 3M is continually producing new and attractive products and building on its company-specific knowledge. Box 2-2 describes a case in point.

Box 2-2

3M
In the 1970s, 3M was one of the first manufacturers of overhead projectors. Unlike other products on the market at the time, these were equipped with high-performance lenses that could also be used in undarkened rooms. 3M's lenses were produced using a process known as microreplication, whereby the microstructure of the lens surface is altered in such a way that light can be better bundled up and transported.

In the 1980s, 3M began to apply its microreplication technology to other surfaces, successfully manufacturing products that reflect light (e.g. textiles), inhibit electric shock (e.g. protective headgear) and adhesives. In 1996, microreplication became the basic technology employed by eight business areas, including reflective materials, adhesives, transport/filter materials and electronics. Central to this success was the combination of technical expertise in the field of microreplication with organizational skills. It was thanks to this organizational knowledge that 3M was able to transfer its technical know-how to the development of other products and restructure the market.

Translated from: Krüger, W./Homp, C. (1997): Kernkompetenzenmanagement. Steigerung der Flexibilität und Schlagkraft im Wettbewerb, Wiesbaden, pp. 130 ff.

The case of 3M shows firstly that there is more to commercial success than simply meeting the existing needs of the customer. Manufacturers must identify new needs and actively promote them to their customers. Several years ago, for instance, 3M invented the "Post-it." Until then, no one had realized how useful such little, repositionable notepads could be. Today, of course, no office would be complete without the ubiquitous "Post-it" note. However, the commonly proffered advice that one should gear one's business to the needs of the customer is not as simple as it may sound, as customers do not generally know today what they may need tomorrow. For companies, this means that even the most carefully conceived strategy of adapting in line with clearly defined customer needs is no more adequate than manufacturing today's products faster, better and cheaper. Instead, one must be ahead of the game and actively create tomorrow's market. The success of this strategy depends on the possession of core competencies, in particular company-specific knowledge.

Secondly, firms must always be acquiring new, firm-specific knowledge. The more technical and organizational knowledge that a firm starts out with, the faster this process will be. In this connection, a company's most important asset is the collective, organizational knowledge it possesses and not individual knowledge, as this can easily be lost if a particular employee goes to work for a rival firm. As such, individual knowledge is not a good basis for sustainable competitive advantage. But where does collective, organizational knowledge reside if not in the heads of individual members of the organization? Besides the technical knowledge and expertise acquired by the various members of the organization, collective knowledge is crystallized and stored in written organizational rules and informal guidelines. This information can be found in a company's software programs, as well as in its procedures, corporate culture and codes of practice under the general heading "the way we do things around here." As a depository for organizational knowledge, the collective wisdom also facilitates the assimilation of new knowledge. A company that already possesses considerable organizational knowledge can more easily assess the value of new information than one that does not.

The development of organizational knowledge is a process based on knowledge that has yet to be explicitly laid down but is still an implicit component of the hierarchical structure of the institution in question. It is important to understand this when it comes to ensuring the transferability and inimitability of the knowledge that a company possesses.

3.1 Explicit and Tacit Knowledge

Explicit knowledge is disseminated by means of books, newspapers, technical drawings, e-mails and the Internet. It may be coded in writing or symbols and can easily be reproduced. Nevertheless, only a small proportion of knowledge is explicit, since we grope for words to tell what we know (Polanyi 1974). As such, explicit knowledge is only the tip of the iceberg in terms of the sum of the knowledge we possess. A far greater proportion is comprised of our so-called *tacit knowledge*. Tacit knowledge, unlike explicit knowledge, cannot be expressed in letters, numbers or symbols. It resides in the heads of those concerned and the skills they possess. It can therefore only be disseminated by people and not by documents, information technology or expert systems. An example is given in Box 2-3.

Box 2-3

XEROX
Xerox has tried to bring together the knowledge possessed by its specialist service and repair staff to create an expert system for installation in its photocopying equipment. This would enable problems to be resolved by telephone, thus eliminating the need for engineers to attend in person to effect the necessary repairs. However, employees were unable to get along with the system. On closer examination, it emerged that engineers transferred knowledge by swapping anecdotes of their experiences of photocopier repair. The expert system developed by Xerox failed to capture the nuances and details of the engineers' accounts. It only captured explicit knowledge.

Hansen, M. T./Nohria, N./Tierney, T. (1999): What's Your Strategy for Managing Knowledge, in: Harvard Business Review (March-April 1999), pp. 106-116.

The use of explicit knowledge in complex situations always depends on tacit knowledge garnered from experience and background knowledge. This means that people possess important knowledge without being able to put it into words, even if they wanted to. This also explains why top managers continue to make as many business trips as ever, despite the widespread use of information technology: face-to-face communication is crucial to the transmission of tacit knowledge.

How is tacit knowledge characterized? *Individual* tacit knowledge consists firstly of cognitive rules and routines of which one is only partially aware. Examples include intuition, natural aptitude or the ability to recognize a face in a crowd. Another aspect is the mastery of physical activities such as riding a bicycle, skiing or walking the tightrope, or the complex, fine motor skills required of a surgeon. Skills of this kind cannot simply be learned from a book, they must almost always be taught. *Organizational* tacit knowledge, on the other hand, consists of tried-and-tested routines and procedures which are commonsensical and function without having to be explicitly agreed by those who carry them out. Both individual and organizational tacit knowledge serve to facilitate the accomplishment of tasks by enabling an established routine to be followed without further thought.

Moreover, the inimitability of resources is closely linked to the mastery of tacit organizational knowledge. This is because tacit knowledge is much slower and more costly to transmit and disseminate than its explicit equivalent, requiring personal cooperation and not merely written rules or information technology tools. That is why tacit knowledge is very difficult to replicate in comparison with written guidelines or knowledge expressed in books. With the exception of copyrights and patents, printed explicit knowledge no longer constitutes a competitive advantage.

3.2 Disseminating Tacit Knowledge

The maxim "If Hewlett Packard only knew what Hewlett Packard knows" or "If Siemens only knew what Siemens knows," as the case may be, leads us to ask how it can be ensured that the valuable asset that is individual tacit knowledge is used optimally by a given company. And how can individual tacit knowledge be turned into collective knowledge that will remain intact even after those concerned have left the company? For instance, how does one go about ensuring that the art of producing a Stradivarius violin does not die out with the last member of the Stradivari family?

The Japanese organizational researchers Nonaka and Takeuchi have constructed a model referred to as the "knowledge spiral," which demonstrates how organizational knowledge can be generated and transmitted. It is their contention that the continual exchange of explicit and tacit knowledge is essential to the generation and transmission of organizational knowledge. In this way, tacit knowledge can be disseminated throughout the entire organization and continually augmented to encompass more complex organizational routines.

In order to generate organizational knowledge, the individual tacit knowledge of the constituent members must undergo a dynamic transmission process. In this way, explicit and tacit knowledge interact during four modes of knowledge conversion: socialization, externalization, combination and internalization.

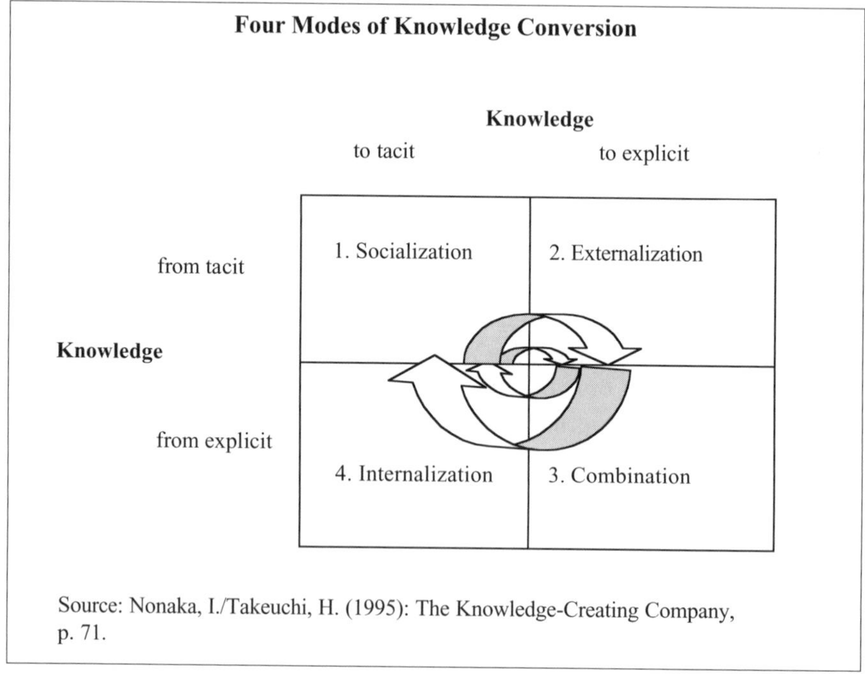

Source: Nonaka, I./Takeuchi, H. (1995): The Knowledge-Creating Company, p. 71.

Figure 2-3

1. *Socialization* entails the transmission of knowledge from "tacit to tacit." In other words, knowledge is transmitted largely without being explicitly expressed. As such, "learning by doing" – through observation, imitation and practice – is the central tenet here. This is, for instance, how children master physical skills such as riding a bicycle, continually pedaling, steering and balancing until they finally get the hang of it. A typical example of socialization as a means of transmitting knowledge in a work environment is the way in which a new member of a team is assimilated into the ethos and activities of the group by simply going through its daily routines. It does not require a written regulation for the individual in question to get acquainted with the corporate culture.

2. *Externalization* converts parts of tacit knowledge into explicit knowledge. However, this is not always possible. The successful transformation of tacit knowledge to explicit knowledge requires intensive personal communication in the form of quality circles or interdisciplinary teams, for instance. Participants endeavor to share the benefit of their experience and exchange the tacit knowledge they have acquired by means of analogies and metaphors.

3. Various forms of explicit knowledge are brought together through *combination.* As the combination of knowledge is not dependent on face-to-face contact, it can be achieved by means of information technology. However, standard IT can really only deal with explicit knowledge transmission. As a result, only a tiny proportion of all the available relevant knowledge is taken into account.

4. In the *internalization* mode, the new body of explicit knowledge is (partially) converted back into tacit knowledge, albeit in an enhanced and more complex form. That is to say, individuals or groups learn to carry out routines that were previously explicitly laid down. Having mastered the relevant routines, less concentration is required and those concerned can effectively carry out complex activities in their sleep.

The more often we go through the knowledge spiral, the more complex the organizational routines become. They are also better mastered by ever more people and continually augmented by newly acquired knowledge. Thus, even if individuals in possession of particular knowledge were to leave the company, its routines would remain intact. The only knowledge lost would be individual tacit knowledge; standard collective knowledge of the relevant routines would be unaffected. From this, we can put forward two reasons why complex organizational routines constitute particularly sustainable sources of competitive advantage.

Firstly, organizational routines are difficult to imitate. The relatively high degree of tacit organizational knowledge on which they are based cannot easily be replicated even if individual employees defect to competitors.

Secondly, organizational routines allow existing organizational knowledge to be transferred to new products and services. An example is a tried-and-tested marketing concept or an efficient process (see Box 2-4 for a case in point).

Box 2-4

The Transferability of Core Competencies: From Gate Gourmet to Rail Gourmet

Gate Gourmet catering service is the most successful division within the Swissair Group. Gate Gourmet has identified and captured a market niche. In the space of four years, Gate Gourmet went from being a dedicated catering supplier to Swissair to become the second largest airline catering service in the world. Today, Gate Gourmet enjoys a strong global position, with subsidiaries all over the world.

Of late, however, Gate Gourmet has encountered a new form of competition, in Europe in particular. In several countries, customers began opting to make short journeys by rail as high-speed trains such as the ICE and TGV offered cheap, reliable alternatives. This trend also took its toll on Gate Gourmet.

However, the company's management came up with a way of putting its skills to use in this new growth market. As more and more business people began taking the train rather than the plane, there was clearly a demand for the type of catering service that they had been accustomed to when traveling by air. At that time, however, no such service was available on the trains. Swissair Relations consequently founded Rail Gourmet to provide catering services of the kind offered on the airlines – but this time geared to the needs of the high-speed rail passenger. Thanks to the agility with which it transferred its knowledge of the airline catering business to the railway service, Rail Gourmet was able to capture a large share of the market.

Knowledge and complex organizational routines are examples of a company's pool resources. They increase the productivity of company members – even of those who have not been involved in creating them. This implies that employees whose motivation is solely extrinsic will only contribute if they are subject to checks or sanctions. But contributions to intangible firm-specific pool resources are extremely difficult to control or calculate. For example, if a team solves a difficult problem or works on a strategy, it is practically impossible to distinguish the respective individual contributions made toward the end result. Moreover, extrinsically motivated employees will be extremely reluctant to relinquish their individual knowledge and the monopolistic benefits it confers. They will free-ride and avoid collaboration wherever possible and play their cards close to their chest if they feel that their contribution is not being duly rewarded. However, teamwork does not function that way. Knowledge-intensive teamwork depends on a common bond or sense of camaraderie, i.e. some kind of intrinsically motivated commitment to work together to accomplish the task at hand. This commonality of purpose is most often to be found in instances where the task in question demands the pooling of the tacit knowledge of the various members of the team.

4. Summary

The resource-based view has changed the emphasis of strategic management. Sustainable, defendable competitive advantages are now sought primarily through inimitable, firm-specific pool resources. These belong to the category of resources whose generation cannot easily be attributed to the efforts of an individual firm member. Such firm-specific pool resources also explain why certain activities are performed within a company and not outsourced or bought on the open market. Tacit organizational knowledge is the building block of these resources. Upon this, a company can build strategically important *core competencies.*

Until now, however, the resource-based view has completely ignored the fact that knowledge management requires the consideration of motivational factors. The management of intrinsic motivation, in particular, has been overlooked. Current management practice also fails to address this issue, focusing on extrinsic financial remuneration systems despite clear evidence that there is no link between variable management pay and corporate performance. If extrinsic motivation is to be prioritized, then the applicable job specifications must be clearly defined. Only then is a contingent remuneration system possible. But if future customer needs have still to be identified or innovative new products developed, then a concentration on extrinsic motivation will not suffice. Creativity cannot simply be conjured up on demand. At the end of the day, innovation and the development of new *core competencies* depend on the exchange of tacit knowledge. Sanctions and formal regulations will be to no avail. In this instance, intrinsic motivation is required.

As we have demonstrated, knowledge management must go hand in hand with motivation management if a company is to generate the strategic resources that build up sustainable and defendable competitive advantages. But the management of intrinsic motivation poses a far greater challenge than its extrinsic counterpart. By its very nature, intrinsic motivation is always voluntary: it cannot simply be commanded. As such, all that one can do is create an environment conducive to the promotion of intrinsic motivation. However, this leads to a degree of tension on the part of management between its role as a kind of external control mechanism and the promotion of intrinsic employee commitment. Against this backdrop, the next four chapters will be devoted to the examination of the conditions under which extrinsic motivation – which is easier to manage – and the more elusive intrinsic motivation should be pursued.

5. Further Reading

The concept of core competencies is elaborated in:

Prahalad, C. K./Hamel, G. (1990): The Core Competence of the Corporation, in: Harvard Business Review (May-June 1990), pp 79-91.
Hamel, G./Prahalad, C. K. (1996): Competing for the Future, Boston.

The market-based approach to strategic management are discussed in:

Porter, M. E. (1998): Competitive Strategy, New York.

For a systematic discussion of the organizational management function, see:

Barnard, C. I. (1938): The Functions of the Executive, Cambridge, MA.

An overview of the foundations of value-oriented business management is provided in:

Rappaport, A. (1998): Creating Shareholder Value. A Guide for Managers and Investors, 2nd edn, New York.

The influence of the shareholder value concept on the behavior of members of an organization and the problems associated with measuring performance in the case of complex activities are addressed in:

Gibbons, R. (1998): Incentives in Organizations, in: Journal of Economic Perspectives 12, pp 115–132.
Osterloh, M. (1999): Wertorientierte Unternehmensführung und Management-Anreizsysteme, in: Kumar, B. N./Osterloh, M./Schreyögg, G. (eds): Unternehmensethik und Transformation des Wettbewerbs, Stuttgart, pp 183-204.
Prendergast, C. (1999): The Provision of Incentives in Firms, in: Journal of Economic Literature 37, pp 7-63.

An overview of research into "extra-role behavior" and "organizational citizenship behavior" may be found in:

Organ, D. W. (1990): The Motivational Basis of Organizational Citizenship Behavior, in: Staw, B. M./Cummings, L. L. (eds): Research in Organizational Behavior 12, pp 43-72.

A comprehensive concept of knowledge management is provided by:

Nonaka, I./Takeuchi, H. (1995): The Knowledge-Creating Company, New York.

The difference between tacit and explicit knowledge is explained in:

Polanyi, M. (1974): Personal Knowledge, Chicago.

Examples of knowledge management in practice are given in:

Hansen, M. T./Nohria, N./Tierney, T. (1999): What's Your Strategy for Managing Knowledge?, in: Harvard Business Review (March-April 1999), pp 106-116.

A prominent researcher who subscribes to the resource- and knowledge-based view writes in:

Grant, R. M. (1996): Towards a Knowledge-Based Theory of the Firm, in: Strategic Management Journal 17, pp 109-122.
Grant, R. M. (1998): Contemporary Strategic Analysis, Oxford, UK.

The development of the knowledge-based theory to a knowledge- and motivation-based theory is described by:

Osterloh, M./Frey, B. S./Frost, J. (1999): Was kann das Unternehmen besser als der Markt?, in: Zeitschrift für Betriebswirtschaft 69, pp 1245-1262.

Part Two

Motivation and Compensation

Chapter Three

BRUNO S. FREY

How Does Pay Influence Motivation?

Introduction

Variable performance-related pay (or "pay for performance") has become an increasingly popular form of compensation. It is also the preferred form from the point of view of economic theory, specifically with reference to the principal-agent theory. In practice it is being used more and more for management grades and other levels of the corporate hierarchy. The key to performance-related pay is that compensation is adjusted to reflect an employee's individual performance. However, research has shown that variable performance-related pay does not lead to a general increase in a company's productivity and earnings. Improved performance only occurs in simple, easily measured activities. In other circumstances, pay for performance can even reduce a person's willingness to perform by "crowding out" the intrinsic motivation to work.

Different types of employees react in different ways to pay for performance. Income Maximizers and Status Seekers will tend to perform better under such a system, while Loyalists, Formalists and Autonomists will tend to react more negatively as their intrinsic motivation to work decreases or disappears altogether. Other forms of motivation – such as praise, commands, participation and autonomy – are more effective with these types of employees. One of the key tasks of "management by motivation" is to apply the mix of monetary and, even more importantly, non-monetary incentives that is most appropriate for each type of person.

1. Contrasting Views

Two completely opposite views of the motivational effect of wages are prevalent today. The first is that an increase in wages will have an incentive effect and induce the employee to work harder. This view is explained in detail in Section 1. The second is that an increase in wages actually undermines motivation and can thus reduce performance. This theory is discussed in Section 2.

We investigate the conditions under which payment of a wage can increase performance (Section 3). We see that the suitability of monetary incentives as a means of raising performance depends on the type of person concerned. Five main types of people are identified. In Sections 4 and 5, we see which types of people will perform better in response to wages, and which will perform worse.

Section 6 shows that there are other motivating factors apart from wages that are particularly appropriate for certain types of people. We distinguish between praise, commands, participation and autonomy. Finally, Section 7 provides an overview and outlook.

According to the principal-agent theory, which is central to an understanding of performance-related pay and which is described in Box 3-1, wages should reflect performance to the greatest possible degree.

If this rule is applied consistently, employees who are only extrinsically motivated will achieve the best performance. But if the wage paid deviates from the performance, employees will exploit the opportunity to earn a higher income without putting in the effort required.

The principal-agent theory draws an unequivocal conclusion with regard to setting wages within organizations. The wage has to be linked as closely as possible to each employee's individual performance. The call for (variable) "pay for performance" thus accords precisely with the demands of modern economic theory.

Box 3-1

How Do Wages Affect Performance? – The "Principal-Agent Theory"
The principal-agent theory poses the following question:
How can managers (principals), as representatives of the organization, best ensure that their subordinates (agents) do what is best for the organization?

There are two problems to address:

- Subordinates act in their own interests and aim to expend as little effort as possible on work.
- Managers cannot accurately observe or check whether their subordinates are completing the tasks allocated to them or if they are performing them in a satisfactory manner. This situation could be described as an "incomplete contractual arrangement with asymmetrical information."

The manager thus has to give his or her subordinates an incentive to act in the interests of the company. In the case of activities whose output can be measured easily, a performance-related wage represents an optimum solution: the wage paid is adjusted as far as possible to the observed performance. The simplest form of this system is piecework, where the employee receives a set amount of money for each unit manufactured.

A performance-related wage enables managers (principals) to elicit the desired performance from employees. This is true not just for the intensity, but also for the orientation of the performance. If performance-related wages are set correctly, employees will carry out precisely the tasks stipulated by their managers. Because any deviation will be directly reflected by a lower income, employees will avoid such deviations.

In recent years, the idea of "pay for performance" has become increasingly popular in practice. For once, then, modern theory and practice are largely in agreement. Fixed basic salaries are declining in significance, while performance-related variable wage components are becoming increasingly important. As well as paying various types of bonuses linked more or less closely to the performance of the individual concerned, today's businesses can resort to a whole arsenal of stock option plans. Some employees have an unconditional right to buy stocks at a preferential price, while others have rights that can only be exercised if the price of the company's own shares is higher than a general share index or an index of comparable companies' shares.

There is no doubt that such performance-related wages often act as an incentive. The cover picture on the August 7, 1999 edition of The Economist shows one way of looking at the relationship between performance-related wages and performance (see Figure 3-1).

Pay for performance is not the exclusive preserve of profit-oriented private-sector companies; it has also been introduced, or at least seriously considered, in the non-profit sector and, especially, in the public sector. One of the central tenets of "new public management," for example, is that wages should be based on the performance delivered.

Table 3-1 shows the extent to which variable pay was used in Switzerland in 1999/2000.

Table 3-1:
Variable Pay in Switzerland 1999/2000

	1st level Executive board members	2nd level Senior managers and divisional heads	3rd level Subdivision and department heads
Recipients (in %)	77	73	71
Percentage of gross salary	18	13	8

Translation from: *Handelszeitung*, No. 26, June 28, 2000, pp. 19-21.

Between 71 and 77 percent of employees received at least part of their salary as a variable component. The percentage of the overall salary may not be very high (between 8% and 18%), but it still makes up a considerable portion of total compensation, especially for executive board members.

The Effect of Incentive Pay

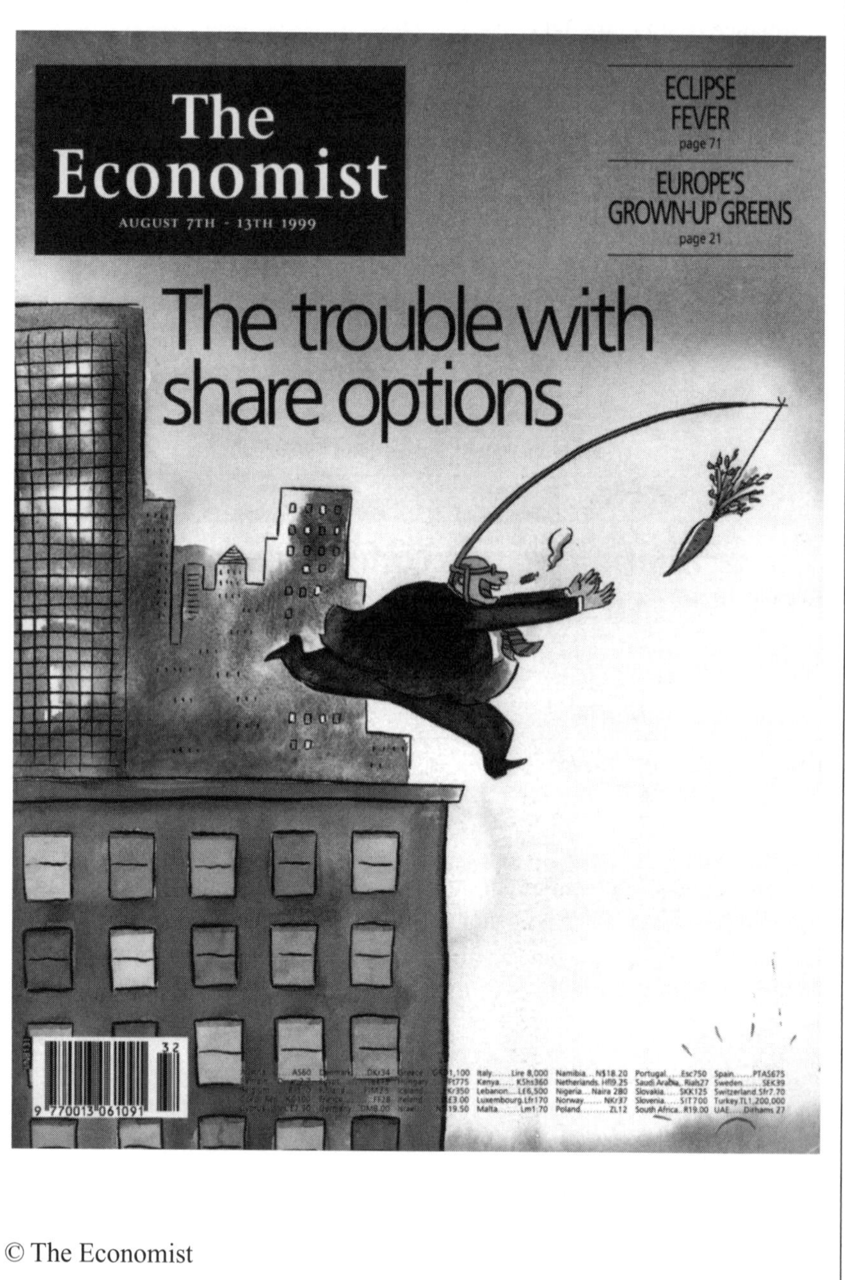

Figure 3-1

Table 3-2 shows the prevalence of variable wages in 1999/2000 in various countries.

Table 3-2:
Management Compensation in Europe
Executives of Internationally Active Companies

Country	Variable compensation	
	Recipients (in %)	Percentage of basic salary
Belgium	44	15
Germany	89	37
France	91	28
United Kingdom	82	27
Ireland	69	18
Italy	80	18
Netherlands	73	25
Austria	64	33
Switzerland	79	22
Spain	61	21

Translation from: *Handelszeitung* No. 26, June 28, 2000, p. 21.

Between 44 percent (Belgium) and 91 percent (France) of managers of internationally active companies receive part of their wages as a variable component. The median is 73 percent (Netherlands). With 79 percent, Switzerland is slightly higher than this median. Variable management wages are much more widespread in Germany (89%) and in France (91%).

The percentage of gross salary accounted for by the variable component lies between 15 percent (Belgium) and 37 percent (Germany). The median value here is 25 percent (Netherlands). Switzerland is slightly lower with 22 percent, while Austria is significantly higher with 33 percent.

Figure 3-2, which gives details for Chief Executive Officers (CEOs) in the United States, shows that performance-related salaries have become much more important in recent years.

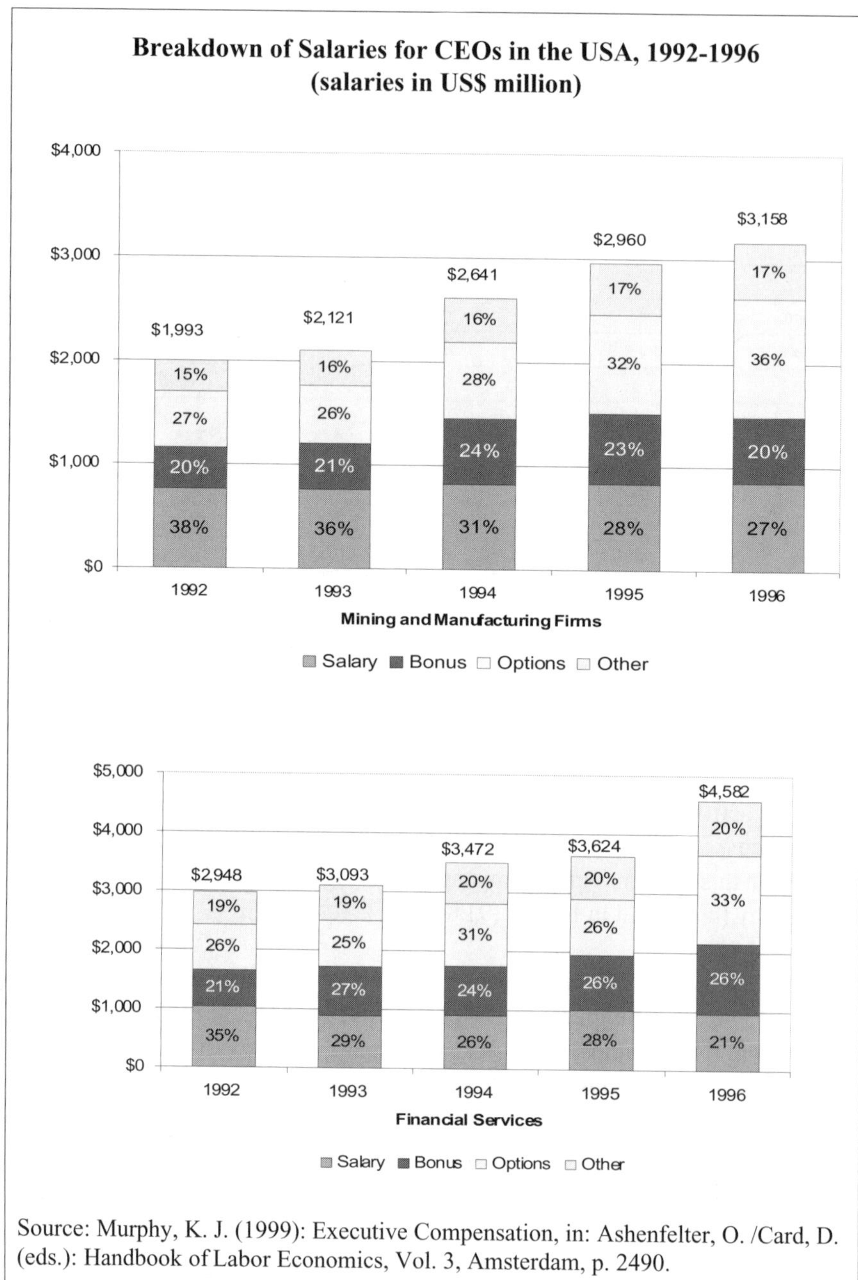

Source: Murphy, K. J. (1999): Executive Compensation, in: Ashenfelter, O. /Card, D. (eds.): Handbook of Labor Economics, Vol. 3, Amsterdam, p. 2490.

Figure 3-2

In mining and manufacturing industries, the percentage of total compensation accounted for by the fixed component fell between 1992 and 1996 from 38 to 27 percent, while the percentage accounted for by bonuses has stayed about the same, and the percentage accounted for by stock options has risen from 27 to 36 percent. The picture is similar for the financial sector, where the portion of overall compensation paid in the form of stock options has gone up from 26 to 33 percent.

One of the consequences of this trend is well known: management wages have increased dramatically, largely as a result of stock options. In Germany, for example, some managers now receive extremely handsome wages. In 1997, the head of Bertelsmann was paid a direct income of DM 7.5 million, while the heads of Volkswagen, BMW and Daimler were all paid between DM 3 million and DM 4.4 million (Manager Magazin 9/1998, p. 216-17). Although top German managers earn several million a year, their income pales in comparison to the wages paid to some American CEOs.

Table 3-3 shows the incomes earned by the top managers of ten widely known American companies in 1998. This list clearly demonstrates that the huge size of these incomes derives primarily from a specific form of performance-related pay, i.e. from the exercise of stock options. The average base salary of these managers is "only" $ 1.3 million per year, plus bonuses of $ 3.04 million per year. The average income of $ 76 million resulting from stock options is almost 60 times as high as the base salary and 25 times higher than the bonuses paid. Thanks to these stock options, some of these CEOs earned in excess of $ 100 million. The head of General Electric earned $ 261.5 million.

Given this explosion in management wages, it comes as no surprise that imbalances in income distribution have become significantly worse. Figure 3-3 shows the growing income imbalance in the United States. In 1970, a CEO earned 25 times as much as a production worker on average. 26 years later, in 1996, the average CEO earned about 75 times as much, if we only take base salaries and bonuses into account. But if we look at income including exercised stock options, the income differential reaches an almost incredible level. The ratio rises from a factor of 25 in 1970 to a factor of more than 210 (!) in 1996.

**Table 3-3:
Income of Top Managers in 1998
Selected Leading Companies in the USA**

Firm	CEO	Base salary in US$ million	Annual bonuses in US$ million	Profit from stock options at end-year in US$ million
American Express	Harvey Golub	1.02	2.40	59.9
AT&T	Michael Armstrong	1.40	1.90	26.67
Boeing	Phil Condit	1.00	0.00	2.63
Chevron	Kenneth Derr	1.28	1.19	22.33
Citigroup	Sandy Weill	1.03	8.50	4.70
Coca-Cola	Douglas Ivester	1.25	1.50	106.48
Disney	Michael Eisner	0.76	5.00	107.22
General Electric	Jack Welch	2.80	7.20	261.54
Johnson & Johnson	Ralph Larsen	1.33	1.30	66.84
Merck	Raymond Gilmartin	1.10	1.45	101.60
Average		**1.30**	**3.04**	**76.00**

Source: *The Economist*, "A Survey of Pay," May 8, 1999, p. 4.

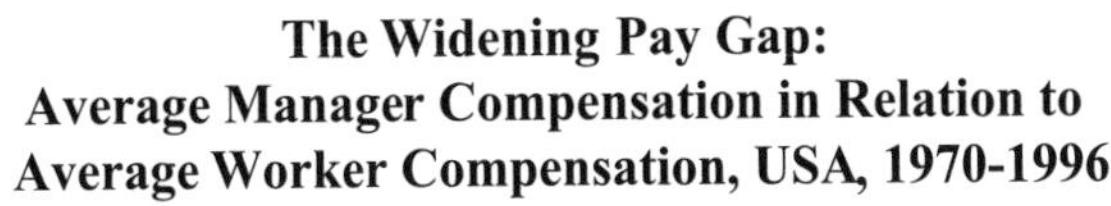

**The Widening Pay Gap:
Average Manager Compensation in Relation to
Average Worker Compensation, USA, 1970-1996**

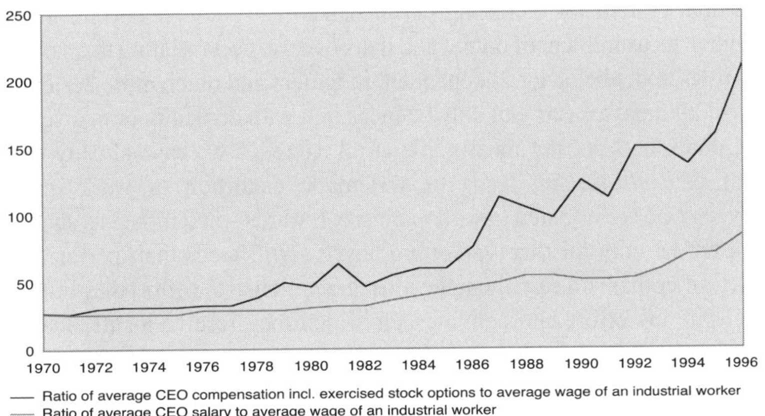

Source: Murphy, K. J. (1999): Executive Compensation, in: Ashenfelter, O. /Card, D. (eds.): Handbook of Labor Economics, Vol. 3, Amsterdam, p. 2553.

Figure 3-3

We can summarize as follows:

Economic theory, or more precisely the principal-agent theory, sees variable performance-related pay as the best way of motivating employees. This view is mirrored by actual practice; performance-related wages are being used more and more, and now form a significant component of many people's wages. Above all, stock options for managers have become very common, leading to an explosion in managerial compensation and to a dramatic increase in income inequality versus other employees.

2. When Do Wages Crowd Out Motivation and Reduce Performance?

The first thing to consider is whether wages can be adjusted to match *individual* performance. Except in the case of very simple activities, this requires a multi-dimensional system for recording performance that goes far beyond the purely quantitative measurement of output and that covers aspects relating to quality, innovation, role-model behavior, independent judgment and much more besides. Most of these additional aspects can only be measured with difficulty or to a very rough degree, and others are not measurable at all. Here, as we have already seen, the problem of *multi-tasking* leads to systematic distortion of work incentives. Employees who are oriented toward monetary rewards – and money is an incentive to work harder only for this type of employee – will focus their performance on those activities that will earn them the most in relation to the effort they put in. They will not put any effort into activities for which they receive insufficient, or no, monetary reward. Such behavior can lead to major problems within an organization.

Box 3-2 describes a case in which one activity (the quantity of goods sold) is well paid, while a second activity (satisfying the buyers' differing needs) is inadequately paid.

Employees will try to sell as many goods as possible even if these goods are not ideally suited to the buyers' needs. As a result, the company is likely to sell fewer goods in the long run, though this is not going to immediately bother the individual salespeople. However, the loss of potential future sales ultimately affects all salespeople, i.e. the general interest is compromised by "free-riding."

A company can, of course, make efforts to avoid the distortions produced by incorrectly set performance-related wages. This is certainly possible in the case of simple activities, but not in more complex cases. However, more complex tasks involving a whole range of aspects are the norm for companies in the modern economy. This is why there are clear limits to the use of performance-related wages.

In addition, it is often difficult to measure the *individual* performance of employees, because many activities are undertaken by a *team*. It is sometimes hard to know which team member contributed what. But teamwork is becoming increasingly important, especially in future-oriented industries. This is another reason why it does not necessarily make sense to use performance-related wages. If the employees involved perceive the attribution of performance input to be unfair, problems can quickly arise and the intrinsic motivation to work can be crowded out.

Box 3-2

Paying Salespeople

Payment by quantity of goods sold:

- Maximizes short-term sales

But ignores
- Customer satisfaction
- Identification of customer desires
- Communication of information
- Adherence to delivery schedules
- Repairs

While
- Reducing cooperation among salespeople
- Compromising inventory management, etc.

As a rule the bonuses and, even more so, the stock option plans that are so popular today cannot be regarded as individual performance-related wages. They are normally based on the overall performance of a division or even of the firm as a whole, and therefore do not reward individual effort (the principal-agent theory speaks of the 1/n-problem, where n is the number of recipients). Such compensation plans may improve employees' identification with the company and general work satisfaction – but this is by no means certain. In any case, such effects do not correspond to the behavior of homo oeconomicus, on which the whole idea of performance pay is founded.

In fact, empirical research has not found any connection between corporate success and performance-related pay. The cherished notion that the introduction of pay for performance raises productivity and earnings has been shown to be incorrect. The main empirical findings are summarized in Box 3-3.

Box 3-3

Management Compensation and Corporate Success:
Does Pay For Performance Increase Productivity and Earnings?

This question has been carefully analyzed by a large number of academic studies.

Findings suggest that:

1. In general there is only a weak link between management compensation and corporate success.
2. Where a (weak) positive link has been established, it is attributed to non-indexed stock options. Such plans do not, however, tend to qualify as performance-related compensation.

Source: Osterloh, M. (1999): Wertorientierte Unternehmensführung and Management-Anreizsysteme, in: Kumar, B. N. / Osterloh, M. / Schreyögg, G. (eds.): Unternehmensethik and die Transformation des Wettbewerbs, Stuttgart, pp. 183-204.

Only one serious study has found any relationship between performance-related pay and corporate success; but even here the relationship is only based on stock options. As we have already established, stock options are not normally given in response to individual performance but in response to the development of the whole company's earnings or stock market valuation (for more on stock options, see the detailed discussion in Chapter 4). This study cannot, therefore, be used as evidence for the effectiveness of pay for performance. In fact, the cause and effect is more likely to be the other way round, i.e. employees simply take a share of the profits that are generated. The higher the profits, the higher the wages, thus producing a positive statistical correlation between profits and wages. However, the profits are not high because performance-related wages are paid. In fact it is the other way round: the wages are high because the profits are high.

The results of the research yield the following two important conclusions with regard to the application of individual performance-related wages.

Performance-Related Wages Increase Productivity in the Case of Simple and Easily Measurable Activities

Box 3-4 describes the case of Safelite, the United State's largest windshield fitting company. Originally, this company paid its employees fixed hourly wages before switching to piece rates.

> Box 3-4
>
> **Effect of Piece Rates on a Simple Activity**
>
> The Safelite Company, headquartered in Columbus, Ohio, is the largest car windshield fitting company in the USA.
>
> In mid-1990 fixed hourly wages were replaced by piece rates (with a guaranteed minimum wage).
>
> Productivity improved by 44% as a result.
>
> Source: Lazear, E. P. (1999): Personnel Economics: Past Lessons and Future Directions, in: Journal of Labor Economics 17, pp. 199-236.

When this company introduced wages directly related to a worker's individual output – i.e. the number of windshields fitted – labor productivity rose by no less than 44 percent. The workers responded strongly to a well-designed performance-related wage plan suited to this type of easily measurable and one-dimensional activity.

Badly Designed Performance-Related Pay Plans Can Have Strongly Negative Effects

Employees are sensitive to the incentives given to them by their employers. Consequently, the company will also suffer if these incentives are set wrongly. History provides us with many examples of companies that have made mistakes in this area. Box 3-5 shows the negative effects of compensation systems at the Heinz Company and at Sears.

The cases discussed here particularly highlight the problem of "multi-tasking." Employees concentrate exclusively on activities for which they receive monetary reward and neglect those for which they receive no money.

Box 3-5

The Damaging Effect of a Badly Designed Performance-Related Pay Plan

H.J. Heinz Company only paid a bonus to managers in individual areas if they managed to improve their profits on the previous year. In response to this plan, managers manipulated profits so that they could always show a year-on-year improvement. They did this by delaying or accelerating deliveries to customers, thus securing payment for activities that had not actually been performed yet. Although in this way the managers were able to secure a pay raise for themselves, it also meant that the future flexibility of the company was severely restricted, thus reducing long-term growth and compromising the value of the company.

At Sears, a badly designed compensation system had even more critical consequences. Mechanics working for the company's car repair operation were paid according to the profits earned on repairs requested by customers. With this incentive in mind, the mechanics talked customers – with some success – into commissioning unnecessary repairs. When this dishonesty was exposed, the Californian authorities threatened to close down all the Sears car repair shops in the state. The company thus abandoned this type of performance-related compensation in 1992.

Sources:

Post, R. J. /Goodpaster, K. E. (1981): H.J. Heinz Company: The Administration of Policy, Harvard Business School Case No. 382-034.

Patterson, G. (1992): Distressed Shoppers, Disaffected Workers Prompt Service Stores to Alter Sales Commission, Wall Street Journal, June 1.

Baker, G./Gibbons, R./Murphy, K. J. (1994): Subjective Performance Measures in Optimal Incentive Contracts, in: Quarterly Journal of Economics 109 (4), pp. 1125-1156.

Incentive contracts can also have negative effects beyond the problem of "multitasking." Chapter 1 provided a detailed description of how intrinsic motivation to work can be crowded out if the relationship between employee and company is conditioned by a performance-related wage. Especially with more complex tasks within a company, pay for performance can thus prove counterproductive.

When the "crowding-out effect" becomes pronounced, the normal monetary incentive effect of the wage is overcompensated. In this case, the employees' performance in general deteriorates when performance-related pay is introduced. The crowding-out effect does not always apply in all circumstances. A monetary incentive in the form of a higher salary can improve performance if the recipient interprets the raise as a sign of support and respect. However, monetary incentives will reduce the willingness to work if they are seen as a sign of the company's controlling power.

The next section distinguishes between the type of person that sees a monetary incentive as supportive and whose motivation will be affected accordingly, and the type that sees it as controlling.

3. Different Types of People

One of the most important management tasks within an organization is to generate and maintain employee motivation appropriate to the tasks that have to be carried out by the employees. In doing this it is useful to distinguish between various types of employees.

Different individuals have different goals in life. They have different wishes and preferences and will therefore react in different ways to incentives imposed from the outside, and in particular to monetary rewards such as bonuses or piece-rate payments. Moreover, they differ with respect to the types of organizations they like to work in.

The dominant element of preference will determine the type of employee as defined in this section. Most people are interested in several goals simultaneously; but, in order to highlight the relationships involved as clearly as possible, we will look only at "ideal" types, i.e. people who concentrate exclusively on a single goal.

3.1 Extrinsically Motivated Employees

We can distinguish between two groups of employees who react primarily to external incentives: Income Maximizers and Status Seekers.

Income Maximizers

This type of person is only interested in earning money. Income Maximizers only derive an indirect benefit from the work itself and the money obtained. Monetary income serves to acquire the maximum quantity of goods and services for consumption. Work is regarded as an unpleasant inconvenience, and effort is expended solely in order to earn income.

The Income Maximizer is a prime example of "economic man" – i.e. of man as defined in economic theory. As mentioned earlier, this concept of the way people act has proven most successful. The concept of "homo oeconomicus" is well suited to the analysis of many aspects of human behavior and, as a key element in the rational choice approach, has also had a telling influence on other social sciences. According to this idea, humans react systematically to external incentives. In particular, they increase their work rate when compensated by a higher wage.

Status Seekers

This type of person is also extrinsically motivated. Status Seekers look to external factors and respond to the evaluation of other people. This type is not interested in consumption for its own sake, but derives benefit solely from comparisons with other people. Behavior is shaped by a concern for the opinion of a reference group composed of neighbors, friends, relatives, schoolmates, fellow students or work colleagues.

Status Seekers are competitive; they seek to set themselves above others in all respects. They are envious of other people's success. This element is particularly prevalent in small, closed communities where people are prepared to work for a position, status, title or other distinction. The term "positional goods" has been coined to describe these perceived benefits. The characteristics of positional goods are detailed in Box 3-6.

Status Seekers also cherish symbolic appreciation; they are therefore less materialistic than Income Maximizers.

Box 3-6

"Positional Goods"
The value of some goods lies simply in the fact that one owns them, while other people do not. If other people acquired them, these goods would lose their exclusivity and attraction.

Examples of such positional goods are titles and other professional distinctions, but also consumer goods such as "exclusive" brands of cars or television sets. If more of these goods become available as a result of economic growth, this kind of exclusivity can be destroyed – the benefit of owning these positional goods thus falls away. If positional goods increase in number, they stop being positional goods.

Goods which are by their very nature exclusive are, therefore, particularly desirable. A parking space close to the company's main entrance is a good example. Achieving such a positional good also clearly indicates the lowlier status of other employees.

3.2 Intrinsically Motivated Employees

There are three types of people whose desires are largely self-determined: Loyalists, Formalists and Autonomists.

Loyalists

These people identify personally with the goals of the organization they are working for. For the most part, their wishes coincide with those of the organization. This sort of utility function is often found among employees who have worked at a company for a long time.

Formalists

These employees have internalized the "right" procedures. Following these procedures has become part of their nature. This pattern can be found in some lawyers and civil servants, but also among technical professions and medical doctors, who are less concerned with the effect of their actions than with the question of whether the correct procedure has been followed. As long as the procedure is not affected, it is difficult to influence such persons with external incentives.

Autonomists

This type concentrates solely on his or her own non-material goals, caring little for other issues and persons. This includes people who want to improve the world in all sorts of ways, as well as those aspiring to self-fulfillment. These people want to reach goals and they use any means they consider correct to do so. This behavior is typical of the esoterically oriented, but also of many scientists and artists. Such persons are strongly intrinsically motivated and react little to outside interventions.

Box 3-7 summarizes the five employee types.

Box 3-7

Employee Types and Their Primary Goals

Extrinsically motivated

1. Income Maximizers	→	Monetary income
2. Status Seekers	→	Position

Intrinsically motivated

3. Loyalists	→	Identification with company goals
4. Formalists	→	Correct procedures
5. Autonomists	→	Pursuit of own ideology

4. Performance-Related Pay Increases Performance

Having defined these different employee types, we can now examine when performance-related pay might be considered an appropriate means of increasing performance in line with company wishes.

Pay for performance, in the sense of variable compensation precisely calibrated to the performance achieved by an individual employee, is certainly suitable for *Income Maximizers.* This type of employee meets all the requirements laid down by neoclassical economic theory and the principal-agent theory. Above all, the direction of causation is clear. A higher monetary incentive induces greater effort and performance because this is a means of increasing monetary income. The interests of employer and employee are made congruent.

Performance wages are best paid out as money (rather than in the form of fringe benefits such as the use of a company car), because money is more flexible: it can be used directly by Income Maximizers to pay for precisely the consumer goods and services they desire. Other forms of remuneration generate unnecessary transaction costs.

Performance-related pay requires a *precise attribution* of compensation to specific performance levels. The relationship between compensation and performance must be clear and must make sense to the employees. If this is not the case, employees will become dissatisfied and/or will start to manipulate the performance-related pay structure. In both cases employee motivation will be reduced and effort will be directed towards unproductive activities, thus reducing efficiency.

The need for precise attribution and full acknowledgement of all appropriate effort means that this system is only effective for *simple tasks,* such as the Safelite Company windshield fitting operation discussed in Box 3-4. The Safelite study also proved that the composition of the company's employees changed considerably once the piece-rate system had been introduced. The percentage of employees who were interested in piece rates, i.e. those that could be considered Income Maximizers, increased substantially.

Status Seekers can also be motivated to perform better by a performance-related wage, as long as this allows them to distinguish themselves from co-workers and other people outside the company. This is often the case. The great economist Joseph Schumpeter emphasized status differentiation – as opposed to size of income – as the main motivating factor for entrepreneurs. Indeed, entrepreneurs are the recipients of the most extreme version of performance-related remuneration: the difference between revenue and costs.

Performance-related wages paid to Status Seekers can differ from those paid to Income Maximizers. The actual *level* of wages has no effect on the performance of Status Seekers. Even if they earn less, Status Seekers will be motivated to work harder by a performance-related system, provided that the wages earned by members of their reference group fall even more.

This aspect is closely related to the tournament theory, which analyzes the incentive effects of career competition. Managers' compensation is seen as being linked to career levels; the compensation earned by a supervisor serves as an incentive for up-and-coming managers. This provides the basis for a theoretical argument that posits a decoupling of performance-related wages and performance. At lower career levels, compensation can be lower than the marginal productivity gain, because this activity is rewarded by an "entrance ticket" to further career levels. The value of this "option" for further advancement reduces as the employee moves up the career ladder. In order to maintain motivation at every career level, employees must therefore be given an additional incentive in the form of a higher salary.

Status Seekers (in contrast to Income Maximizers) do not have to be compensated with money alone. In many cases other types of compensation are even more effective than money because they more clearly indicate status. Such compensation may be in material form (such as a more spacious office or a parking space close to the main office entrance), or may be largely symbolic (selection as "employee of the month," for example). As far as many outsiders are concerned, such performance incentives can sometimes appear a little ridiculous; but they work well with Status Seekers. However, such compensation must be closely linked to *specific* performance goals – a requirement that is sometimes difficult to fulfill when using incentives such as a better office.

Summarizing, we may say pay for performance undoubtedly works well with income-maximizing employees. Nevertheless, a correct, motivation-enhancing application of performance-related pay is only possible in a very limited area, i.e. only where simple activities are involved. Such activities are, however, becoming less and less important to the modern economy. They certainly do not feature prominently in today's typical workplace. The normative proposal put forward by the principal-agent theory is correct – but of limited relevance to modern companies. For Status Seekers, the proposed monetary performance-related pay does encourage greater effort, but many useful alternatives in the form of non-material compensation can also be used to motivate such employees. Furthermore, the level of compensation does not influence Status Seekers' motivation to work.

5. Performance-Related Pay Reduces Performance

The relevant literature discusses various reasons why performance-related pay often fails to motivate employees to produce the desired performance. The major reasons identified are the practical problems of application that we have already discussed. If the performance is assessed incompletely (the "multi-task" problem) or incorrectly, the employees' incentives are distorted. The principal-agent theory thus deduces that *performance measurement* needs to be improved. If an unbiased quantitative measurement of all the relevant performance aspects proves impossible, one must turn to subjective evaluation. However, the principal-agent theory does not tell us how performance-related wages should be set.

The existence of the crowding-out effect leads to completely the *opposite* conclusion. Under certain empirically identifiable conditions, performance-related pay actually *reduces motivation.* In such a case, the motivation to work can be maintained and strengthened by *decoupling* compensation from the desired performance.

Box 3-8 describes a practical example from the American aircraft industry.

Box 3-8

Performance-Related Pay Is Inappropriate: Delayed Aircraft Departures, USA

Two different approaches can be taken to reducing delays in aircraft departures:

- The source of the errors is *identified precisely* and the responsible parties are punished.

In response, the employees concerned invest a great deal of energy and resources in passing the blame onto others.

- The *"whole team"* is made responsible.

As a consequence, there is a sharp reduction in delays – there are now far fewer delays than at other airlines.

Source: Austin, R. D. /Hoffer Gittell, J. (1999): Anomalies of High Performance: Reframing Economic and Organizational Theories of Performance Measurement, Harvard Business School, Harvard University.

This case deals with the problem of how managers should deal with delayed aircraft departures.

It would seem reasonable to first inquire who exactly is responsible for the delays. The employees concerned should be confronted with their shortcomings and made responsible for them. Their poor performance should be reflected in a wage cut. This approach would accord with the principal-agent theory because it attempts to link wages as closely as possible to individual performance. This is exactly the approach taken by the American airline industry. But it is only modestly, if at all, successful. Singling out particular employees as the "guilty parties" results in a defensive attitude – especially since salary levels are at stake. Employees thus spend a lot of time and effort on pinning the blame for delays on others. They also make sure right from the start that any possible delays can be attributed to someone else's actions.

However, one airline decided to adopt a completely different strategy. Delays were declared to be a problem for *all* employees, and therefore *all* of them were asked to seek improvements. Responsibility for shortcomings was thus attributed to the team as a whole. This strategy has turned out to be very successful and delays have been reduced to a considerable degree. They are now much less frequent than at comparable airlines.

In the case of the three intrinsically motivated types of employees, pay for performance does not raise performance, and it can often reduce it.

Loyalists

Loyalty cannot be bought; it is a result of intrinsic motivation. Loyal employees interpret strictly performance-related pay as a signal that the company considers their work to be inadequate. Such an intervention is perceived as being damaging to self-respect, and as such it undermines the intrinsic motivation to work. Well-managed companies are aware of this problem and shy away from subjecting long-serving employees to a performance-related pay plan. Empirical research confirms that the longer a manager works for a business, the less his or her salary is determined by individual or company performance.

Formalists

For people who attach great importance to correct procedures, performance-related pay tends to be counterproductive. Such employees carry out their work correctly and appropriately out of an inner conviction. If a performance-related plan is introduced, they might start to feel that the company thinks that they are not doing their work properly, i.e. they will see the plan as an unwelcome controlling intervention, and their intrinsic motivation to work will suffer.

Autonomists

People who see work as part of their self-fulfillment very quickly lose their intrinsic motivation to work when subjected to performance-related pay. Their very concept of work is put in doubt, which can reduce or even destroy their intrinsic motivation. Many artists and scientists see self-determined activity as essential, and this way of thinking is not compatible with a wage that is paid for a specific performance determined from the outside. Indeed, a performance-related wage is counterproductive for artists and scientists because it reduces or even destroys their creativity. This conclusion is well supported by the life histories of great artists and scientists. Psychological researchers have gathered much evidence to suggest that intrinsic motivation is fundamental to creative performance.

Thus we see that performance-related pay only leads to increased performance in the case of Income Maximizers (and only then if simple tasks are involved). Pay for performance is less well suited to Status Seekers; and with loyal, formal and autonomous employees, performance-related pay actually reduces performance because of the crowding-out effect.

We have to remember that the typical employees described here do not actually exist in this pure form in reality. Elements of all these types can be found to widely varying degrees in most people. Pay for performance is thus not very well suited to improving performance if employees are intrinsically motivated and want to earn an income. Conversely, a carefully calibrated performance-related wage can minimize loss of performance among employees who are otherwise intrinsically motivated.

6. Motivation Beyond Wages

Employees must, of course, be paid. People have to earn at least as much as they need to maintain their standard of living. This principle is just as true for non-profit organizations, such as monasteries and charities, as it is for commercial enterprises. The question, though, is how far compensation should be used as a motivator for specific individual accomplishments in the way envisaged by the performance-related pay concept. We should acknowledge that there is a broad spectrum of alternative forms of motivation above and beyond wages. Today, however, there is no doubt that wages are all too often the only aspect considered.

We will now look at four alternative forms of motivation. They are actually quite well known, even if they are rather neglected today. Box 3-9 gives an overview of the motivators to be discussed.

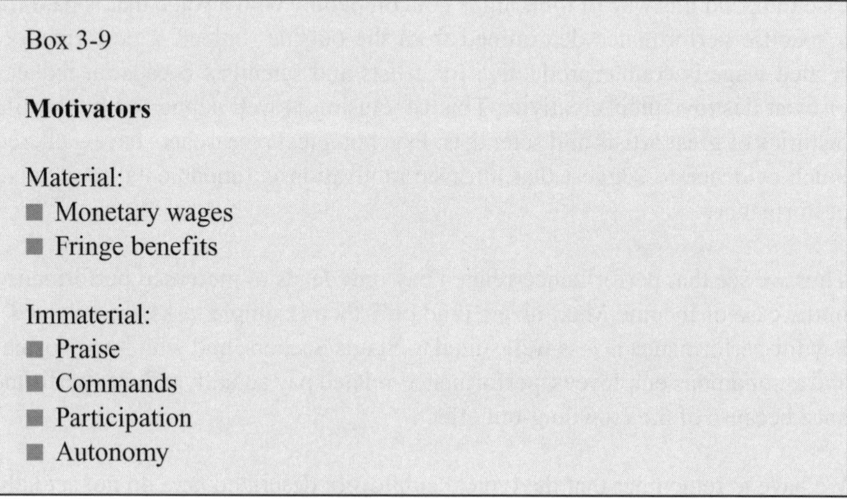

Box 3-9

Motivators

Material:
- Monetary wages
- Fringe benefits

Immaterial:
- Praise
- Commands
- Participation
- Autonomy

The first two immaterial motivators, praise and commands, are addressed specifically to each individual employee.

1. Praise:

Many organizations use praise extensively to motivate employees. Praise may take many different forms. Ceremonies are held to honor particular workers or departments, citations – such as "employee of the month" – are awarded, and incentive travel and other gifts are offered. As long as praise is perceived as supporting an employee's sense of personal worth, it can bolster intrinsic motivation and willingness to perform. But praise can also be perceived as controlling when it is not given in earnest. It also loses its motivating effect if it is taken for granted.

Status Seekers respond in a strongly positive way to this kind of appreciation because it sets them above others. Their motivation and performance are improved. Loyalists are also responsive to praise because it emphasizes the special relationship to "their" organization. By contrast, Income Maximizers reject praise because they "can't buy anything with it." Autonomists also react negatively because they can easily perceive praise as an attempt to absorb them into the organization. Formalists are not much impressed by praise as they are "only doing their duty." With these last three employee types, the motivation to work is reduced and the crowding-out effect comes into play.

2. Command:

Hierarchical organizations are founded upon *commands* and upon *sanctions* that are imposed if the commands are not followed. Commands (just like performance-related wages) constitute an outside intervention, which is perceived to be controlling and which can therefore crowd out intrinsic motivation. But commands can have very different effects depending on the type of employee involved. Income Maximizers and Status Seekers, but also Loyalists and Autonomists, see commands as a controlling restriction of their opportunities for self-determination – an obstacle to the achievement of their goals. For these types of persons, commands crowd out intrinsic motivation. As with monetary incentives, however, the countervailing incentive effect must also be taken into account. The net effect on performance is thus hard to assess. Autonomists and Income Maximizers in particular interpret commands as controlling, meaning that crowding out and reduced performance are likely to be particularly pronounced with these employee types.

Formalists, on the other hand, do not see commands as restrictive, but welcome them as a helpful guide. With this type of employee, commands can lead to improved performance.

Box 3-10 describes an empirical analysis of 116 medium-sized Dutch companies. The analysis shows that even in profit-oriented companies, where one would expect to find a high proportion of Income Maximizers, the exact nature of the command relationship is of considerable importance.

Box 3-10

The Counterproductive Effect of Tight Controls
An econometric study investigated the behavior of 116 managers in mid-sized Dutch businesses with between 100 and 30,000 employees in 1986. The companies came from various branches of industry.

Type of control exerted on manager		*Effect on effort (hours worked)*
■ Impersonal, less intensive control through parent company	→	Significantly *positive*
■ Impersonal control through board of directors	→	No significant difference
■ Personal control through CEO	→	Significantly *negative*

Source: Barkema, H. G. (1995): Do Executives Work Harder When They Are Monitored? In: Kyklos 48, pp. 19-42.

By contrast with the two forms of motivation described above, the following two motivators are applied generally across a workforce rather than to each individual employee.

3. Participation:

With this form of motivation, employees from different levels of an organization discuss the goals to be achieved and the means to be used, and, to a certain extent, they take decisions jointly.

Autonomists can be motivated by such a system because they feel that their own goals are being taken seriously. Income Maximizers (and also some Status Seekers) view such discussions as superfluous or even as a waste of time because these types are extrinsically motivated and not interested in the work itself. Empirical research shows that participation raises intrinsic motivation because it bolsters perceived self-determination (see also the detailed discussion of participation as a motivating instrument in Chapter 8). As Box 3-11 shows, in the world of politics the institutionalized participation that is central to Switzerland's direct democracy (popular initiatives and referenda) raises intrinsic motivation in the form of civic pride. This greater sense of belonging manifests itself in, among other things, a lower level of tax evasion.

Box 3-11

Effect of Participation in the Political Process

The 26 Swiss cantons involve their citizens to varying degrees in the process of government decision-making. According to an econometric study, the greater the opportunity people have for direct co-determination on real issues (through popular initiatives and referenda), the greater the identification with the state, and the lower the level of tax evasion.

Source: Frey, B. S. (1997b): A Constitution for Knaves Crowds Out Civic Virtues, in: Economic Journal 107, pp. 1043-1053.

4. Autonomy:

Employees may be given plenty of scope to make their own decisions, the expectation being that they will make these decisions in the interests of the organization. For Loyalists such freedom is essential if their motivation is to be maintained and increased. By contrast, this kind of autonomy is inappropriate for extrinsically motivated Income Maximizers and Status Seekers, but also for Formalists, because of their lack of focus on the organization's goals.

The four forms of performance motivation discussed here affect the various types of employees in different ways. While the different responses to pay for performance are largely determined by whether an employee is extrinsically or intrinsically motivated, responses to praise, commands, participation and autonomy are completely different. Thus, for example, extrinsically motivated Income Maximizers as well as intrinsically motivated Autonomists react negatively to praise and tend to reduce their efforts accordingly.

Box 3-12 gives an overview of the expected effects of the various forms of motivation on employee performance.

Box 3-12

The Effect of Different Forms of Motivation

Form of motivation	*Dominant influence on performance*	
	Crowds out	Crowds in
(A) Praise	• Income Maximizers • Autonomists	• Status Seekers • Loyalists
(B) Commands	• Income Maximizers • Status Seekers • Loyalists • Autonomists	• Formalists
(C) Participation	• Income Maximizers	• Autonomists
(D) Autonomy	• Income Maximizers • Status Seekers	• Loyalists

7. Outlook

Variable pay for performance *can* increase employees' performance, but this only happens in *very limited circumstances.* Two prerequisites are particularly important:

1. The activity concerned has to be simple and easy to measure. If the performance achieved by an employee is incorrectly recorded or attributed, the incentive effect is distorted. This makes the activity less valuable, or even damaging, for the company.

2. Employees have to be motivated in such a way that extrinsic incentives actually do encourage greater effort. This is the case with people who are only interested, or primarily interested, in monetary income and, possibly, social status. People who are motivated in a different way, especially those who feel a loyalty towards "their" company, or who are concerned about following correct procedures, or who want their work to provide them with self-fulfill-

ment, tend not to respond well to a variable performance-related wage, because it undermines their intrinsic motivation. One of the foundations of high productivity, especially in the case of complex tasks, is thus removed. Within a modern, knowledge-based economy it is vital that employees show commitment and think and act in the best interests of their company. However, these qualities cannot be measured directly, meaning that the intrinsic motivation of employees has to be taken on trust.

Consequently, management has to recruit the right kind of people as employees. "Management by motivation" does not just mean achieving the appropriate combination of extrinsic and intrinsic motivation among current employees, but also selecting the types of people who are best suited to the work done at the company. This is not an easy job, since it is difficult to identify the various different types. Apart from anything else, the potential recruitees can try to pass themselves off as a different type if they think that doing so will improve their conditions of employment. An applicant who is perfectly capable of loyalty might thus present himself as an Income Maximizer in order to push up his wage offer. However, corporate managements can use a whole range of techniques to correctly evaluate job candidates. These include assessment centers, but also, perhaps more importantly, the experience they have gained over time in dealing with employees.

It is clear from the points that we have discussed that managements should avoid using remuneration as the sole or even the main incentive to perform. Obviously they have to pay competitive wages if they want to attract suitable people, but these wages should never be the only form of reward. Unfortunately, however, this often seems to be the case these days. One of the most important tasks facing corporate managements is to add appropriate doses of praise, commands, participation and autonomy to the mix. In doing this, they should pay due attention to both extrinsic and intrinsic motivation.

8. Further Reading

The state of economic theory with regard to companies and the principal-agent theory is discussed in:

Gibbons, R. (1998): Incentives in Organizations, in: Journal of Economic Perspectives 12, pp 115-132.

Prendergast, C. (1999): The Provision of Incentives in Firms, in: Journal of Economic Literature 37 (1), pp 7-63.

For the empirical link between performance-related pay and corporate success:

Murphy, K. J. (1999): Executive Compensation, in: Ashenfelter, O./Card, D. (eds.): Handbook of Labor Economics, vol 3, Amsterdam, pp 2485-2563.

Osterloh, M. (1999): Wertorientierte Unternehmensführung and Management-Anreizsysteme, in: Kumar, B. N./Osterloh, M./Schreyögg, G. (eds.): Unternehmensethik and die Transformation des Wettbewerbs, Stuttgart, pp 183-204.

Backes-Gellner, U./Geil, L. (1997): Managervergütung and Unternehmenserfolg – Stand der theoretischen and empirischen Forschung, in: WISU, vol 5, pp 468-475.

Two articles in *The Economist* are also useful and very informative:

The Economist. “A Survey of Pay: The Best ... and the Rest.” May 8, 1999.

The Economist. “The Trouble With Share Options.” August 7, 1999.

The study of wage systems at Safelite, which is referred to here several times, is presented in:

Lazear, E. P. (1999): Personnel Economics: Past Lessons and Future Directions, in: Journal of Labor Economics 17, pp 199-236.

The effect of allocating responsibility in the airline industry is investigated in:

Austin, R. D./Hoffer Gittell, J. (1999): Anomalies of High Performance: Reframing Economic and Organizational Theories of Performance Measurement, Harvard Business School, Harvard University.

The influence of different forms of supervision on managers’ performance is subjected to econometric analysis in:

Barkema, H. G. (1995): Do Executives Work Harder When They Are Monitored?, in: Kyklos 48, pp 19-42.

Chapter Four

MATTHIAS BENZ, MARCEL KUCHER
AND ALOIS STUTZER

Stock Options for Top Managers – The Possibilities and Limitations of a Motivational Tool

Introduction

Relying solely on extrinsic motivational incentives creates both problems and unintentional results. This chapter will demonstrate this, using the example of stock options for top managers. The widespread practice of granting stock options is based on the idea that managers will thus be motivated to gear their interest and activities toward increasing the value of their company. Until now, this connection has been hard to document. In our empirical research, we find that stock options moreover have an unintentional negative impact. They enable top-level managers who are not sufficiently supervised to amass large incomes at the owners' expense. Stock options allow managers to act in a selfish manner and may even encourage such behavior. Therefore, the complex task of motivating managers cannot be reduced to simple extrinsic incentives. On the contrary, new, alternative motivational tools should be actively sought out.

The belief that external incentives should be used to motivate managers dominates the current discussion of management motivation. It is very closely related to the recommendation that performance-based salaries should increasingly be paid out in the form of stock options. Most management consultants and economists agree that this is a motivational tool capable of encouraging managers to take a keen interest in the value of their company.

In this chapter, we demonstrate that stock options cannot live up to these high expectations. What's more, they produce side effects that are unexpected. Based on a study of the 500 largest companies in America, we show that stock options have enabled top managers to amass large incomes. This is the more so, the less supervised managers are. For example, where the board of directors and management overlap, senior managers are better placed to sway salary decisions in their favor.

Our study focuses on compensation for top-level managers, which has been the prime topic of discussion with regard to performance-related pay. The results we present can only be partially applied to lower management levels. Generally, it is only top managers who have the opportunity to lobby for better compensation. We will show that the more opportunity managers have in this respect, the greater the dysfunctional effect of stock options. However, we do not assume that top managers are exclusively motivated by extrinsic values. Without a doubt, they do possess a significant amount of intrinsic motivation to do their job. Even so, by promoting the use of stock options, the monetary aspect of the relationship between a company and its managers is intensified, which affords managers the opportunity to act selfishly, and might even encourage such behavior.

1. Extrinsic Incentives and Management Motivation

Motivating managers is a challenging task. How should companies go about fostering entrepreneurial spirit, or at least encouraging the type of behavior advantageous to the company, if managers rarely exhibit the traits of the classic entrepreneur?

In order to analyze this question, economic theory focuses on the distinction between the shareholders who own the company (principals) and the company's management (agents). The approach championed by principal-agent theory is explained in detail in Box 3-1 in Chapter 3. It implies that the interests of the two parties generally do not correspond. The owners or shareholders are primarily interested in a high company value, while the managers often pursue their own interests, which can be in direct conflict with this objective. For example, large corporations operating in prestigious sectors of the economy are not necessarily successful. The desire for status achieved through corporate takeovers or the construction of a business empire often means lower returns for shareholders. The contrast between shareholders and managers creates no problems as long as the principal is able to easily supervise the agent. If, however, the shareholders only hold a very small percentage of the outstanding shares, as is generally the case with publicly held corporations, they have neither the opportunity nor the incentive to deter managers from pursuing their own personal objectives. Principal-agent theory suggests that the solution to this supervision and incentive problem is to cast managers in the role of shareholders as far as possible. This can be achieved by paying senior managers in stocks and stock options.

2. The Structure and Level of Managers' Salaries

Most management consultants and economists recommend that stock options be used to direct managers' attention to the value of the company. This recommendation has fostered an income trend which has turned many a top manager into a top earner. Several examples are given in Table 3-3 in Chapter 3. Stock options are responsible for the massive increase in managers' incomes over the past few years and also for the growing gap between managers' salaries and those of the average employee (see Chapter 3). Box 4-1 shows the general development for an average company, in several major industrialized countries and in different years. These figures clearly demonstrate that managers in the United States have benefited the most from higher compensation.

Box 4-1

The Evolution of Total Compensation Packages for Top Managers in 5 OECD Countries, 1984-1996

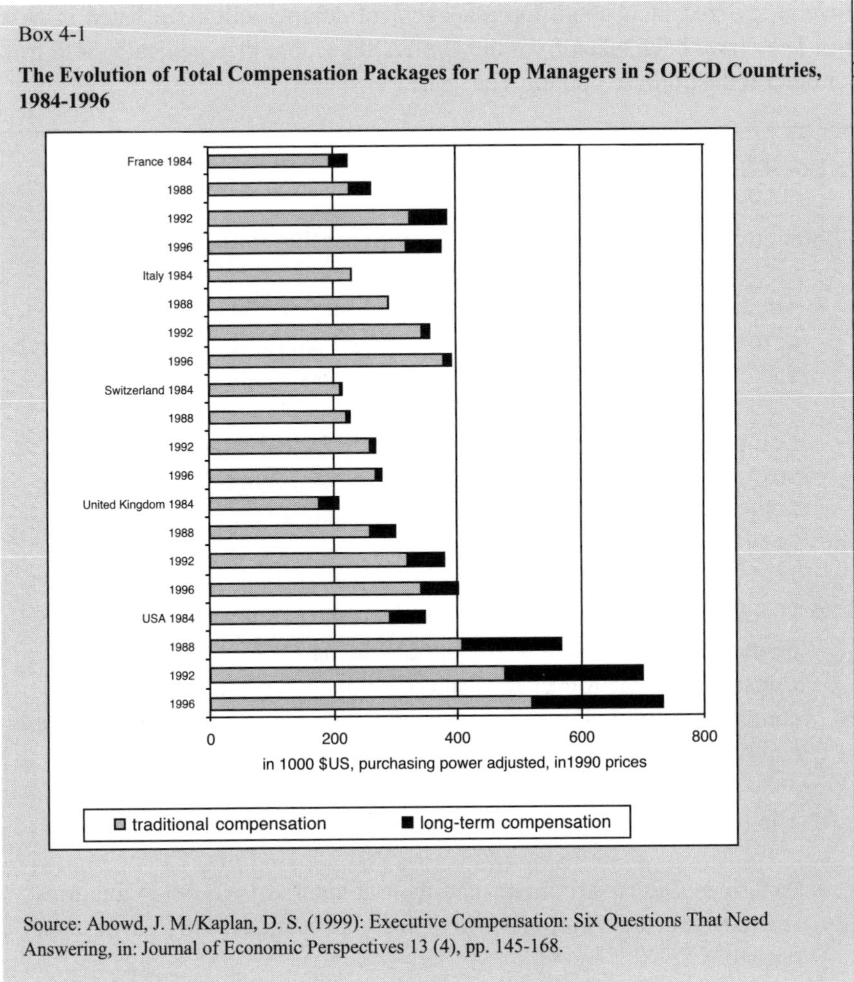

Source: Abowd, J. M./Kaplan, D. S. (1999): Executive Compensation: Six Questions That Need Answering, in: Journal of Economic Perspectives 13 (4), pp. 145-168.

Managers' compensation is comprised of several other components in addition to stock options. Generally a distinction is made between base salary, annual bonus, other benefits and long-term compensation, with the latter usually composed of stock options, blocked shares and stock plans. The base salary is defined as monetary compensation determined at the beginning of an annual compensation cycle. Bonuses are determined at the end of the cycle and paid out in cash. They are linked to a manager's performance, which in most cases is measured in financial terms. Benefits correspond to the company's expenses for pension plans, health insurance premiums and other fringe benefits. They are usually included as annualized current value in the calculation of total compensation, as is long-term compensation.

Several stylized facts about top management compensation are listed in Box 4-2. They have been taken from the United States, but they generally hold true for other industrialized countries as well.

Box 4-2

Structure and Level of Executive Compensation in the U.S.A.

- The salary level of CEOs differs from industry to industry. Top managers in the financial services sector earn more than those in manufacturing and even more than those in utility companies.
- Compensation for top managers increased by leaps and bounds in the 90s. The average salary for a CEO (1996 prices) in the manufacturing industry rose by 55% from 2 million dollars in 1992 to almost 3.2 million in 1996.
- Higher salaries are largely due to the increased number of stock options granted (with the value of the options being measured at grant date). Consultants Pearl Meyer & Partners estimate that the 200 largest U.S. companies promised stocks and stock options in incentive plans at the end of 1998 amounting to 13.2% of their share capital.
- The larger the company, the higher the CEO's compensation.
- American CEOs earn more than their counterparts in other countries and receive a larger proportion of their compensation in the form of stock options.

Obviously, stock options are of primary importance both for the salary structure (proportion of variable remuneration) as well as for the high level of compensation. Can these observations be interpreted as a breakthrough for shareholder interests? Do stock option grants make for a more successful business?

3. The Relationship Between Management Compensation and a Company's Success

On the basis of the principal-agent theory (see above), the impact of stock and stock option plans at the highest managerial level on a company's success has been analyzed in a great number of studies. A list of related literature is given at the end of the chapter. These studies focus on the relationship between the amount of compensation managers receive and shareholder returns. Early studies only established a weak correlation. In 1987, an increase of US$ 1,000 in shareholder wealth was associated with an increase in CEO wealth of only US$ 3.25. The authors concluded that CEO salary policies contained too few incentives to be compatible with principal-agent theory. Actually, these results can be attributed to the fact that only few CEOs owned stocks at the time the study was conducted. In the 90s, this changed dramatically. Calculations for 1994 thus show a much larger correlation between pay and performance – US$ 1,000 in additional shareholder wealth meant an increase in the average CEO's wealth of US$ 25.11.

In addition to these studies which focus on the entire compensation package, numerous researchers have also conducted detailed analyses of the impact of stock options on stock returns. Several of them have found correlations between such financial incentives and stock returns.

None of these studies, however, provides any insight into the actual impact of stock options. Even if a positive relationship between stock options and company value can be established based on these facts, it still remains unclear as to how it should be interpreted. Do stock options truly provide a greater incentive to improve performance, reflected in higher stock returns or additional shareholder wealth? Or does this connection simply mean that successful companies offer their top managers better compensation? There is a great deal of evidence in favor of the latter interpretation.

An increase in a company's stock price, which boosts the value of top-level managers' stock options, is more often a result of outside factors rather than management's efforts. For example, it was economic growth in the United States in the 90s which was primarily responsible for the booming stock market. In addition, companies try to influence their own share prices. Company executives who own a large number of stock options may for example decide to retire shares, which are bought on the stock market with company money in order to support ailing share prices. Furthermore, the correlation between success on the stock market and the value of stock options can result in a self-fulfilling prophecy. According to a large-scale survey by the consultants Pearl Meyer & Partners, financial analysts often include in their assessments the compensation schemes applied to the top executive level. Stock option plans are positively reflected in the analysts' suggestions to investors. The introduction of a stock option plan can be interpreted as a signal for the management's belief in bright prospects. Stock prices can also rise when dividends are cut. It has been shown that the more stock options managers receive as compensation, the lower the dividends a company distributes (Lambert, Lanen and Larcker 1989).

As the examples mentioned above demonstrate, it is difficult to show by means of capital market data whether or not stock options work as incentives that make managers care more for their company's success. There are, however, other weighty arguments that militate against strong motivational effects. First and foremost is the assertion that results, i.e. changes in company value, cannot be attributed to individual managers. Corporate earnings are usually achieved by the joint efforts of a large number of key players. According to the assumptions of the principal-agent theory, which the stock option proposition is based upon, one would expect individual managers to free-ride to a certain extent in precisely these situations. Managers may devote less time to transferring their experience and knowledge to other members of the team, for example. Thus, there is justifiable skepticism as to whether stock options actually provide any motivation whatsoever when company success is to some extent a public good. Moreover, the motivational effect of stock options may be totally lost on some managers. With a suitable hedging strategy, they may largely free themselves of corporate risk. In the United States, there is evidence that managers use comprehensive derivative financial instruments to hedge against bad news from their own company.

The previous arguments question the disciplinary impact of stock option plans on managers and demonstrate that it is a very fragile empirical basis indeed upon which the justification of option-based incentive mechanisms is founded. Kevin J. Murphy, a leading economist in the field of management compensation and advocate of incentive-oriented tools remarks,

"Although there is ample evidence that CEOs (and other employees) respond predictably to dysfunctional compensation arrangements, it is more difficult to document that the increase in stock-based incentives has led CEOs to work harder, smarter, and more in the interest of shareholders" (Murphy 1999, p. 2555).

The question then remains why, in the face of such evidence, stock options have gained such prominence.

4. Managers' Interest in Stock Options

Stock options have taken on such importance in the last few years because *they are in the best interest of top managers.* Wherever possible, managers will opt to receive a greater proportion of their pay in the form of share options. This reflects management's natural interest in higher compensation.

This view diametrically opposes that of the principal-agent theory, which finds that, as an instrument of discipline, share options run contrary to the interests of management. The principal-agent theory assumes that managers are risk averse, which means that, all other things being equal (and given the same total compensation in particular), they would prefer a fixed income because this reduces their exposure to pay fluctuation. Therefore, they are only interested in having as few stock options as possible as a component of their total income.

In reality, however, such conditions rarely exist. Stock options are seldom a substitute for a given percentage of managers' base salaries, but rather a top-up. Thus, senior managers can generally only benefit from the introduction of share options. The sharp rise in managerial salaries in the United States which we mentioned at the beginning of this chapter is largely based on the additional earnings made possible by the introduction of stock option plans.

Even if the stock market does not continue its strong upward trend, this presents little risk for managers. In reality, managers hardly ever face downside risks; thus stock options are a relatively riskless way of increasing total compensation. They can hedge against falling share prices or heavy risks with suitable derivative financial instruments. In other cases, the companies themselves implement risk minimization measures. The widespread practice of "repricing" means that the strike price for an option is often subsequently lowered if the share price fails to catch up to the strike price. However, this makes a mockery of the notion of putting top managers in the shareholders' shoes via stock options. As the influential business journal "The Economist" (August 7, 1999, p. 20) puts it, "[...] the fact that firms reprice managers' options reduces to nonsense the comparison of bosses with owners, who cannot write off downside risk so blithely."

Further evidence of the advantages of stock options for top-level managers can be found in the lobbying activities employed by American companies in 1995 to prevent the introduction of new accounting standards. The proposed new standard was to offset the cost of option plans against companies' profits. However, the lobbyists vehemently and successfully opposed such transparency. A study by Smithers & Co. for 1998 shows that on average reported corporate earnings are as much as 50% too high once liabilities with regard to option plans are offset against profits. Stock options are still not included in the balance sheet, which makes it all the easier for top managers to earn additional income without attracting undue attention. Stock options also offer certain tax advantages.

All the reasons outlined above suggest that managers have an interest in the introduction of (additional) stock options. We can assume that they will pursue this interest provided no obstacles are put in their way.

Does this paint a negative picture of top managers? We would argue it does not, as it simply assumes that senior managers would prefer an increase in their salary as opposed to a decrease. This assumption is likely to apply to all employees. Top managers are, however, in a better position to influence their salary than their non-managerial counterparts. The extent to which they are actually able to exert this influence depends very much on the constraints imposed upon them.

5. How Many Stock Options Per Manager? The Influence of the Management Environment

The most important constraints on top-level managers exist in the management environment, which takes into consideration the fact that management does not act in isolation, but is part of a multi-layered environment. Various institutional conditions act as controls and constraints on managers' behavior. We will focus on three central aspects:

- The board of directors as a direct instrument of management control
- The shareholders as an additional instrument of management control
- Competitive pressure on the main product market as a constraint imposed by the market

5.1 The Role of the Board of Directors

As representatives of the shareholders, the board of directors controls management and generally determines managers' compensation[1]. Various studies have examined how the different characteristics of a board affect the type and amount of compensation for managers. One of the more recent studies is presented in Box 4-3.

Box 4-3

Structure of the Board of Directors and Management Compensation
The composition of the board of directors has a considerable impact on the type and amount of compensation managers receive. Corporate governance structures which do little to limit the managers' leeway lead to significantly higher managerial salaries and to a larger percentage of performance-related pay. This is the case when the CEO is also the chairman of the board of directors. The larger the board is, the more external directors are appointed by the CEO, and the more "grey directors" are on the board (who themselves or whose employers receive payments from the company over and above their salary as a member of the board).

Source: Core, J. E. et al. (1999): Corporate governance, chief executive officer compensation, and firm performance, in: Journal of Financial Economics 51, pp. 371-406.

Any dual representation of persons in management and on the board of directors weakens the board's control function. Managers who also sit on the board are, in effect, responsible for controlling themselves. This gives them greater scope to sway decisions in their favor. Thus the following hypothesis can be deduced.

Hypothesis 1:

The value of stock options granted to managers increases if they are also a member of their own board.

---

1 In the U.S.A., this function is performed by compensation committees. Part of the board of directors, these committees are comprised solely of external board members and have the task of making proposals for salary policies for approval by the entire board. When determining management salaries, very informal processes often play an important role in the decision. Salary recommendations which have been previously sent to top management for review and approval are usually submitted to the remuneration committee by the Human Resources department. Senior management, Human Resources, the remuneration committee and the board make many compromises and carry out negotiations which may result in the creation of compensation plans that are in the best interest of management. Exactly this process is illustrated by an interview with Alex Krauer, the Chairman of the Board of Directors of UBS, a large Swiss Bank, in the *Neue Zürcher Zeitung* on April 15, 2000. "It is a package comprising one-third stocks, blocked for five years, one-third cash and one-third options, blocked for three years. I receive suggestions from the CEO. Then we discuss them in the Compensation Committee, which is limited to the top echelons of the company. The committee also decides for the board, with the persons concerned automatically being excluded from the voting."

5.2 The Influence of Shareholder Concentration

Which shareholder structure offers the most control over a company's management? A wide distribution of shares or a single major shareholder? Recent research on the subject suggests that the answer is not clear-cut: neither of the two situations is ideal. Dispersed ownership with a low degree of share concentration cannot ensure effective supervision due to the "public good" problem. None of the minor shareholders has sufficient incentive to participate in the supervision process, and the interests of these dispersed shareholders are difficult to coordinate. On the other hand, for one or more major shareholders (higher concentration level), effective supervision is worthwhile as it has a direct bearing on the value of their stocks. This incentive to supervise, however, is offset by an *entrenchment effect.* Major shareholders can join forces with management or appoint their preferred candidates to managerial positions in order to profit from the company other than through increased share value. For example, they might induce the company to pump large sums of money into causes close to their heart such as sponsoring sports or cultural events, or have the company pay excessive amounts for goods or services provided by other companies in which the major shareholders have a controlling interest. Finally, a major shareholder may grant certain managers excessive compensation in exchange for the implementation of that shareholder's own visions and ideas.

Thus, the higher the concentration of shares, the greater the incentive for individual shareholders to engage in management supervision. At the same time, however, the countervailing entrenchment effect also increases, which results in weakened supervision. From a specific level of concentration onwards, this entrenchment effect may even predominate. The chart below provides a graphical description of this hypothesis (see Figure 4-1).

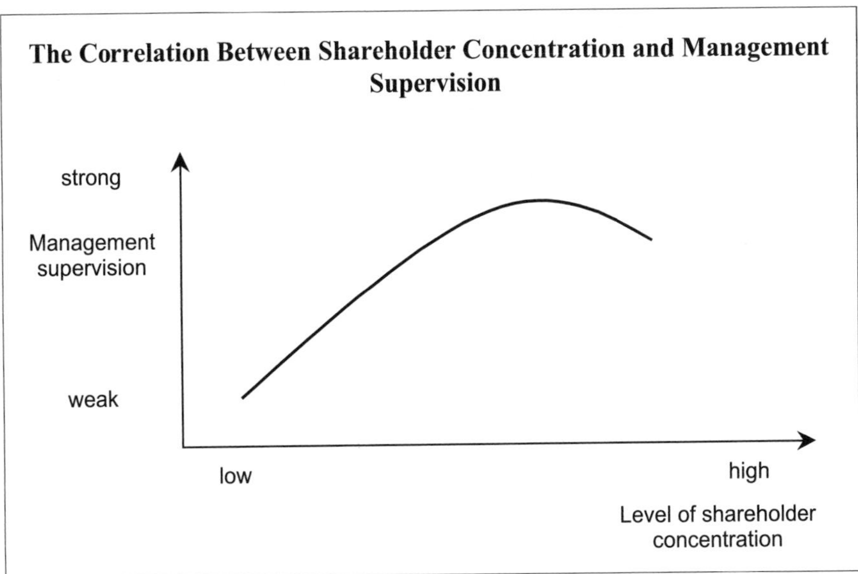

Figure 4-1

Stricter supervision by the shareholders results in managers having less power to promote their interests. Thus it follows that top managers' newly acquired stock options decrease in value. Figure 4-2 demonstrates the correlation between the level of shareholder concentration and the value of stock options granted (the curve is the exact opposite of Figure 4-1).

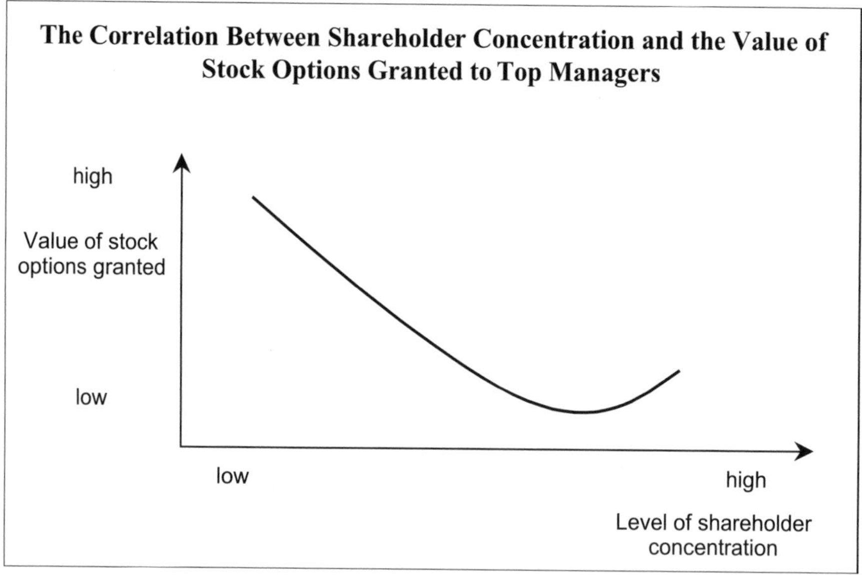

Figure 4-2

The hypothesis in this case can be summarized as follows.

> Hypothesis 2:
>
> The higher the concentration of shareholders in a company, the lower the value of stock options top managers receive as compensation. This may change at a certain concentration level if the entrenchment effect predominates.

5.3 Competitive Pressure in the Main Product Market

The influence of the market environment on managers' compensation has not been intensively researched in the past. Yet the competitive situation in a company's main market assuredly represents one of the greatest constraints on management. Tough competition not only forces management to take more notice of consumer wishes, it also requires that management find ways of making production more cost-effective. Managers subjected to fierce competition find it more difficult to pursue matters of self-interest than a management in a monopoly situation. Therefore, it is to be expected that managers of companies facing intense competition will receive fewer stock options because otherwise the competitiveness of the company would be reduced.

However, a countervailing effect could very well weaken the correlation in this situation too. Companies in highly competitive markets rely on talented managers, since they alone are in a position to ensure success in a complex and challenging environment. However, top-flight managers require greater remuneration. Which of these two effects is the more dominant is quite difficult to determine from a theoretical viewpoint. We assume that the restrictive effect of competition is all the more important.

These considerations produce the same correlative graph as for shareholder concentration in Figure 4-1 and Figure 4-2. Figure 4-3 demonstrates what effect competitive pressure on a company's main product market has on the value of the stock options received by top managers.

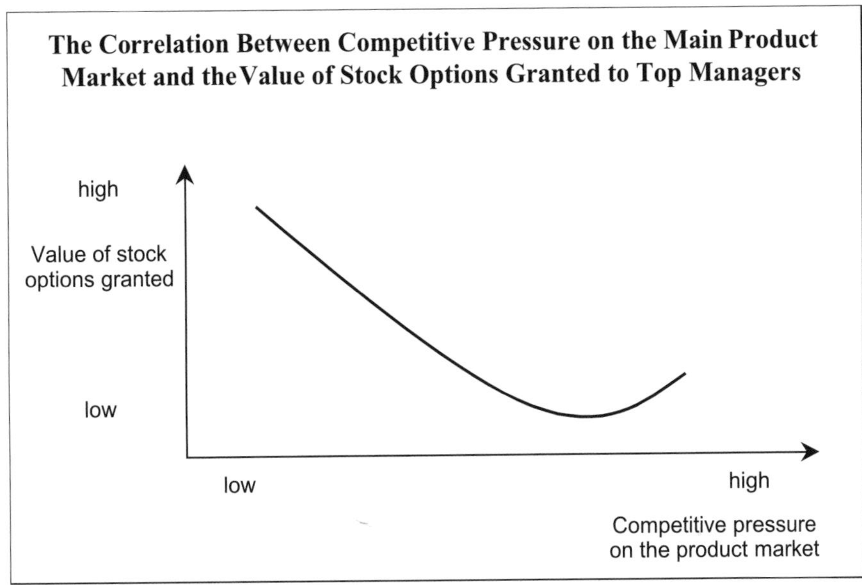

Figure 4-3

The hypothesis here can be summarized as follows.

Hypothesis 3:

The greater the competitive pressure (or the lower the market concentration) on a company's main product market, the fewer stock options a top manager will receive. This correlation becomes weaker as competitive pressure increases, however, because highly qualified, well-paid managers then become increasingly important to the company.

The three hypotheses above show how the management environment affects the compensation of top managers. Stock options will be granted more frequently where the environment (board of directors, shareholders, main market) only places slight constraints on top-level managers. So do these three hypotheses hold water?

6. A Concrete Test: The S&P 500 Top Managers

6.1 Descriptive Analysis

The empirical test of the proposed hypotheses is based on "Executive Compensation", a data set collected by Standard & Poor's (S&P). This is the data set upon which most scientific research on management compensation is founded. "Executive Compensation" contains detailed information regarding the amount and composition of pay packages for top executives from the 500 U.S. blue chips featured in the S&P 500 Index. In addition to compensation data, "Executive Compensation" provides information about the executives' function and the firms they work for. As the institutional setting, as well as the performance of the firms, is of crucial importance for our study, we have added selected data on the firms from Standard and Poor's "Compustat"[1], and data on market concentration from the U.S. Bureau of Census.

Stock options have become significantly more important, particularly in the last few years; therefore, the analysis is based on the latest available data for 1992-1997.

1 "Compustat" is a database, primarily used by financial analysts, providing detailed information on firm performance and ownership structure of exchange-listed US firms.

The U.S. blue chips used in the study are compiled by S&P according to market capitalization, liquidity and sector, providing a good overview of the U.S. economy. Generally, only the very top managers of these companies are included in the "Executive Compensation" data set. On average, it covers five managers, which amounts to a theoretical figure of roughly 15,000 observations for the six years under review. Unfortunately, however, key information is missing for a large number of managers, which lowers the number of observations to approximately 12,250.

The focus of this chapter is compensation in the form of stock options. The managers included in the data set received stock options averaging US$ 1.3 million per annum (valuation based on the Black-Scholes method). The highest sum went to Henry R. Silverman of the Cendant Corporation (Avis, Days Inn, Ramada), who received stock options worth almost US$ 257 million in 1997.

It is worth noting that, in absolute terms, the amount of options granted escalated from some US$ 720,000 in 1992 to over US$ 2.2 million in 1997, as illustrated in Figure 4-4 below.

Stock options average out to around 41.0 percent of the total income of the managers analyzed, with this percentage continuing its upward trend, rising from 35.8 percent in 1992 to 49.0 percent in 1997. Moreover, the base salary accounted for just under 24 percent in 1997. Figure 4-5 demonstrates the weighting of the other salary components, with (performance-related) bonuses playing a particularly important role alongside stock options and the base salary.

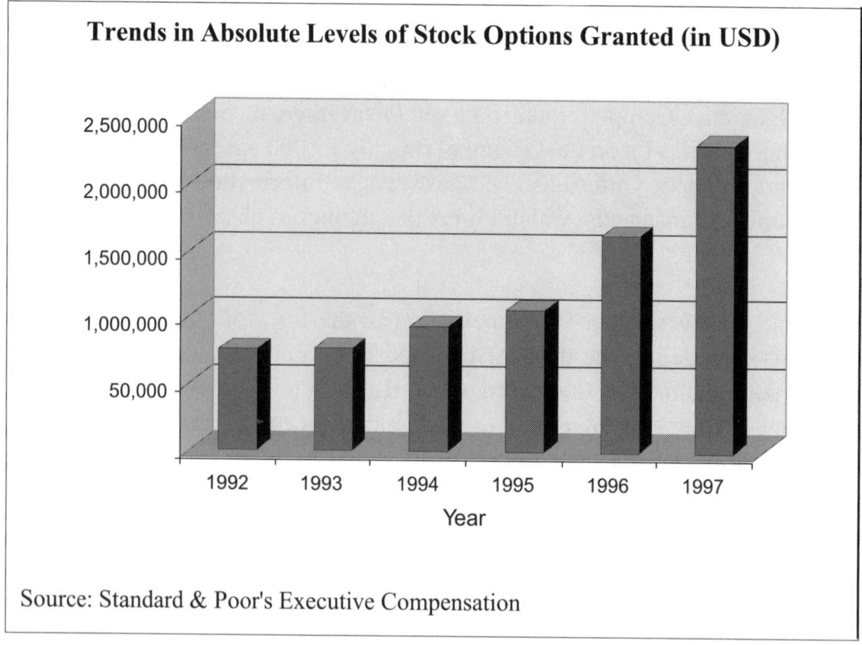

Source: Standard & Poor's Executive Compensation

Figure 4-4

As outlined in the previous section, we attribute the extraordinarily high value of stock options granted in some cases primarily to the lack of supervision of management, which in turn is due to the institutional setting. Three types of constraints on management form the focus of our empirical research: the overlap of personnel between the board of directors and management (hypothesis 1); shareholders' varying influence due to differences in ownership structures (hypothesis 2); and finally, the varying severity of market constraints as a result of differences in competitive pressures (hypothesis 3).

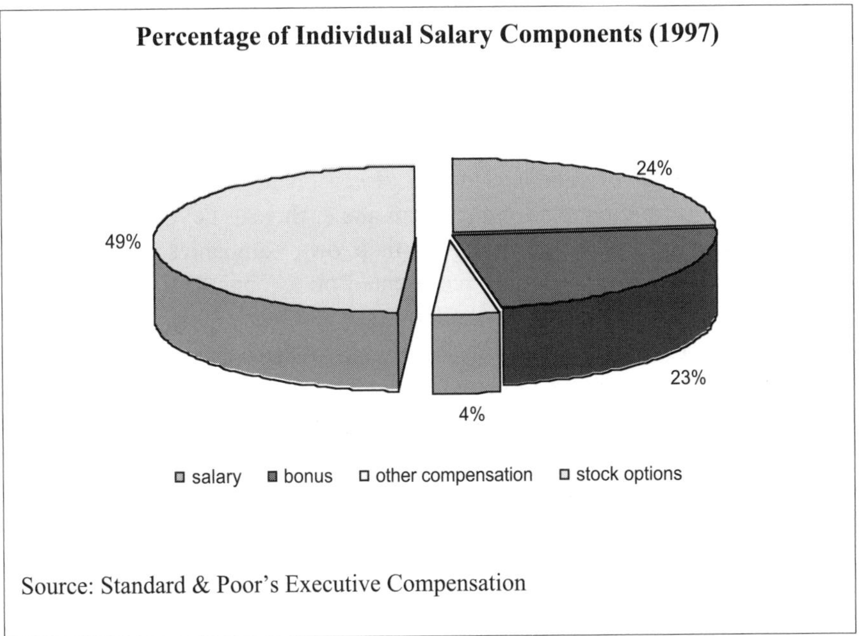

Figure 4-5

If a company's *board of directors* has a large management contingent, the control function of the board is weakened. This is especially true of those managers who also sit on the board, and thus effectively regulate themselves. We use two variables on board composition that measure the entanglement between the management and the board of directors: (i) a variable *member of the board of directors* that indicates whether a manager also sits on the board of his or her own company; (ii) a variable that indicates the *absolute number of managers who are sitting on their companies' board* in a given year.

The first variable *(member of the board)* serves as a measure for entanglement on an individual level. Managers who have themselves been appointed members of the board are, in actual fact, responsible for controlling themselves. Compared to managers not sitting on the board, they have larger possibilities to influence their own compensation. Hence, we expect a higher amount of option-based pay for these managers. In fact, managers who are members of the board of directors (43 percent of the managers in our data set) earn on average US$ 2.4 million in stock option grants, while those who are not members get only a third of that amount (roughly US$ 0.8 million). However, these differences could possibly be attributed to other factors. It is quite conceivable, for example, that particularly successful managers tend to be elected to the board of directors and therefore earn more. Certainly, the variable *member of the board* partly reflects such differences in individual productivity of the managers. We therefore include a second variable on board composition in the analysis that estimates entanglement effects irrespective of individual productivity.

The variable *number of managers on the firms'* board indicates the absolute number of executive directors for each firm and each year, i.e. the number of a firms' top managers who are sitting on their own companies' board. If the management of a firm is strongly represented on the board of directors, the controlling function of the board is undermined, and rent-seeking activities can be expected to be more successful. We thus hypothesize that the larger the absolute number of executive directors is, the larger are stock option grants for the managers in a firm. In the data set used, there are on average 2.31 managers sitting on their companies' board.

The different *types of ownership structure* are reflected in the number of shares the average shareholder owns. If this number rises (thus increasing shareholder concentration), then it is more profitable for individual shareholders to pursue their own interests (and those of their fellow shareholders). This diminishes managerial freedom, and stock options are likely to decline in importance. Among the companies that we examined, the average shareholder owns about 0.014 percent of the total capital stock. From 1992 to 1997, the importance of the individual shareholder fell sharply, with the average stockholding dropping from 0.04 to 0.001 percent. According to hypothesis 2, this increase in managers' freedom should lead to an increase in the amount of income paid in stock options. On the surface, this hypothesis would appear to be endorsed by the fact that, as stated above, in the six years under review, the level of income paid in the form of stock options rose enormously. Of course there are also numerous other possible reasons that could be cited, which means only a detailed statistical analysis, as will be conducted in the next section, can clear up the facts.

The U.S. Census Bureau (http://www.census.gov) assesses the *competitive environment* in the various sectors on a regular basis. Concentration rate 4 (CR4), i.e. the proportion of total sector turnover generated by the four largest companies, is considered a primary indicator of the market power of a company. The CR4 data we use in our analysis refer to the four-digit level of the Standard Industrial Classification (SIC) of sectors. The average market share for the four largest companies in the sectors examined is approximately 36 percent. Comprehensive studies of the CR4 for all sectors are rarely carried out, which is why the data used refers to 1992. As data is only available for one year, no trends can be identified for the period in question. A high CR4 corresponds to slight competitive pressure, which in turn means fewer market constraints on management; high salaries thus have fewer negative implications, as the costs can be more easily passed on to the consumer and higher returns can also be achieved, which are then handed over to managers (at least in part).

In addition to the institutional setting, several other factors have a bearing on the popularity of stock options and on total management incomes. There are three types of control variables: (1) the personal characteristics of the manager, (2) the size and growth rate of the company and (3) the financial success of the company.

The personal characteristics of the manager. "Executive Compensation" offers little information about the managers themselves. There are, however, two known factors which may possibly influence the amount of option-based pay: whether the manager is CEO of the company in question and the manager's gender. Some 15 percent of the managers in our data set are CEOs and only a little over two percent are women.

The size and growth rate of the company. A number of studies show that company size is a key determinant of salary levels – large companies generally pay higher wages. The number of employees, sales and total assets are the three factors according to which a company's size is classified. On average, the companies in our data set record sales of around US$ 7.9 billion and have about 37,000 employees. Assets are usually somewhere around US$ 15.8 billion. And the companies post average annual (nominal) sales growth of 12.5 percent and hire approximately 6.8 percent more employees each year.

The financial success of the company. A company's financial success should be a decisive factor when it comes to management compensation levels. We have tried to record this success using four variables – return on assets, earnings per share (EPS), dividends per share and the P/E ratio as an indicator of a company's market valuation. Generally, the return on assets of a company is around 5.5 percent, with the figure standing at 5 percent in 1992, reaching almost 6 percent in 1994 and then falling back again to just over 5 percent in 1997. Earnings per share looks more or less the same. It rose from a little more than one dollar per share in 1992 to about US$ 2.5 in 1994, then making its descent back down to US$ 2.2. This results in an EPS of around 2 dollars, about half of which (US$ 0.95 to be exact) was passed on to shareholders in the form of dividends. As an average share of the companies under observation cost just under 50 dollars, these dividends give a direct return of about 2 percent to the shareholders.

6.2 Statistical Analysis

Previous descriptive analysis fails to take into account that certain factors simultaneously affect the level and composition of a manager's compensation. It may be assumed that financially successful companies also pay higher compensation, that CEOs tend to be paid in options, etc. However, controls need to be carried out for these additional factors if general statements are to be made about what specific influence the institutional setting has on the compensation of top managers.

A multiple regression analysis keeps the influence of other factors on compensation constant. The method enables all relevant factors to be included in the estimation equation. The results can then be easily interpreted. The effect that is determined for a single variable applies *ceteris paribus,* meaning that the influence of all other variables remains constant. The effect of the individual variables can thus be isolated.

Table 4-1 provides the results of an ordinary least-squares regression. This regression explains the absolute amount of options granted to a manager by means of several factors. Included in the regression are the institutional conditions of particular interest to us here, namely shareholder and market concentration and managerial membership in the board of directors. There are several other factors taken into account which might explain the differences in the amount of options granted. These are the three criteria mentioned earlier – the personal characteristics of the manager, the size and growth rate of the company and its financial success. Moreover, the regression corrects for firm-specific and annual effects (technically, this is a regression with "fixed effects" on the company level). "Fixed effects" take into account that the compensation practices of the S&P 500 firms might vary greatly for reasons beyond the scope of what the variables we include in the regression can capture. For example, a firm might put little weight on option grants because it is part of its long-standing corporate culture. For every firm, the regression computes a firm-specific effect that reflects compensation practices that do not change over time. Annual effects, on the other hand, account for time-related effects, such as inflation or the general market trend. Therefore, firm-specific charateristics or time trends do not distort the results. This ensures that the results obtained present an unbiased picture, i.e. that the results reflect only the influence of the factors in question.

As the index for market concentration applied in this chapter exhibits no variance over time, and as the firms considered do not switch market sectors, this measure cannot be included in a regression with firm-specific fixed effects. Therefore, we have to take two steps. In Table 4-1, the upper part presents the results of the first step: a fixed-effects regression excluding market concentration data is run. In a second step, we try to explain the firm-specific compensation practices we have computed in the first step by market concentration and its square (results are in the lower part of Table 4-1).

As previously mentioned, the regression is based on approximately 12,250 observations. The quality of the regression is reflected in the number R^2. This denotes what percentage of the variance in the absolute level of options can be explained by the variables used. The estimation accounts for some eight percent of the variance, as can be seen in Table 4-1. This may not seem to be much at first glance, but for empirical research that deals with individual salaries, it is a good value. Particularly so since quite a lot of information about the managers is missing, their age or educational background, for instance.

Table 4-1:
The Influence of Institutional Controls on Management Compensation

	Absolute value of options granted	
	Estimate (t-value)	Absolute change in compensation: if member of the board of directors, for every additional manager sitting on the board, or given an increase in the medium concentration rate of 50 percent
Member of the board of directors	735.17** (15.81)	USD + 735,170
Number of managers on the board	200.21** (3.39)	USD + 200,210
Shareholder concentration	-3.26e+6 ** (-5.18)	USD - 210,000
Shareholder concentration (squared)	9.46e+3** (4.41)	–
No. of observations	12,243	
R^2	0.08	

Comments:

In addition to the variables listed above, the following control variables are included in the regression: CEO, gender, company size, sales, number of employees, assets, return on assets, earnings per share, dividend per share, P/E ratio and fixed effects for each firm and year.

** denotes a statistical significance of 99%.

	Firm-specific fixed effects for the absolute value of options granted	
	Estimate (t-value)	Absolute change in salary given an increase in the medium concentration rate of 50 percent
Market concentration (CR4)	15.81** (3.39)	USD + 270,000
Market concentration (squared)	-0.05** (-10.04)	–
No. of observations	422	
R^2	0.06	

6.3 Interpretation of the Results

In the left-hand column of Table 4-1, the estimated coefficient and the t-value of the coefficient is given for each explanatory variable. The latter provides information about the statistical reliability of the coefficient. A t-value of more than three indicates a 99% degree of significance, i.e. we can be 99 percent sure that the established correlation is not coincidental and would not change if other managers were selected. As the coefficients are in some cases difficult to interpret due to the estimation process, we compute absolute changes in compensation and provide them in the right-hand column. This allows us to directly illustrate in US$ the effects of membership in the board of directors, of every additional manager sitting on the board of his or her own firm and of a fifty percent increase in the average value of both market and shareholder concentration rates.

As can be seen from the tables, all three hypotheses are supported. We discuss the regression results for each of the three institutional variables in turn.

Board structure. On average, managers who sit on the board of directors receive around US$ 735,000 more in options. We would like to once again stress that for the purposes of our calculations, numerous influential factors were kept constant. This means that this increase cannot be linked to the relevant company's particular success, its rapid growth or any other such factors, but that it is actually a result of membership on the board of directors. Over and above that, every additional manager sitting on the company's board results in an increase in stock option compensation of roughly US$ 200,000. The more managers are appointed members of the board, and are thus essentially responsible for supervising themselves, the higher the amounts of option-based pay.

Shareholder concentration. A higher shareholder concentration lowers the absolute value of options paid out to managers. The simple term is negative, which means that the curve is shaped according to theoretical expectations illustrated in Figure 4-2. As the squared term is positive, the curve begins to rise again at a certain point. This point is reached when an individual shareholder owns an average of more than 0.17 percent of the company's shares. This is a very large percentage, and only about one percent of the companies in our data set demonstrate such a high degree of shareholder concentration. Thus the curve corresponds exactly to theoretical expectations. If the average shareholder concentration rises by fifty percent, then managers receive an average of US$ 210,000 less in options.

Market concentration. The higher the market concentration, the less competition there is in the sector and the more options are granted to managers. In line with theoretical expectations, the effect is diminished by increasing market concentration, which is expressed by a negative squared term. The squared term, however, only predominates with a market concentration of more than 100 percent; and is hence of no relevance for the sectors analyzed here. All things being equal, a rise in the average market concentration by fifty percent increases the options granted to the average manager by US$ 270,000.

The coefficients of the control variables (not shown) are significant and in line with previous research - CEOs receive more options and women managers less in absolute terms. Large and successful companies grant more options. For successful companies, however, reversed causality may be assumed as their stock prices usually show stronger growth, thereby generating a disproportionate increase in the value of stock options granted. Nevertheless, it is important to control for measures of profitability in the regression. This assures the result that, all other things being equal, similarly successful managers are granted more stock options when there is less control in a firm's institutional environment.

7. Summary

In this chapter, we dealt with the question of whether top managers can be additionally motivated by stock options. We asked whether this form of performance-related compensation fosters stronger commitment in the interest of shareholders. It can be demonstrated that the task of management motivation cannot be reduced to the use of simple instruments such as stock options. The management motivation argument does not justify the huge sums top managers receive in stock options.

The empirical evidence on the relationship between performance-related pay and stock returns is rather weak and the direction of causality is unclear. Thus, there is room for alternative explanations of current levels of stock option compensation. We focus on institutional determinants of stock option grants. It is argued, and empirical evidence is offered, that weak institutional restrictions have allowed top managers to collect rents in the form of stock option payments in a bullish stock market environment. Three institutional restrictions are analyzed: the composition of the board of directors, the concentration of shareholders and market competition. The empirical results presented for the S&P 500 firms and the years from 1992 to 1997 show that the more managers are exposed to supervision, the less compensation they receive in stock options in absolute value.

In addition to the effects of higher compensation on the performance of top managers as analyzed here, the impact of the increasingly uneven distribution of salaries on the motivation of other employees requires investigation. It would be particularly interesting to see how middle management reacts, as it stands to gain little from a boom. They may regard the growing discrepancy in salaries as unfair, which could dampen their motivation.

Based on these results, we would like to conclude by proposing a number of institutional reforms which might lead to a corporate pay policy that is better geared to shareholders' interests.

1. The clear division of responsibilities with regard to the compensation structure for top-level management. This means fewer managers holding a seat on the board of directors.

2. No restrictions on external major shareholders in publicly owned corporations, as they are more motivated to exercise control. In return, greater disclosure of cross-holdings involving related interests would be required.

3. Ensuring competition in the main product market by means of a strong competition authority so that competitive pressure makes the payment of so-called "fat cat" salaries more difficult.

In general, there is a dire need for more transparency. Stricter guidelines should be introduced for top management with regard to income transparency and reporting requirements. Accounting guidelines should include an obligation to offset stock options against reported earnings with a view to improving shareholders' rights to information and representation. Corporate tax breaks on stock options should also be abolished.

Institutional reforms should be implemented so that senior managers are subject to effective controls. Such reforms are also necessary to turn our attention to alternative motivational instruments once more. At the end of the day, stock options alone do not seem to be able to instill entrepreneurial spirit in managers.

8. Further Reading

The latest information on management motivation via financial incentives can be found in:

Murphy, K. J. (1999): Executive Compensation, in: Ashenfelter, O./Card, D. (eds): Handbook of Labor Economics, vol 3, Amsterdam, pp 2486-2563.

Influential earlier works on the link between management compensation and corporate success can be found in:

Murphy, K. J (1985): Corporate Performance and Managerial Remuneration: An Empirical Analysis, in: Journal of Accounting and Economics 7 (1-3), pp 11-42.
Deckop, J. R. (1988): Determinants of Chief Executive Officer Compensation, in: Industrial and Labor Relations Review 41 (2), pp 215-226.
Jensen, M. C./Murphy, K. J. (1990): Performance Pay and Top-Management Incentives, in: Journal of Political Economy 98 (2), pp 225-264.
Hall, B. J./Liebman, J. B. (1998): Are CEOs Really Paid Like Bureaucrats, in: Quarterly Journal of Economics 111 (3), pp 653-691.

An international overview with the latest figures can be found in:

Abowd, J. M./Kaplan, D. S. (1999): Executive Compensation: Six Questions That Need Answering, in: Journal of Economic Perspectives 13 (4), pp 145-168.

For a broader critical study of the discussion and research in Europe, see:

Osterloh, M. (1999): Wertorientierte Unternehmensführung und Management-Anreizsysteme, in: Kumar, B. N./Osterloh, M./Schreyögg, G. (eds): Unternehmensethik und die Transformation des Wettbewerbs. Shareholder-Value – Globalisierung – Hyperwettbewerb, Stuttgart, pp 183-204.

The influence of corporate governance structures on management compensation has been examined in numerous new, and some as yet unpublished, studies:

Finkelstein, S./Boyd, B. (1998): How Much Does the CEO Matter? The Role of Managerial Discretion in the Setting of CEO Compensation, in: Academy of Management Journal 41 (2), pp 179-199.

Core, J. E./Holthausen, R. W./Larcker, D. F. (1999): Corporate Governance, Chief Executive Officer Compensation, and Firm Performance, in: Journal of Financial Economics 51, pp 371-406.

Bertrand, M./Mullainathan, S. (2000): Do CEO's Set Their Own Pay? The Ones Without Principles Do, NBER Working Paper No. 7604.

Chapter Five

IRIS BOHNET AND FELIX OBERHOLZER-GEE

Pay for Performance: Motivation and Selection Effects

Introduction

Does pay for performance increase productivity? The answer has to be, "Yes, but..." Larger ex gratia payments, bonuses and commissions do motivate employees to put in more effort, but at the same time they provide an incentive for less qualified people to carry out activities that are rewarded by performance-related pay. Consequently, the overall effect of a greater focus on performance is ambivalent: if the motivational effect dominates, output per employee will go up; if the selection effect has the upper hand, output per employee will fall. The trick is to create a compensation structure that exploits the motivational potential of monetary incentives without encouraging inefficient activity. In this chapter we use an empirical study of employee suggestion plans in more than 1,400 companies to show how this is possible. We find that companies that pay higher rewards for suggestions do not receive more useful ideas. The quality of suggestions does not rise because a relatively larger number of less qualified employees take part in generating the ideas. Companies that pay lower amounts but which focus these payments on the best suggestions achieve much greater cost savings. The significance of the motivational and selection effects is not, of course, limited to suggestion plans.

1. Introduction

Performance-related pay has become more prevalent in recent years. Ninety percent of Fortune 1,000 companies report that they use incentive plans which tie pay to some measure of individual output (see also Chapter 3). Ninety-three percent of the largest 460 European companies state that performance-based pay has become more important at all levels over recent years. Following the success of "new public management" in New Zealand, people are even beginning to wonder whether public-sector employees, such as civil servants and teachers, could be better motivated if their pay depended on their individual performance. Performance-related incentives do not just change employees' motivation, however. They also influence who chooses to perform which tasks. This *selection effect* is often forgotten when companies introduce compensation systems based on performance. However, unless selection effects are taken into account, it is impossible to exploit the full potential of performance incentives.

In this chapter, we demonstrate the importance of selection effects by analyzing how different compensation systems affect the production of *employee suggestions* for improvements in companies. Many companies encourage their employees to think beyond the immediate parameters of their own jobs and come up with ideas about how the business's products and processes could be improved. In most cases, employees who suggest genuine improvements can expect to be rewarded. Employees typically receive some percentage of the cost savings achieved as a result of their suggestion. This type of *ideas management,* once seen as rather old-fashioned, is currently experiencing something of a renaissance. According to the German Institute for Business Administration in Frankfurt, the number of companies that employ formal evaluation procedures for suggestions has increased dramatically in recent years. Among the most successful industries are the electrical and auto industry. These industries make use of 80 percent of all suggestions that employees produce. Managers in Germany estimate that suggestion systems contributed to cost savings on the order of DM 2 billion in 1999 alone (Handelszeitung, 01/20/2000).

But are the performance-related incentives used in ideas management as effective as many managers believe? Our empirical study of more than 1,400 Swiss companies between 1989 and 1998 suggests that the answer is, "Yes, but…". On the one hand, larger rewards do induce employees to work harder at producing more valuable suggestions. This *motivational effect* explains why more generous companies receive more, and often better, suggestions. On the other hand, larger rewards also have an undesirable *selection effect:* because of the large rewards, employees with little talent for the development of new ideas turn in suggestions just as often as those who really do have an eye for potential cost savings. As a result, companies that increase the average reward per suggestion receive a much larger number of useless proposals. Our study shows that the negative selection effect and the positive motivational effect basically cancel each other. The net result is that, on average, *larger rewards do not lead to more valuable suggestions.*

Box 5-1

One of the Most Successful Ideas: "Post-it" Notes
The small yellow stickers that decorate offices all over the world are the result of an employee suggestion made at 3M. The company is known for the incentives it gives to employees to think up good ideas. Until recently, 3M's divisions expected 25 percent of sales to come from products that were introduced in the past five years. Today, innovations are even more important and the firm now expects to make 30 percent of its revenue from products launched in the past four years.

"Post-it" notes resulted from two ideas: Spencer Silver developed a special glue, while Art Fry noticed how glue and paper could be combined to produce a note. It was not pure chance that Fry realized this opportunity. An active member of a church choir, Fry was often annoyed because traditional bookmarkers would fall out of his hymnbook. Having invented "Post-it" notes, Fry is now not only a member of the choir, but also of the "Carlton Society," 3M's elite club for outstanding innovators.

Source: Bartlett, C. A. and Ghoshal, S. (1995). Rebuilding Behavioral Context: Turn Process Reengineering Into People Rejuvenation. *Sloan Management Review* 37, pp. 11-23.

This chapter is organized as follows. Section 2 explains why performance-based pay produces motivational and selection effects. In Section 3, we present the results of the study into how employees react to different incentives as applied to "ideas management" suggestion plans. Section 4 discusses how managers can design more effective incentive plans. It goes without saying that the relations between motivational and selection effects that we analyze here do not apply only to ideas management. Finally, Section 5 summarizes the most important insights resulting from our empirical analysis.

2. Performance-Related Pay - The Perfect Solution?

2.1 Drawbacks of Pay for Performance

So far, this book has discussed two reasons why companies should treat incentive pay with a degree of skepticism. As outlined in Chapter 1, performance pay can crowd out employees' intrinsic motivation. This may be costly for a company since it is impossible to contractually specify every possible contingency that may arise in the workplace. In many situations, businesses have to rely on their employees' common sense, trusting that workers have the interests of the company at heart even if their behavior can neither be observed nor rewarded. If employees are intrinsically motivated, they will try to meet their obligations even in unpredictable and thus non-contractable circumstances. However, if performance pay crowds out intrinsic motivation, overall productivity can be negatively affected, even if incentive pay increases performance levels in individual areas.

Companies should also be cautious about performance incentives in areas where employees are carrying out a variety of tasks and where these different tasks are measurable to varying degrees. Holmstrom and Milgrom (1991) were the first to analyze this problem of "multi-tasking" (see also Chapter 1). The use of performance incentives obviously depends on how well performance can be measured. It is comparatively easy, for example, to measure how often the telephone rings before a salesperson picks it up. It is much harder to measure how helpful and polite the person is on the phone. If companies introduce performance-related pay in such multi-tasking environments, hard-to-measure tasks are not normally rewarded (at least not adequately). As a result, employees focus mainly on the aspects of their work that can earn them money while neglecting tasks that offer weaker incentives. Again, productivity as a whole may decrease even if the incentives are successful in a narrower sense.

2.2 Different Abilities

In this section, we focus on a third aspect that can decrease or even destroy the effectiveness of performance pay. This problem arises when different employees have *different abilities* to handle a task. Consider the following example. Mary, a salesperson working for a used car dealer, is very successful at convincing customers to buy cars. She expects to close a deal with every other customer. Tom, on the other hand, is not quite as talented. He expects one in ten customers to purchase a vehicle. At this dealership, all employees earn a commission of 10 percent on the sales they make. Obviously, the job is more attractive for Mary than for Tom. She expects to make five times as much money as he does. Realizing the dire prospects of such a job, Tom decides not to join the sales team of this dealership.

What will happen if the owner of the car dealership decides to introduce larger rewards? Assume he increases the commission rate to 20 percent. Undoubtedly, Mary will now work harder because it is twice as rewarding to sell a car. This *motivational effect* of stronger incentives results in an *increase* in the number of cars sold per salesperson. However, Mary is not the only one adjusting her behavior. Less talented Tom now also finds the job more attractive, possibly attractive enough to quit his current job and become a used car salesperson. The fact that larger rewards also attract the less talented leads to an undesired *selection effect.* In contrast to the motivational effect, selection effects *decrease* the number of cars sold per employee unless management takes countermeasures. Whether higher commission rates lead to more or fewer cars being sold thus depends on the relative weighting of the motivational effect and the selection effect.

2.3 Incentives and Suggestion Systems

When companies use incentive plans to motivate employees to come forward with new ideas and suggestions, both motivational and selection effects can be important. Figure 5-1 depicts the relationship between performance pay and the number of suggestions received.

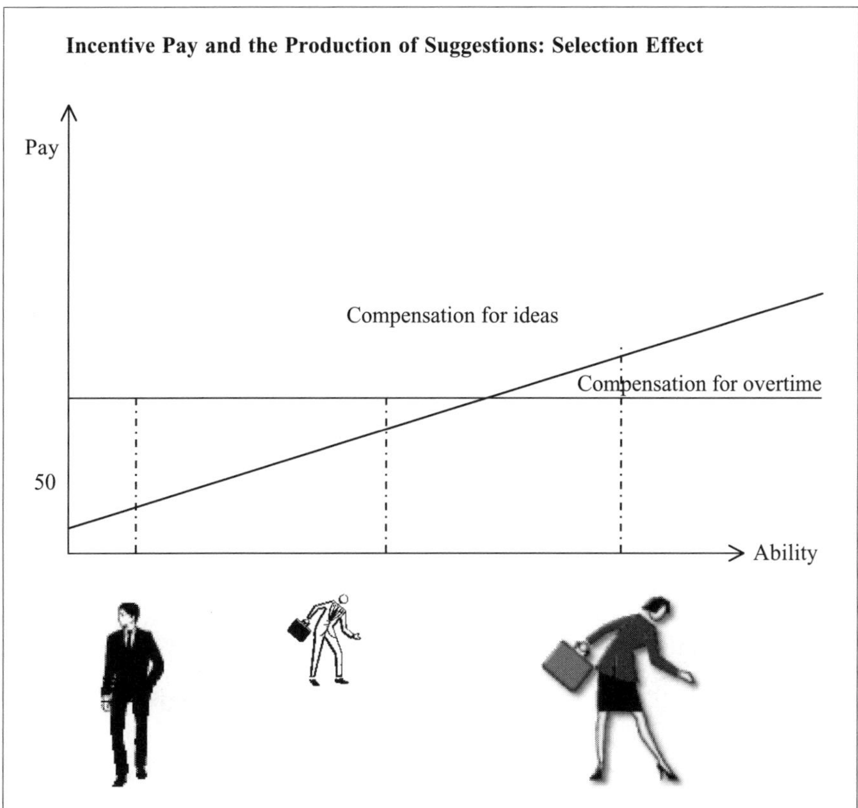

Figure 5-1

The horizontal axis shows the ability levels of three employees. The gentleman in the dark suit is the least talented, the woman with the briefcase has the best ideas. They all have two ways of increasing their pay: they can either work overtime, earning a fixed hourly wage (the horizontal line in Figure 1), or they can try to develop new ideas. The company pays a fixed reward of $ 50 for every idea. In addition, employees making suggestions are also paid 20 percent of the cost savings that result if the idea is implemented. Developing new ideas is, therefore, more attractive for more talented employees. In Figure 1, a reward of 20 percent (represented by the upward-sloping line) only motivates the lady with the briefcase to come up with ideas. Her colleagues are financially better off working overtime. But what happens if the company increases the reward in order to motivate employees to produce more ideas? Figure 5-2 presents the resulting effects.

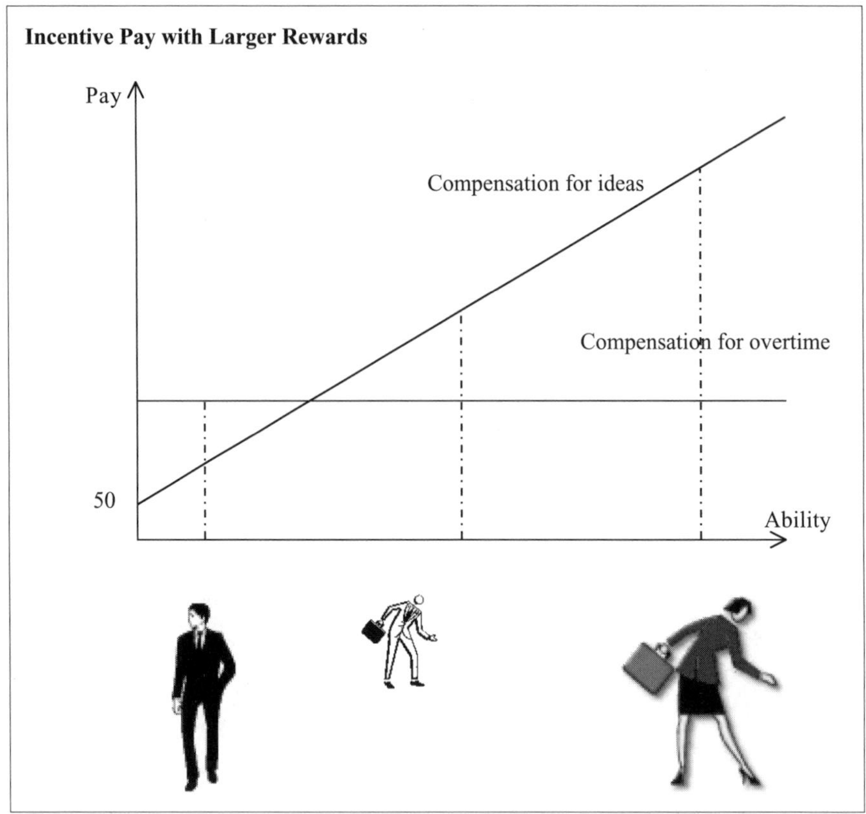

Figure 5-2

If rewards increase, say, from 20 to 40 percent, the lady will provide even better ideas. This again represents the desired *motivational effect.* In contrast to Figure 5-1, however, the gentleman in the white suit, who is less talented than the lady, now also starts contributing ideas. This has positive and negative effects. On the one hand, the company now receives more suggestions, some of which it might even be able to implement. On the other hand, the ideas submitted by the gentleman in white come at a cost for the business. Every suggestion must be evaluated and a fixed reward of $50 is paid. *Such fixed costs make it undesirable to have less talented employees participate in the generation of ideas.* The rewards themselves represent only a (small) portion of the overall costs associated with suggestion systems. For instance, UBS, a Swiss bank, reports that the personnel and the information technology used for the evaluation of ideas account for 65 percent of the total cost of its suggestion system. The payment of rewards is only responsible for 35 percent (Handelszeitung, 01/20/2000).

2.4 Consequences for the Company

The most effective incentive plans do not encourage *all* employees in *all* areas to perform better. They discourage workers from taking on tasks for which they lack education or experience. Even if worthless ideas did not cost the company money, there are opportunity costs – the employee could have spent his or her time doing something else (in the example above, working overtime) which would have added more value than generating ideas.

Employees themselves often help to ensure that resources are allocated sensibly within a company. If they face similar incentives for various tasks, they will automatically select the areas in which they are likely to be most productive. As employees know their own strengths and weaknesses, they will always be financially better off performing the tasks which they master best. When designing compensation plans, the greatest danger is thus that managers *focus on some tasks in isolation.* A typical reaction might be, "We receive fewer cost-cutting ideas than our competitors. Therefore, let's increase the rewards we pay for ideas." This argument overlooks the fact that raising the level of rewards paid for suggestions makes it more attractive for employees to submit an idea even if the producer of the idea would have been much more productive doing something else.

The relevance of selective incentives can be demonstrated empirically. We expect higher rewards to have the following two effects:

- Companies that pay higher rewards receive *more* suggestions.
- More generous businesses do not necessarily receive *better* suggestions. If the selection effect is stronger than the motivational effect, the average quality might even decrease.

The following section tests these two hypotheses using data collected from suggestion plans used by Swiss companies.

3. Testing the Selection Effect

Another reason why suggestion systems provide us with an interesting test case for this theory is that many academics and practitioners believe that economic incentives do not affect creativity. Teresa Amabile of Harvard Business School, for example, concludes, "Money doesn't necessarily stop people from being creative, but in many situations, it doesn't help" (Amabile 1998, p. 79). Skepticism about economic incentives is also typical in the German-speaking world. A publication on suggestion systems by the state government of Bavaria, Germany, concludes, "Ideas generate money, but money does not generate ideas" (Frey et al. 1996, p. 67). Sprenger (1993) talks about "de-motivation through rewards" and other scholars propose that rewards are certainly not the most important determinant of new ideas (Bumann 1991, Etienne 1997, Losse and Thom 1977). Most of these statements seem to be based on the psychological insight that creativity is an innate ability (see Box 5-2) that cannot be influenced by performance-related pay. However, this analysis ignores the fact that people with other skills can put more or less effort into the development of good ideas. While monetary incentives do not change abilities, at least in the short run, they affect the likelihood that employees will work hard to come up with ideas that lead to significant improvements.

Box 5-2

Creativity as an Ability

Research on creativity emphasizes that personal characteristics are crucial to a person's creativity. Creative people are noted for their self-discipline, willingness to take risks, stamina, tolerance of frustration, independence and lack of interest in social recognition. According to the frequently used personality test devised by H. G. Gough, the "Creative Personality Scale," the following adjectives are good indicators that a person is creative: clever – inventive – risk-taking – original – unconventional – informal – humorous – self-confident – sexy – snobbish. Using this scale, an attempt was made to predict the number of suggestions made at two U.S. industrial companies employing a total of 200 employees. They found that employees doing complex work who, according to this measure, were creative, submitted more suggestions than employees who were rated as less creative.

Source: Cummings, A./Oldham, G. R. (1997): Enhancing Creativity: Managing Work Contexts for the High Potential Employee, in: California Management Review 40, pp. 22-38.

3.1 The Data

The data referred to here is based on a survey conducted by the Swiss Association for Suggestion Systems.[1] Every year, more than 100 companies report on the structure and the success of their systems. The average company examined here has 2,715 employees and receives 65 suggestions per year, resulting in average cost reductions of about Sfr 100,000 per year. Annual rewards are on the order of Sfr 11,000 in the average company. The largest sum of rewards paid in any year by a single company in our sample was Sfr 437,661. The largest single reward was Sfr 131,057.

Two aspects of our data should be noted. First, all of our information comes exclusively from companies that run formalized suggestion systems. It is reasonable to assume that these companies chose to have such a system for good reason, meaning that they could well differ systematically from Swiss companies in general. For instance, our sample might consist of companies that find it particularly easy to motivate their employees. Our results thus apply to companies with existing suggestion systems only, and the insights gained in our study cannot easily be applied to companies in general.

Secondly, not all companies that are members of the Association for Suggestion Systems respond to the survey every year. This is problematic, since it is quite possible that the survey is more likely to be returned in "good" years when the company receives a large number of suggestions. In fact, the data shows that companies which completed the survey only once between 1989 and 1998 reported a surprisingly large number of ideas. In order to avoid such distortions, our sample consists of companies which completed the survey at least three times between 1989 and 1998. Following this adjustment, we are left with 1,472 observations for this 10-year period.

3.2 Empirical Analysis

The first aim of our tests is to clarify *how many ideas* a company receives. Hypothesis 1 suggests that the employees of companies that offer more generous rewards will submit a greater number of ideas. In order to study how the *structure of rewards* influences the production of ideas, we will look at the highest

[1] We thank the president of the SAV/ASS, Mr. H. Grob, for allowing us to use the data. This work would not have been possible without his generous support.

rewards offered by a company. The following thought experiment helps to illustrate the issues involved.

Take two identical companies with the same suggestion systems. Both receive the same number of new ideas. We now allow company 1 to change the structure of its rewards system, albeit with the restriction that the total sum of rewards has to remain constant. For example, the company can increase the largest reward, but for the sum of rewards to remain constant, the company then has to decrease some of the smaller rewards. How would such a change impact the number of suggestions that company 1 receives? Only the most talented employees with a realistic chance of submitting a really good idea will benefit from an increase in the largest reward. Figures 5-1 and 5-2 above suggest that these employees are likely to have submitted ideas even prior to the change in the structure of rewards. At the same time, however, the decrease in the level of smaller rewards, which is necessary to hold the total sum constant, impacts on the less talented, such as the two men in our illustration. They will be less likely to produce ideas in company 1 than in company 2. Thus, we expect *the number of ideas to decrease as the largest reward increases.*

Results: The Number of Ideas

The results of the analysis indicate that more generous companies with a larger *overall sum of rewards* really do receive more suggestions (the statistical information behind all the points discussed here is collated in Table 5-1 in the appendix to this chapter). If the total sum of rewards increases by Sfr 1,000 per year, employees will submit almost three additional ideas on average. If the company raises the reward for the *best idea* by Sfr 1,000 (keeping the overall sum of rewards the same), it receives fewer suggestions (minus 2.63). These results accord with our expectations. Companies that concentrate rewards on the best ideas discourage less talented employees who know that they do not stand a chance of winning the big prize. As a consequence, the overall number of suggestions received decreases.

But just how robust are these results? We can test our model further by checking for extraneous factors that might influence the number of suggestions that a company receives.

Industry. We first check for industry characteristics (ten different categories). Our results indicate that the number of ideas submitted does not generally depend on the industry. Two exceptions are the engineering industry, where employees submit a significantly larger number of ideas, and the public sector, where few new ideas are put forward. Our model predicts that a company in the public sector will receive 89 fewer ideas on average than an otherwise comparable business in another industry.

Year. 'Year' effects could arise if employees are found to submit more ideas during recessions when unemployment rates are high and they feel that they have to fight for their jobs. The results show sizable fluctuations from year to year, and overall there seems to be a general time trend: suggestion systems appear to have experienced a boom during the last ten years. Today, companies receive a good 40 ideas more annually than they did ten years ago.

Characteristics of the company. "Fixed effects" are a statistical tool with which we can allow for unobservable company characteristics that remain constant during the period under review. This is particularly important since corporate culture, management style and the importance attached to suggestion systems all undoubtedly vary from company to company. In fact, our results change noticeably as soon as we take factors such as corporate culture into account. *If the sum of rewards increases by Sfr 1,000, the company receives just one additional suggestion; but if a company rewards the best idea more generously, it will receive 6.28 fewer ideas on average.* The better we can adjust for observed and unobserved factors, the more pronounced this key relationship – that companies which emphasize rewards for the very best ideas receive fewer suggestions – becomes.

Results: The Quality of Ideas

The quality of ideas is obviously more interesting than the sheer quantity. We measure quality by assessing the costs that the company saves per submitted suggestion (details of this statistical analysis are shown in Table 5-2, which can also be found in the appendix to this chapter). The effect is as expected: *a Sfr 1,000 increase in the overall sum of rewards does not lead to an improvement in the quality of the ideas submitted.* In fact, most assessments suggest that the influence is negative, though so small that it is virtually neutral. This indicates that the motivational effect of an increase in the overall reward pool is more or less balanced out by the selection effect. When promised higher rewards across the board, all employees, both the talented ones who have already been submitting suggestions and the less talented ones, try harder to come up with new ideas. While the number of suggestions increases, the higher level of participation among less talented employees ensures that the average quality does not improve, despite the higher rewards offered.

Of course, it could be argued that the lack of a clear positive effect results from the fact that monetary incentives do not influence creativity. However, the results of our study of the largest reward offered suggest that this argument does not apply. If a company decreases the rewards for less valuable suggestions and uses the resulting savings to finance an increase in the largest reward by Sfr 1,000, *it does receive more valuable ideas* (average cost savings increase by Sfr 829). This is a huge gain, considering that the average company in our sample receives 65 suggestions.

As expected, we do not find any significant differences between large and small companies with regard to the quality of ideas. In fact none of our other control variables influence the value of ideas. In general, it seems to be quite difficult to account statistically for the fact that some companies receive better ideas than others. While rewarding the best suggestions more generously always results in an economically relevant and statistically significant increase in quality, our other variables do not correlate with average cost savings. Overall, our model probably only accounts for two percent of the variation in our sample.

Note, however, that even though many other factors may potentially affect the results, our main hypothesis stands: selection effects critically influence how effective monetary incentives are. Employees do respond to the reward structure set up by their company. If the pie is larger, more people try to grab a piece. If there are fewer but larger slices, only the best participate and work harder. Merely increasing the size of the pie is thus not the most effective solution. It is more important to divide it up "correctly."

4. More Effective Compensation Systems

Our analysis certainly sheds light on the question of how compensation systems can be better structured. The most important insights relate to the three elements of the rewards paid: maximum rewards, the fixed percentage of savings passed on to employees, and minimum rewards.

Maximum rewards. Many companies limit the size of rewards that employees can receive. Audi, the car manufacturer, for example will not pay rewards in excess of DM 100,000. Such maximum limits do not produce a selection effect, because it is only the most talented employees who can reasonably expect to compete for these big prizes. However, maximum rewards do limit the positive motivational effects among precisely this group of talented employees. Thus, maximum limits on rewards have no place in an effective compensation system.

Percentage of savings passed on to employees. Nearly all companies reward ideas with a fixed percentage of the total savings made when these ideas are implemented. This fixed rate typically lies between 10 percent and 30 percent. The main argument in favor of this type of reward structure is its perceived fairness. All employees are treated the same. Some companies even set a relatively higher rate for worse ideas and a lower one for more valuable ideas. There is no doubt that fairness contributes a great deal to individual motivation and a positive working environment. However, our study suggests that fairness of this sort can be quite expensive for the company. Recall that taking Sfr 1,000 in rewards for small ideas and allocating it to the best idea increases the value of every idea by Sfr 800. In view of this effect, managers would do well to carefully consider the cost of "fair" compensation systems. Would any harm be done to the desired corporate culture by starting the scale of rewards at 20 percent for less good ideas and then gradually increasing it to 25 percent for the most valuable suggestions?

Of course there are all sorts of ways of awarding disproportionately high rewards for the best ideas, and it is not difficult to combine such a policy, in the interest of fairness, with opportunities for employee participation. For instance, companies could have an "Idea of the Year" competition based on the five most valuable suggestions submitted over the course of the year. Employees would be asked to pick the idea that they think has done most to further the company's development. This type of competition increases incentives for the most talented without generating undesired selection effects.

Whatever adjustments managers make, it is important that they ensure that the changes are perceived as gains rather than losses. Psychological studies show that a loss of Sfr 100 has a much greater negative impact than the positive impact produced by a gain of Sfr 100. Changes to an existing linear reward structure should thus ensure that in future the best ideas are rewarded more generously. A simple redistribution of rewards from the less talented to the best would probably cost the company more dearly than the current, less effective fixed percentage reward system.

Minimum rewards. The arguments in favor of minimum rewards are similar to those for fixed percentage rates. Companies acknowledge the good intentions of employees by rewarding suggestions of little economic value. There is no doubt that the mutual acknowledgment of good intentions is a key component of good working relations (see Chapter 1, and also Fehr and Gächter, 2000). Whether or not minimum rewards make sense depends on the associated costs. The Sfr 50 given for each reward is not the main cost; the main cost is the selection effect that leads to *employees submitting ideas purely because they hope to receive the minimum reward.* Managers who believe that this selection effect does not cause a problem in their company can leave the minimum reward system in place. However, those that suspect that the selection effect could be significant may want to dilute the system, perhaps by converting the monetary minimum rewards into some form of symbolic recognition. A bottle of wine, a letter of appreciation from the executive board, or a meal with the manager can be as valued by employees as much as a small sum of money.

5. The Effectiveness of Performance Incentives

Pay for performance creates both selection and motivational effects. More generous compensation strengthens the motivation of employees to perform well. At the same time, activities that bring generous rewards also become more attractive for less talented individuals. The overall effect of stronger incentives is, therefore, ambivalent. Where the motivational effect prevails, average output per employee will increase. But if the selection effect is more pronounced, average output per employee will fall.

In this chapter we have demonstrated this relationship by looking at the example of suggestion systems used by Swiss companies. If the rewards for valuable suggestions increase, the company will receive more ideas, but these ideas will not be of a better quality. The quality of suggestions does not improve because many less talented employees, who typically would not submit proposals if the rewards were lower, start submitting ideas when the incentive becomes greater. The most effective compensation systems are those that exploit the motivational effect of monetary incentives to the full without increasing the selection effect.

Our results show that the value of the average new idea increases by Sfr 800 if companies lower the rewards for less valuable ideas by Sfr 1,000 and increase the rewards for the best suggestion accordingly. In economic terms, this represents a very significant improvement, given that the employees in our sample submit more than 60 ideas per year on average. Companies that pay out fewer rewards, but concentrate resources on the best suggestions achieve far greater cost reductions.

The lesson to be learned from this study is simple: monetary incentives work. Paradoxically, these incentives sometimes work all too well. They motivate *everyone* to put in greater effort, even those whose effort is unlikely to produce valuable results. Thus, pay for performance can bring about greater efficiency, but it can also lead to economic inefficiencies. Successful managers know how to exploit the motivational potential of monetary incentives without at the same time encouraging inefficient activities.

6. Further Reading

How managers can design more effective incentive plans is shown in:

Lazear, E. P. (1998). *Personnel Economics for Managers.* New York: Wiley.

Interesting ways of influencing creativity are discussed by:

Amabile, T. (1998). How to Kill Creativity. *Harvard Business Review,* September-October: pp 77-87.
Bazerman, M. H. (1994). *Judgment in Managerial Decision Making.* New York: Wiley.

The management of suggestion systems in Switzerland was studied by:

Büsch, K.-H. and N. Thom (1982). Kooperations- und Konfliktfelder von Unternehmensleitung und Betriebsrat beim Vorschlagswesen. Betriebliches Vorschlagswesen 4: pp 163-181.
Etienne, M. (1997). *Grenzen und Chancen des Vorgesetztenmodells im Betrieblichen Vorschlagswesen: Eine Fallstudie.* Bern: Lang.
Frey, D., R. Fischer and O. Winzer (1996). *Mitdenken lohnt sich - für alle! Ideenmanagement durch Vorschlagswesen in Wirtschaft und Verwaltung.* Bayerisches Staatsministerium für Arbeit und Sozialordnung, Familie, Frauen und Gesundheit (publ.). Munich.
Post, H. and N. Thom (1980). Verbesserung und Ausbau des Betrieblichen Vorschlagswesens: Erkenntnisse einer Befragungsaktion. *Betriebliches Vorschlagswesen* 3: pp 114-136.

7. Statistical Appendix

In Table 5-1, we show *how many* ideas a company receives. Besides the overall sum of rewards and the size of the largest reward, we control for additional variables which may have an effect: the number of employees, the industry, the year, the Swiss canton in which the company is located, and finally the company's unobservable characteristics that remain constant over time. The further right in Table 5-1 the results appear, the more factors are held constant.

Table 5-1:
Why Do Companies Receive More or Less Ideas?

	Number of ideas	Number of ideas	Number of ideas	Number of ideas	Number of ideas
Sum of rewards + 1000	2.80 (0.20)**	2.70 (0.19)**	2.72 (0.19)**	2.68 (0.19)**	1.01 (0.28)**
Largest reward + 1000	-2.63 (1.20)*	-3.13 (1.18)**	-3.03 (1.18)**	-3.50 (1.15)**	-6.28 (1.22)**
Number of employees +1000	4.06 (0.63)**	6.20 (0.78)**	6.24 (0.78)**	5.66 (0.79)**	2.22 (3.29)
Controlled for industry?	no	yes	yes	yes	yes
Controlled for year?	no	no	yes	yes	yes
Controlled for canton?	no	no	no	yes	yes
Company fixed effects?	no	no	no	no	yes
Constant	36.08 (5.58)**	19.50 (11.99)**	41.22 (20.87)*	18.62 (58.37)	80.97 (27.13)**
Number of observations	856	856	856	850	850
Corrected R^2	0.33	0.33	0.36	0.37	0.10

Note: ** p≤0.01, * p≤0.05, standard errors in parentheses.

The results in Table 5-1 can be interpreted as follows: if a company increases the sum of rewards by Sfr 1,000, it receives 2.80 more suggestions. ** indicates that this effect is statistically significant.

Table 5-2:
Why Do Companies Receive Better or Worse Ideas?

	Quality of ideas	Quality of ideas	Quality of ideas	Quality of ideas	Quality of ideas
Sum of rewards ÷ 1000	-55 (37)	-55 (38)	-56 (38)	-58 (39)	45 (69)
Largest reward ÷ 1000	742 (229)**	740 (230)**	758 (231)**	731 (238)**	829 (303)**
Number of employees ÷1000	-107 (120)	-132 (155)	-129 (155)	-103 (167)	-435 (850)
Controlled for industry?	no	yes	yes	yes	yes
Controlled for year?	no	no	yes	yes	yes
Controlled for canton?	no	no	no	yes	yes
Company fixed effects?	no	no	no	no	yes
Constant	2953 (1094)**	1070 (2395)	2654 (4196)	832 (12045)	-3520 (6946)
Number of observations	795	795	795	789	789
Corrected R^2	0.01	0.01	0.01	0.01	0.02

Note: ** p≤0.01, * p≤0.05, standard errors in parentheses.

Part III

Motivation and Work Organization

Chapter Six

JETTA FROST AND MARGIT OSTERLOH

Motivation and Organizational Forms

Introduction

How a company is organized has a significant impact on the motivation of its employees. In fact, the motivation of employees working in participative team structures differs from that of employees in an organization with several hierarchical levels and strict rules of delegation. In this chapter, we investigate the relationship between motivation and organizational forms. We discuss Taylorism, overlapping group organizations and the profit center organization, and how they affect motivation.

In this chapter we show that the structure of organizations has been closely associated with motivational issues since the beginnings of organizational research. Frederick Taylor, architect of the assembly line, was interested in the relationship between efficient organizational structure and effective work incentives. However, he focused solely on extrinsic motivation. In the 1920s, a group of psychologists at Harvard University conducted the so-called Hawthorne experiment. They discovered the significance of informal organization and concluded that good performance would ensue only if employee satisfaction is maintained. In the following years, this conclusion was contested and considered naïve by many researchers. They argued that organization should be viewed as an institution in which employees derive satisfaction from the performance of their tasks. This places the emphasis on intrinsic motivation. But what about extrinsic motivation? Until now organizational theories have tended to concentrate either on intrinsic or extrinsic motivation. But we know from the previous chapters that both types of motivation are relevant.

In the first section of this chapter, we look at Taylorism, a traditional form of work organization based on the principle of extrinsic motivation. Then, in the second section we discuss Likert's overlapping group structures, which focus on the promotion of intrinsic employee motivation. In the third section we examine the current phenomenon of the profit center organization and ask whether this form of organization can produce a balance between extrinsic and intrinsic motivation. Focusing on one of the most important of competitive resources, knowledge, we then highlight the connection between the generation and transmission of explicit and tacit knowledge and the need for extrinsic and intrinsic motivation.

1. Organization and Extrinsic Motivation: Taylorism

Frederick W. Taylor (1856 - 1915), an engineer by profession, was among the first theorists to investigate the relationship between organizational structure and motivation. His *scientific management* approach became known the world over as *Taylorism*. In 1911 he published his book, "The Principles of Scientific Management." Taylor's scientific management theory was the product of a new kind of professional factory management which was emerging at that time.

Taylor wanted to increase the efficiency of human labor in mechanized operations. His proposition centered on the idea that increases in productivity could be achieved through an efficient system of dividing and performing the tasks at hand without increasing the workload of the individual employee. Taylor's "scientific management" was based on the following methodical principles:

- The work processes involved were divorced from the skills of the workers, i.e. tasks were simply divided into several very small steps *(horizontal specialization)*. At the same time intellectual tasks were completely separated from manual tasks *(vertical specialization)*. As a result, all the employees were able to learn how to perform the task at hand in a very short space of time, while affording maximum control over the entire work process.

- *A material stimulu* – a piece-rate system – was also needed in order to promote the willingness of workers to perform.

- Taylor was the pioneer of the *science of labor management.* New workplaces were created to promote employee performance, with optimal light, proper arrangement of the machines and well-adjusted climatic conditions. Work times were short, with several breaks in between, aimed at enhancing work intensity. Moreover, methodical studies of the tasks performed and the time span required to perform them were undertaken in order to find the best physiological method of executing the tasks.

- The systematic standardization of the objects worked on made *total planning and control* of the workflow possible.

Taylor's vision enthusiastically described a production system encompassing both men and machines that functioned as efficiently as a well-designed, well-oiled machine. This demanded a functionally-oriented organizational form.

One of the best-known examples of the application of Taylor's concept was in the workshops of Henry Ford (1863 to 1947). In the workshops at River Rouge and Highland Park, the famous T-model was manufactured. Ford applied Taylor's ideas to the new industrial production techniques, which essentially involved mechanized mass production on assembly lines. In the Ford concept, employees were no longer controlled by their supervisors but by the repetitive assembly line steps. These involved only one or two manual actions. The Ford production system introduced a whole raft of innovative ideas that were completely new in their day: a continuous flow of production based on a rational workflow system, the standardization of individual parts, the vertical integration of manufacturing components, and the use of mass production to achieve economies of scale.

The fact that Ford and many other firms adopted Taylorism was a consequence of the industrial revolution. Mechanization at that time made mass production possible. Labor was also cheap due to the massive inflow of unskilled rural workers into the cities. Moreover, the view of human beings at the time of the industrial revolution was a fervently mechanistic one. The organization was determined by the production flow of the machines and the rhythm of the assembly line. Work was thus driven by external forces. *Intrinsic* motivation did not play a role in Taylorism. Workers were simply production factors without any particular needs other than the wages they earned. It was assumed that they did not have any interest in the tasks they carried out. Thus, control and performance-based compensation were used to *extrinsically* motivate them to work.

However, Taylor's system of work organization led to unexpectedly high control costs. This was exacerbated by the so-called *control paradox:* the workers only worked when they were controlled. The feeling of being controlled, however, led to reduced satisfaction at the workplace and, as a consequence, a reduction in the willingness to perform. Control mechanisms were therefore increased, which further reduced satisfaction, and so on, becoming a vicious cycle. This control paradox is illustrated in Figure 6-1. It can be viewed as an early demonstration of the crowding-out effect: heavy control mechanisms in the workplace reduce the satisfaction of initially intrinsically motivated employees.

Taylorism: The Control Paradox

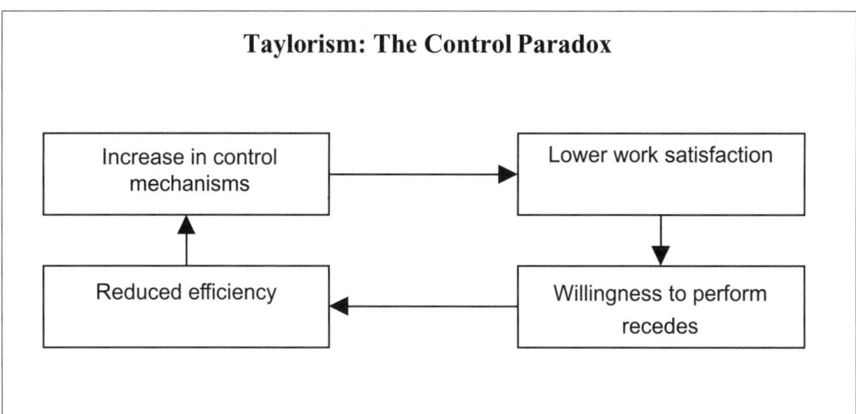

Figure 6-1

2. Organization and Intrinsic Motivation: Likert's Group Organization

Rensis Likert (1961, 1967) was one of the first researchers to investigate the relationship between organization structure and (intrinsic) motivation, although he did not use this term. His model of the group organization, first published in the 1960s, has become the most well-known of organizational forms, the aim of which was self-determination in the workplace. Today Likert's group organization has lost none of its modernity.

Likert was a proponent of the human relations approach to organizations. This argues that personality development, stimulating work, recognition, responsibility and participation are relevant factors in the workplace. If such factors are taken into consideration, then the readiness of employees to perform will increase. A reverse of the control paradox could possibly ensue as illustrated in Figure 6-2.

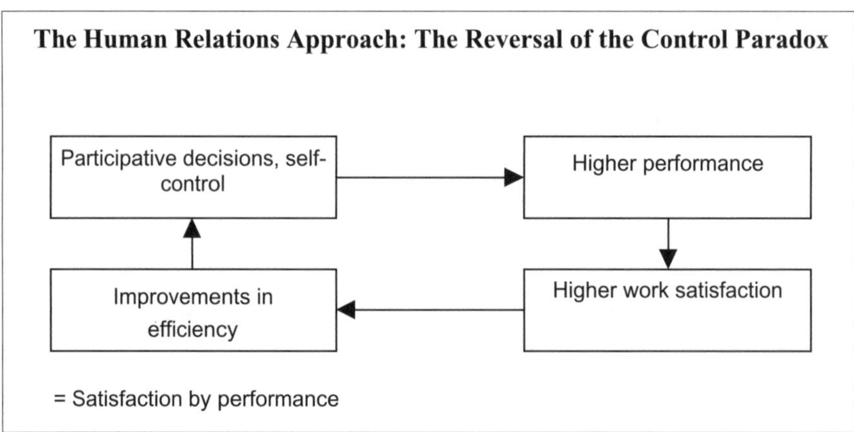

Figure 6-2

Likert developed his group organization concept on the basis of empirical research undertaken with colleagues from the University of Michigan. They investigated management behavior, group processes and the significance of communication. Likert was essentially interested in the crucial differences between efficient and inefficient organizational departments. He concluded from his research that the type of management principles adopted determine the productivity or non-productivity of departments. Less productive departments tended to have authoritative management styles. These Likert classified as System 1. Similar to Taylor's scientific management, System 1 is also characterized by as much division of labor as possible. Consequently, management has to provide a detailed description of the various tasks to be accomplished. There is then minimal communication between managers and their subordinates. Systematic incentives are used to improve performance. Productive departments on the other hand typically adopt *participative management systems.* Likert labeled this form System 4. These systems follow principles that are compatible with cognitive evaluation theory and the theory of psychological contracts discussed in Chapter 1.

The Principle of Supportive Relationships

In Likert's concept, the principle of supportive relationships characterizes the behavioral conduct between managers and their subordinates. This means a cooperative relationship exists between them, with the recognition of each other's worth. Managers have faith in the abilities of their subordinates. They also support the further development of their skills and learning. In line with the theory of psychological contracts, the principle of supportive relationships depends on managers and employees having respect for the reasons behind each other's actions.

The Principle of Group Decision-Making

Central to Likert's concept is the establishment of teamwork within the different divisions of a firm. Participative management systems demand a high level of communication. Intensive decision-making processes take place within the group. (For more on participation, see Chapter 8.) The basic idea is that all members of a work group participate as much as possible in all the relevant decision-making tasks. The important thing is for participants to be able to exert influence on how decisions are made and what is decided, while also being responsible for the smooth functioning of the cooperative undertaking. Teamwork has several advantages over traditional hierarchical structures:

- The fact that the team includes a wide range of different employee skills ensures that the quality of the decisions is enhanced.

- The sense of belonging to the team brings about a higher level of satisfaction, lower absenteeism and minimal employee turnover.

- Participative decision-making reduces resistance when decisions are implemented, since the different opinions have already been incorporated in the decision-making process. Those affected by implementation of the decisions will identify with the change because they had a part in the decision-making.

The underlying assumptions of the two principles of supportive relationships and group decision-making are the basis for Likert's concept of overlapping group structures. This can be applied to the whole organization.

The Multiple Overlapping Group Structure

Throughout the whole organization and all the hierarchical levels, work groups should be linked with each other in such a way that they overlap at several points. This ensures that tacit knowledge for the joint development and use of pooled resources can be exchanged throughout the company regardless of the boundaries separating each department. The overlapping of the groups may take any of the following three forms:

Vertical Overlapping

The individual work groups are enmeshed with each other over several different hierarchical levels. This is achieved by a member of each group – normally the group head – belonging simultaneously to the next higher level of hierarchy as the "linking pin." This scheme ensures that there is sufficient communication between the different hierarchical levels. Representing the group, the head can communicate the suggestions and ideas of his or her group to the next-higher group. He will then also convey to the rest of the group the decisions made by the higher group, which are then discussed. If the exchange of ideas is to function properly, it is important that the decisions are really taken by the group.

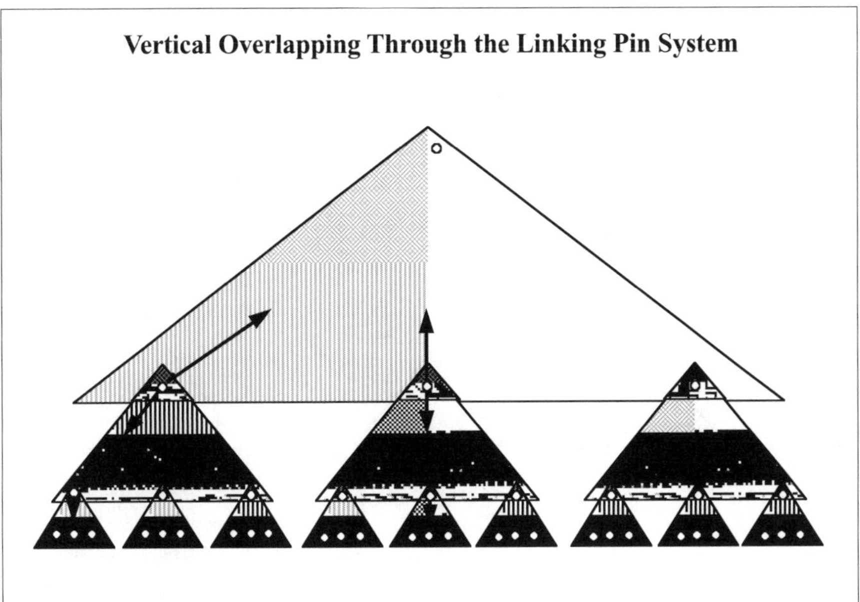

Figure 6-3 (Likert 1967, p. 50)

Horizontal Overlapping

Within the same hierarchical level, Likert likewise proposes that groups overlap through a member's simultaneous participation in two teams. This allows collaboration to take place between departments and simplifies the coordination dynamics of the whole firm. So-called "cross-function work groups" are formed with members coming from the different work groups. The cross-function work groups are then led by one of the heads of the work groups. As in matrix organizations, dual management functions arise, with team members reporting to two different heads, thereby creating the need to remove overlapping areas of authority. The aim is to anchor communication and coordination processes clearly in the structure of the firm. Decision-making processes can then be better coordinated and the quality of decisions will improve. By adding new dimensions via cross-functional relationships the aim is to broaden the view of the problems to be solved. That is the advantage of this organizational form. Nevertheless, there are disadvantages: with employees belonging to two different groups, coordination difficulties and role ambiguities can arise. Each organizational interface is a potential source of organizational irresponsibility. Moreover, the situation creates dual loyalties, which demands a strong ability to deal with and tolerate conflict, especially with conflicting management pressure coming from two different sources.

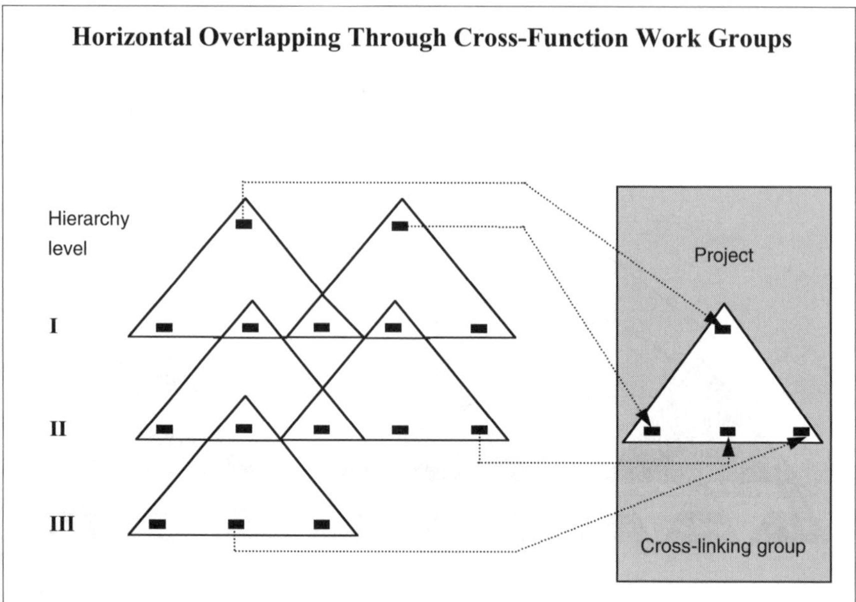

Figure 6-4 (Likert 1967, p. 160)

Lateral Overlapping

Another type of enmeshed system is created by lateral interaction between "cross-function groups." It differs from horizontal overlapping in that membership in two different teams is not confined to a single hierarchical level. This overlapping concept ensures coordination across various functions and different hierarchical levels: in other words, lateral integration. Lateral groups function in the same way as project teams. Specialists from various departments and hierarchical levels are involved. And regardless of their status within the organization, the team members seek to solve complex problems together. Although in this system too a formal group head is present, Likert considers it absolutely essential to take decisions by consensus.

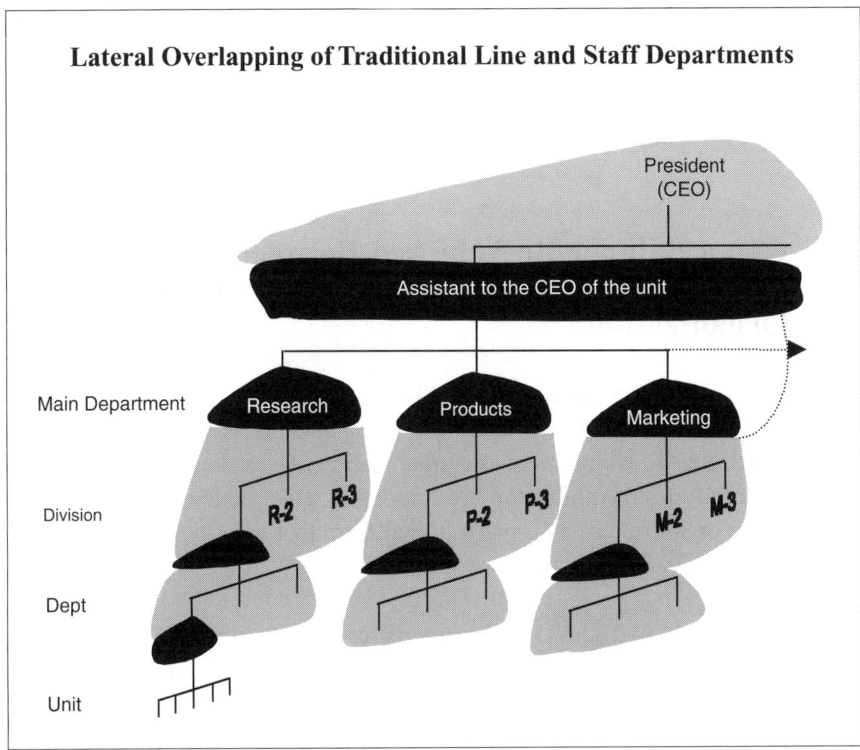

Figure 6-5 (Likert 1967, p. 175)

The group organization presupposes intrinsic motivation of its members. They are willing to share their knowledge with other members and make the goals of the organization their own. However desirable, group members active at the interfaces cannot be forced to share their knowledge by directive anyway. As a result, this organizational structure is particularly suited to promoting the exchange of tacit knowledge. The link pins ensure that the teams are connected vertically, horizontally and laterally and that information and knowledge is thus freely transferred.

However, Likert's group organization has been criticized on two grounds.

Firstly, it ignores aspects of *extrinsic* motivation completely. Monetary impulses are not deemed significant. In Chapter 1, we have seen that extrinsic motivation of the organization members does play an important role. *Secondly,* the decision-making process involved is extremely time-consuming. Building a consensus takes much longer than when directives are simply issued by management.

Both these disadvantages may be the reasons why group organizations are not very often applied in reality. What we have seen is the use of quality circles or task forces in some companies.

3. Can a Balance Be Achieved Between Extrinsic and Intrinsic Motivation Through the Profit Center Organization?

From the discussions in Sections 1 and 2 we have seen that Taylorism is founded solely on extrinsic motivation, whereas group organizations require only intrinsic motivation from the members of the organization. As explained in Chapter 1, however, both types of motivation are important. This section will discuss the profit center organization, an organizational form that tries to secure a balance between extrinsic and intrinsic motivation.

In Section 3.1 we will discuss the characteristics of a typical profit center organization. In the process, it will be shown that this organizational form is not totally without its problems, but has two areas of conflict. In Section 3.2, we will discuss the conflict between (intrinsic) motivation and the coordination mechanism of transfer pricing. Thereafter, we will discuss the conflict between (extrinsic) motivation and knowledge.

Nowadays, restructuring in firms increasingly takes the form of allowing more market forces to function within the firm. The basic idea is to set up an internal market within the firm, with different organizational units both providing and purchasing internal services at a certain price determined by market forces. As a result, internal markets and prices will gradually replace the (hierarchical) coordination mechanisms of directives, instructions and rules. The profit center organization embodies the concept of internal market mechanisms.

3.1 The Typical Profit Center Organization

A *profit center* is an organizational unit for which a *specific periodic profit* can be calculated. With the profit center organization, divisions, subsidiaries and units can be organized according to individual products, services, product groups or major projects. The distinctive feature is that grouping is based on the unit's output. This leads to the specification of service quality levels and prices in "service level agreements." Within a firm, the profit centers pay only for the services that they have actually used. Those providing services gear themselves to serving the needs of their (internal) customers. The internal market pressure educates the profit center heads to behave entrepreneurially because prices:

- determine the profit contribution of each unit to the corporate outcome,
- provide the basis for profit-based performance assessment, and
- exercise control on the basis of the delivered output.

The work processes in profit center organizations do not need to be controlled in the same way as under Taylorism. Only the results achieved matter. As a "firm within a firm," profit centers encourage *entrepreneurship.*[1]

Ideally, the profit center organization will use market prices as a means of coordination. Price competition is used to evaluate the output and productivity of the profit centers. For this the following three conditions need to be fulfilled:

- *Availability*. This means that an external market must exist for the goods and services. Otherwise, it will not be possible to determine a market price for the services provided by the profit centers.
- *Exchange autonomy.* This means that the buying unit should autonomously decide whether the goods or services it needs should be sourced internally or externally. Moreover, the competitive conditions between the profit centers should be the same as those applying in the external market. In this case, transactions occur only when they are agreed upon by managers both in the buying and the selling roles.
- *Standardized goods and services.* The more similar the goods and services among rival firms are, the more easily these offerings can have an "objectively" set and contractually laid down price. Standardized goods and services are transferable and can be bought and sold with little difficulty. Firm-specific pool resources, such as core competencies (the nature of which we discussed in Chapter 2), do not belong to this group of services because they cannot be easily transferred. They cannot be bought in the outside marketplace and must be developed by the company itself.

1 The following points apply mainly to managers of profit centers because of the bonuses and incentives they receive. Only they are paid performance-related variable salaries, whereas their subordinates normally receive fixed salaries. As a result, it is not possible to assess their motivational effects definitively.

If the aforementioned conditions could be fulfilled, then the profit center organization would truly produce substantial *extrinsic* and *intrinsic motivational effects*. There are two reasons for this:

- Market prices encourage efficiency. The profit center heads will behave as if they were managing autonomous firms. If they earn a high profit, their monetary rewards will also be large. Profits are the measure on which performance-related pay or the awarding of bonuses are based. In this way, extrinsic motivation is fostered.

- Market prices also promote intrinsic motivation. This is because the decentralization of the different divisions allows for a great deal of autonomy with a high degree of decentralization of authority and responsibility. The profit center heads are accountable for their endeavors. The orientation is toward results, and there is thus greater scope for independent action and decision-making than is possible when detailed instructions and regulations are dictated from above. Moreover, market prices are considered fairer than other transfer prices because they have been "objectively" determined and are thus less susceptible to manipulation. For instance, the market price does not depend on the information advantage that individual profit center heads possess.

It might be inferred from this that the profit center organization is the ideal organizational form from the point of view of motivation management. The promotion of both extrinsic and intrinsic motivation is taken care of. This only occurs, however, when the autonomy of the individual profit centers is great enough for genuine market mechanisms to actually work in dealings between the profit centers.

The question then is: What *organizational* advantages do profit centers stand to gain from staying within a corporate structure? If the profit centers indeed act as if they were independent firms within a large complex organization, why not actually allow them to operate on their own? If profit centers seek to maximize their own results even at the expense of other profit centers, why should they remain together at all? What distinguishes decentralized profit center organizations from the outside marketplace? In Chapter 2, we have said that firms exist because within them firm-specific pool resources can be developed and used, which cannot be found in this form on the market. Such pool resources cannot be generated by an individual member of the organization. They arise from the collaboration between various members belonging to different units and divisions of the organization. Thus, firm-specific pool resources are strongly intertwined with the whole organization itself. They cannot be traded and cannot be specified exactly in contracts. This is the real reason why not all activities can be performed or priced by the market.

However, a *conflict* ensues from this:

- *On the one hand,* we know that the profit centers ought to behave like independent firms. Each transaction between the profit centers should then have a set price based on market prices. The profit centers compete with each other for capital and other resources on the basis of performance. For this to be possible, services should be comparable to the services of external firms. As a result, prices will also be comparable to the prices set by external firms. But the profit centers will have to be granted *a high degree of exchange autonomy* if they are to properly price their services and earn their own profit for a particular period. This is essential for determining their contribution to the company's revenues and granting appropriate monetary incentives.

- *On the other hand,* complementary firm-specific pool resources should generate *synergy effects* for the firm as a whole. Internal market competition, however, leads to disinterest in working collaboratively with other units. If contributions to the firm-specific pool resources are difficult to ascribe to a particular unit, profit centers will not be interested in providing them. They will seek to maximize their own results, even though this may be at the cost of the success of the firm as a whole. Owing to this, limits need to be set with regard to a profit center's autonomy or its decision-making power. This will promote cooperative undertakings, but will be at the expense of individual profit center goals. Thus there are limits to the use of market mechanisms within profit center organizations.

In the following two sections, we proceed to discuss this conflict extensively: firstly, as a conflict between motivation and the coordination mechanism of transfer prices (Section 3.2) and, secondly, as a conflict between motivation and the transfer of knowledge (Section 3.3).

3.2 The Conflict between Motivation and Coordination via Transfer Prices

We will discuss in this section the relationship between motivation and coordination via transfer prices. The previous section highlighted the trade-off between the use of market coordination mechanisms and the realization of synergy effects, especially in terms of the development and use of firm-specific pool resources. To ease this conflict, profit center organizations have tended to use other coordination mechanisms, namely internal *transfer prices*.

Transfer prices serve to enable a unit to report a profit when profit center autonomy is diminished by the enmeshment of services and interdependencies or by the need to promote cross-divisional collaboration. In these cases the profit centers cannot influence all the critical success factors of their business areas independently as they are not responsible for all the levels of the value-added process of a product or service. This problem can be alleviated by using internal transfer prices to create *virtual internal markets.* This means that the customer-supplier relationships between profit centers are only simulated. Often, the internal transaction partner is not really free to decide whether he or she wants to source internally or to cooperate with other units or not. As a result, the units do not negotiate like external market partners. They use other methods of evaluating deliveries. We will investigate the effects of the two most well-known forms of transfer pricing – cost-based and negotiated transfer prices – on motivation and collaboration.

Cost-Based Transfer Prices and Their Effects on Motivation and Coordination

Cost-based transfer pricing focuses on the cost of producing an internal service. As a rule this is easy to determine, because the relevant cost data can simply be taken from the accounts. The actual costs incurred can be easily calculated. Nevertheless, the unit requiring the goods or services has no influence over the cost structure of the unit providing it. Figure 6-1 provides an overview of three different methods of cost-based transfer pricing: full cost, marginal cost and the cost-plus method.

For the following two reasons, cost-based transfer prices bring little in terms of *extrinsic* and *intrinsic motivation:*

1. If the selling unit can charge the full cost of production to the unit requiring the goods or services, then there will be no incentives that promote efficiency. This would be necessary, however, if *extrinsic* motivation is to be enhanced.

2. Cost-based transfer prices entail a certain degree of illusion as regards autonomy. Since no pure market price exists, transfer prices are determined under guidelines established by higher-level managers: a notional internal price is fixed, called an adjusted market price. It reduces the authority of profit center managers to determine transfer prices themselves. This is often viewed by profit center managers as unfair, especially if they feel that they have to source their requirements from a unit that operates inefficiently. *Intrinsic* motivation in this case is reduced. Furthermore, the fact that autonomy in the decision-making process is limited also impairs intrinsic motivation.

Table 6-1: Cost-Based Transfer Pricing

Full Cost	Marginal Cost	Cost-Plus
• Represents the actual *full costs* of the providing unit • Problem I: determining the proportion of fixed costs and general overheads • Problem II: no pressure to save costs • Problems I and II can be alleviated by the use of *standard or marginal costs.* • Practical relevance	• *Marginal cost* = incremental cost of every additional unit produced • Overall profit is maximized when transfer price = marginal cost • Conditions: technological interdependence and demand interdependence • Problem: transfer price, i.e. MC, must be determined centrally; no decision-making autonomy for the units • Of little practical relevance	• Full cost plus an *additional markup* (notional market price), normally as a percentage • Profits are ascribed to the providing unit • Same problems I and II as with full cost method • Problem III: motivation for the units providing the service; costs are high (danger of autonomy illusion) • Very popular in business practice

In addition, cost-based transfer pricing has a limited *coordination effect.* The central planning unit will frequently intervene since the cost and revenue curves of the units concerned need to be coordinated in order to produce correct budget figures. The coordination effects that transfer pricing was originally intended to produce are also radically diminished by the continuing need to resort to other central coordination mechanisms of the hierarchical system. The coordination effort between the different units is substantially higher because generally accepted standards first need to be agreed on, e.g. the criteria for systematically structuring the costs incurred. This causes transfer prices to lose their relevance as an indicator of the profitability of the unit. As a consequence, cost-based transfer prices will only be useful for long-term internal sourcing of goods and services. This does not allow much flexibility.

Negotiated Transfer Prices and Their Effects on Motivation and Coordination

Given the limitations of cost-based methods, enthusiasm for negotiated transfer prices is expressed when perfectly competitive markets do not exist (Kaplan/Atkinson 1989). The fundamental idea behind negotiated transfer pricing arrangements is to establish a "service- or product-level agreement" by direct negotiation between the units involved. This is an agreement on which products and services are to be provided at which price level. Underlying this is the notion that there should be a balance between marginal cost and marginal utility, thereby ensuring that the profit of the whole firm is maximized.

But the effects on *intrinsic* motivation *cannot* be clearly identified for two reasons:

1. Negotiated transfer prices can *enhance motivation.* Independent negotiations between different departments increase the autonomy of the units involved. Moreover, the opportunity to participate in the decision-making process can lead to a higher acceptance level of the results. Thus there is a positive effect on *intrinsic* motivation.

2. However, the obligatory transfer of goods and services between different units can lead to a monopoly situation for a particular unit, thereby limiting the scope for negotiation. For example, if the annual budget process has already defined the potential volume of internal services to be exchanged, then there is naturally an obligation to source goods and services internally. If the stronger negotiating partner exploits its bargaining power, the negotiated transfer price will be considered unfair by the counterparty. In this case, *intrinsic* motivation is reduced. An empirical study has even shown that profit center managers prefer to negotiate with external market partners, because they are then dealing with comparable and specific prices that can be specified in contracts. Internal negotiations, on the other hand, are often perceived as difficult and unfair (Eccles 1985).

The effects on extrinsic motivation cannot be clearly evaluated either. It is unclear whether an internally negotiated transfer price will produce the same motivational effects on the profit center managers as an external market price. In seeking to manage extrinsic motivation this problem is of importance.

Similarly, the *coordination effects* of negotiated transfer prices remain uncertain. No final word can be said on this. If the units involved are given the freedom to determine the transfer prices themselves, this will eliminate the costs of having to determine transfer prices centrally. In this case, transfer prices have a positive effect on coordination between the units. On the other hand, the danger exists that the negotiating units will agree on prices which are detrimental to third parties. They will set what they believe to be the best transfer price for them. This may, however, not be optimal from the point of view of the company as a whole. To compensate for this, other coordination mechanisms will have to be used, which usually means that the company's executive management will have to intervene. In addition, negotiations tend to take a lot of time.

All in all, the conflict potential between motivation and coordination via transfer prices can be summarized as follows: both cost-based and negotiated transfer prices reduce the autonomy of the profit centers. This results from the use of notional internal market prices instead of real market prices. As a rule, internal market prices only create an illusion of autonomy and have to be supplemented by central coordination mechanisms. Moreover, if profit center managers feel that the transfer prices are unfair, intrinsic motivation will be reduced.

3.3 The Conflict Between Motivation and Knowledge Transfer

In this section we will discuss the conflict between the promotion of extrinsic motivation and the organization of knowledge transfer. *On the one hand,* the transfer of knowledge – most especially of tacit knowledge – between organization members and different organizational units is a prerequisite for the development of firm-specific pool resources. *On the other hand,* if the profit center is only evaluated on the basis of the profits it achieves, then there will be an incentive for it to implement decisions even when the undertaking is at the expense of other units or problematic consequences could be expected for the company as a whole. The more autonomously the profit centers are organized and the more external motivational stimulators are used, the greater is the risk of departmental egoism. This inhibits the development of common organizational knowledge as a key complementary pool resource. Internal market control mechanisms or traditional "command and rule" coordination mechanisms are not effective here.

At this point we would like to return to the argument put forward in Chapter 2 that motivation and knowledge are the most important strategic resources for competitive advantage. Then we link intrinsic and extrinsic motivation with the transfer of tacit or explicit knowledge. Combining motivational and knowledge requirements leads to a typology of organizational forms, as presented in Table 6-2. (For a detailed differentiation between tacit and explicit knowledge, see Chapter 2.) We will discuss which organizational forms can best enable the transfer of explicit or tacit knowledge with respect to the required extrinsic or intrinsic motivation.

Table 6-2: Combining Motivational and Knowledge Requirements with Organizational Forms

		Knowledge Transfer	
		Tacit	**Explicit**
Motivation	**Intrinsic**	2 Knowledge-based production teams Likert's group organization	3 Knowledge-producing teams e.g. task forces, quality circles
	Extrinsic	4 Individualists	1 Profit centers

Quadrant 1: This quadrant covers organizational forms like *profit centers,* spin-offs or legally independent holding companies. It describes the situation commonly considered by economists when they suggest running a firm as "if it were a set of markets." As we have explained, in profit centers (transfer) prices are used as the preferred coordination mechanism for eliciting efficient extrinsic motivation. This means, however, that the exchange of knowledge *between* the individual profit centers occurs on the basis of internal contracts, in which the prices and the goods and services to be provided are established. The components or modules exchanged must be specified exactly. *Either* the knowledge to be transferred between the decentralized units is explicit and attributable *or* such knowledge is incorporated in tradable product components or modules, which can be assembled or used with the help of instructions. Similar to driving a car, where the driver does not need to know how the car functions in order to drive, all that is needed are the right instructions. In both cases the price and the product are contractually agreed. *Intrinsic* motivation is unnecessary, because what each party wants of the other is clearly established, and the goods and services can be readily attributed and reported as profits of the unit.

However, extrinsically motivated competition between the profit centers hinders sharing knowledge with one another and prevents the flow of tacit knowledge across unit boundaries to where it is needed. The members of an independent unit have no incentive to give up their individual competitive advantage as long as they are compensated according to the unit's profitability. Thus, the organizational form described in Quadrant 1 will only be efficient if we are dealing with the transfer of explicit knowledge or with an exchange between independently produced goods and services between units. Only then is the use of prices as a coordination mechanism effective and there will be no need for intrinsic motivation. Note however that it is not possible to establish any sustained competitive advantage in the relationship between the decentralized units because imitation is facilitated by the fact that everything is defined explicitly in contracts.

Quadrant 2 represents *"knowledge-based production teams"* or the *"Likert group organization."* Knowledge-based production teams are those whose members attempt to integrate not only their explicit knowledge but also their tacit knowledge, thereby enabling the organization to offer a unique and difficult-to-imitate product in the market.

Examples include the production of a top-class wine, the manufacturing of a complex technical installation or the development of software. In these cases, we are dealing with products or services incorporating the tacit knowledge of various specialists.

The knowledge of wine specialists remains tacit even when the wine bottle is on the table. The applied know-how cannot be made explicit through "reverse engineering" either. That is one reason why wine is so expensive. Reverse engineering is when a product is broken down to reveal the underlying production expertise. This is impossible to accomplish when tacit knowledge is an "ingredient." Tacit specialized knowledge is not tradable individually or in association with other knowledge. It can only be sold as an integral part of a product or service. This integration in the product makes it a critical success factor. The effect of synergies or complementary strengths inherent in teams is a key factor in their success. This concept can be extended to the entire firm and as such corresponds to Likert's principles of group organization. Through their cross-functional activities employees in different units work with each other face to face and thus have the opportunity to exchange tacit knowledge with one another, thereby integrating it into the whole.

In the case of wine production, for instance, not even the specialists can specify which tacit knowledge is necessary. Nor do they have much idea what each one of them has contributed to the product. They simply play their part in building firm-specific pool resources. For this reason, the tacit knowledge that is paid for in the price of the wine cannot be attributed proportionally to the individuals involved in its production. Within the team, it is impossible to measure the contribution of individuals, which can motivate opportunistically oriented members of the team to free ride at the expense of the others. To avoid this, *intrinsic* motivation needs to be promoted. Fortunately, the work environment for many specialists working in teams is conducive to intrinsic motivation. The key factors here are collective decision-making and problem-solving, individual responsibility, tasks that enable and promote identification with the end product, team spirit, shared norms and qualitative feedback from colleagues. Likert has summarized this principle in the notion of participative management, which is the basis for implementing an overlapping group structure.

Although, in the cases described, only intrinsic motivation has been described as absolutely necessary, extrinsic motivation nevertheless plays an important role. This typically applies to situations where a person makes a decision to join a certain team or firm. The granting of stock options in many "new economy" companies, for instance, is an attractive alternative for potential employees in comparison to traditional compensation packages. (See also the discussion on remuneration policy at ING Barings in Chapter 9.) Marc and Simon (1958) pointed out the significant difference between "motivation to participate" and "motivation to produce."[2]

Quadrant 3 encompasses organizational forms in which parts of tacit knowledge are converted into explicit knowledge, but where intrinsic motivation is required for the conversion. *Quality circles* with voluntary participation or *task forces* provide some fitting examples. The members of quality circles or task forces contribute their knowledge inputs (which are often only tacitly available) via the problems dealt with. They attempt to make explicit suggestions for the improvement of the system that will then be transmitted to the manager concerned. In contrast to the tacit knowledge involved in the wine production team in Quadrant 2, explicit knowledge is produced, albeit specific to the firm. The team members are not concerned with ambitious concepts but with normal day-to-day questions. However, intrinsic motivation is necessary, if tacit knowledge is to flow and be imparted to others. Since the sharing of tacit knowledge cannot be commanded, quality circles more often than not arise voluntarily. In this sense, the knowledge production in Quadrant 3 is similar to that in Quadrant 2. What distinguishes them is that the output of a quality circle or task force is explicit. It can be both observed and measured. However, this explicit knowledge cannot be attributed to an individual working in these teams and can only be used in the context of its generation.

2 March, J. G./Simon, H. A. (1958): Organizations, New York/Oxford.

Box 6-1

Quality Circle at Volkswagen

The quality circles in the automobile industry are particularly well-known. For example, there was a quality circle at Volkswagen in Wolfsburg which set itself the question: "How can we reduce night shifts at the Volkswagen Golf works?" Different teams consisting of six to nine skilled and assembly line workers from the production areas involved were formed to come up with a solution. They were presided over by a foreman with training in moderation techniques. The teams met each week at a fixed time during working hours. At the beginning of the first meeting, a member of executive management explained in person what the purpose of setting up the quality circle was. During the sessions which followed, the team members then began to look for possible solutions. Possible causes of problems were allocated to the individual sections of the manufacturing process. Then the team members considered at which of these stages in the production process they would be able, on the basis of their own experience, to intervene themselves or find a remedy. In the final meeting, a poster showing the results was drawn up. It was found that the main problems were caused by inadequate cleaning of dirty tools, inefficient management of useful waste or scrap, and bad lighting between two presses. Collectively, they then decided upon the possible solutions to recommend to their managers.

The suggestions for improvement proposed by the team members of the Volkswagen quality circle are explicit. Most of the knowledge of the production process remains tacit. The knowledge that has been produced by the quality circle only acquires value through Volkswagen-specific contextual knowledge. The suggestions for improvement are thus only useful for Volkswagen. This knowledge cannot be sold as there is no market for it. In this way, the difference between explicit knowledge and this type of knowledge is made clear. Explicit knowledge can be transferred from profit center to profit center (see Quadrant 1). But in contrast with Quadrant 1, the explicit knowledge produced for a specific company cannot be paid for via (transfer) prices. At the most it can be rewarded by a special group bonus for the collective effort.

It follows from this that the level of intrinsic motivation needed within quality circles or task forces differs from that outside the team. *Within* the teams, intrinsic motivation is indispensable. Tacit knowledge will only be contributed if the team members are intrinsically motivated. Otherwise, members will tend to dodge making a contribution. This intrinsic motivation is usually described as team spirit, esprit de corps or group identification. *Outside* the teams, i.e. in terms of the team's contribution to the firm as a whole, intrinsic motivation is also needed. This is often described as identification with the goals of the company. Group bonuses can be used where the share of knowledge that can be made explicit is high. But caution is needed: group bonuses can also result in crowding-out. "Group egoism" would then surface and knowledge would not be imparted if there is no corresponding payment offered for it. It is therefore wiser to pay group bonuses as a symbolic act of recognition, i.e. as feedback, rather than apply external mechanisms.

Quadrant 4 involves situations where tacit knowledge is transferred under conditions of extrinsic motivation. This holds for *individualists,* e.g. star salespersons in insurance companies. The value of the tacit knowledge transferred to the customer cannot be measured directly, but profits can be. This can then be directly attributed to the salesperson. Their success can be rewarded by the transfer of ownership rights or monetary reward. Individualists may be supported by other employees of the firm. But if the individual's knowledge is to remain attributable to them alone, they cannot be dependent on intermediate input in the form of the tacit knowledge of their team members. The disadvantage is that the tacit knowledge of individualists can easily be lost to the company, i.e. if the person leaves the company and makes their tacit knowledge available to a competitor. This happened at ING Barings, as described in Chapter 9. Companies seek to protect themselves from such an outcome by paying individualists above-average salaries. But for employees who are only extrinsically motivated, this can encourage blackmail tactics.

4. Concluding Remarks

This chapter has shown the relationship between motivation and organizational structure. Whereas Taylorism focuses on extrinsic motivation, the group organization of Likert is based exclusively on the need for intrinsic motivation of organization members. However, both types of motivation are important. This is why many consider the profit center organization as the ideal form of organization, seeking as it does to balance extrinsic and intrinsic motivation. The prerequisite is that the autonomy of the individual centers is great enough to promote the operation of "real" market mechanisms between the profit centers.

A closer look at profit center organizations, however, reveals that they are laden with conflict: the more companies are reliant on internal markets, the more difficult it will be to generate firm-specific pool resources across the different profit centers. Internal market competition forces the profit centers to make their knowledge explicit. This knowledge will consequently no longer be a source of sustainable competitive advantage. By making it explicit and contractible, it can be easily imitated by competitors.

To generate sustainable competitive advantage, a firm should pursue the procurement of core competencies, which are difficult to imitate. These competencies should preferably be based on a pool of intangible common resources not amenable to contract. There will be no market for these. Core competencies are created solely via non-market mechanisms. Because of the aforementioned considerations, there will generally be limits to the autonomy of the market-oriented profit centers and the granting of extrinsic incentives. This applies specifically to those areas where profit centers are required to work together to generate core competencies, which only become difficult-to-imitate resources in the context of their overall configuration. In other words, the price mechanism within the profit center organization should be supported by non-market mechanisms, most especially that of intrinsic motivation. Intrinsic motivation is indispensable when tacit knowledge needs to be generated or transferred.

However, these considerations should not be taken to mean there is a need for all-encompassing integration or centralization of the different organizational divisions and functional departments. No company consists purely of core competencies. Companies generally also own sections of the corporate value-added chain. Within this chain, knowledge is incorporated into the tradable product components and modules and can be compared with the service offered by external suppliers. In this environment, thinking in terms of products and prices forces the different organizational divisions to exactly specify their internal products and services and the consideration to be paid for them. This can then promote dialogue between the different divisions about the quality of these products and services.

As a result, motivation management in profit center organizations could be said to involve finding the right balance in the contradictory relationship between market and non-market mechanisms. Organizations must aim to combine the economies of scale and scope and the advantages of market power and pooled core competencies enjoyed by large organizational units with the advantages of smaller units such as flexibility, reduction of bureaucracy and close market control to develop superior long-term organizational capabilities and firm-specific pool resources in relation to their competitors.

5. Further Reading

The discussion on scientific management was initiated by:

Taylor, F. W. (1911): The Principles of Scientific Management, New York.

A critical review of the fundamental principles of Taylorism is provided by:

Piore, M. J./Sabel, C. F. (1990): The Second Industrial Divide: Possibilities for Prosperity, reprint edn, New York.

Among the most prominent supporters of the human resources approaches are:

Argyris, C. (1964): Integrating the Individual and the Organization, New York.
Herzberg, F./Mausner, B./Snyderman, B. B. (1959): The Motivation to Work, New York.
Maslow, A. (1954): Motivation and Personality, New York.
McGregor, D. (1960): The Human Side of Enterprise, New York.

The concept of overlapping group organizations stems from:

Likert, R. (1961): New Patterns of Management, New York.
Likert, R. (1967): The Human Organization: Its Management and Value, New York.

Transfer pricing – from an accounting point of view – is discussed in:

Kaplan, R. S./Atkinson, A. A. (1989): Advanced Management Accounting, 2nd edn, Englewood Cliffs, New Jersey.

Transfer pricing – from an organizational point of view – is discussed in:

Eccles, R. G. (1985): The Transfer Pricing Problem. A Theory for Practice, Lexington, Massachusetts.

Chapter Seven

ANTOINETTE WEIBEL AND SANDRA ROTA

Fairness as a Motivator

Introduction

In their jobs, people often attach less importance to the absolute amount of their income than to the observance of norms of justice and fairness. Both distributive fairness (in terms of results) and procedural fairness (how decisions are made and people are treated) play a role. These aspects are investigated in the research conducted into the concept of justice.

We describe here what is understood by justice and fairness in companies. We show the effects that perceived justice and fairness can have on the attitudes and behavior of employees. And we look into the connection between fairness and "organizational citizenship behavior." It becomes clear that perceived fairness has a definite effect on intrinsic motivation.

Researchers investigating issues of justice in the legal system have long known that people react to injustice. The race riots in Los Angeles in April 1992 are a good example of the radical effect that perceived injustice can have. Three police officers were accused of the brutal beating of black motorist Rodney King. The incident was recorded on amateur video and broadcast around the world. The officers were eventually acquitted, which triggered an eruption of violence in which 54 people were killed and over 2,000 injured, and over 900 million dollars' worth of property damage was caused. What happened? In the eyes of many, the court's decision was unfair in terms of its outcome. But a deciding factor was also that the *trial in itself, i.e. the procedure,* seemed unfair too. The proceedings had been shifted to a (predominantly white) suburban area. The jury was also regarded as being police-friendly and conservative.

Those studying the different aspects of management have come to recognize that fairness plays an important role within companies too. Many of the findings made in legal research on justice have been applied successfully within companies, and some new discoveries have also been made. It is becoming increasingly clear what a major impact fairness has on employee motivation. Perceptions of fairness alter attitudes and thus alter the direction of and momentum driving the behavior of employees, i.e. they affect intrinsic motivation.

1. Distributive and Procedural Justice

The question "What is fair?" has been a rich source of debate through the ages. In the research conducted into the concept of justice, the question is approached in two distinct ways. The one approach asks when a judgment or decision is perceived as being unfair in terms of its outcome. Thus, studies on justice within companies look at when the results of the distribution of different goods, in particular wages, are seen to be fair. The focus here is on *distributive justice.* The other approach examines the procedure which leads to a judgment or outcome. In companies, aspects of *procedural justice* come into play in areas such as staff selection, wage determination, handling of complaints, setting of objectives, performance appraisals and termination of contracts.

1.1 Distributive Justice

The research into *distributive justice or fairness of outcome* is dominated by the idea that it is not the absolute amount of a person's income which is the determining factor in whether the distribution is perceived to be fair. Rather, fairness is judged primarily through comparisons with other people. More specifically, employees compare their own ratio of inputs to outcomes with that of other people. They will regard a monthly starting salary of 3,000 dollars as fair if other people who are just starting earn about the same amount. However, the comparisons which employees make are rather more complicated than this, as many other input factors such as education, age and effort can be included in the equation, as well as many possible results such as the prestige of the job, responsibility and opportunities for promotion. Research into distributive justice has been heavily influenced by Adams' "equity theory," the main ideas of which are outlined in Box 7-1.

Box 7-1

The Theory of Distributive Justice (Adams' Equity Theory)
According to Adams, there is no objective measure of distributive justice. Rather, people compare their ratio of inputs to outcomes with that of other people.

If employees find they are subject to unfairness, they will try to reduce it. There are various ways they can do this:

- By altering outcomes – e.g. employees demand an increase in pay.
- By altering inputs – e.g. employees reduce their work effort.
- By choosing another person with whom to compare themselves. Instead of comparing themselves with Mrs. Smith, they choose Mrs. Jones as the new person with whom to compare themselves.
- By leaving the "field". Employees resign or try to get a transfer.

Source: Adams, J. S. (1965): Inequity in Social Exchange, in: Berkowitz, L. (ed.): Advances in Experimental Social Psychology 2, New York, pp. 267-299.

Thus, according to the equity principle, we should get what we deserve, or what we have earned. Equity is the best understood principle of distributive justice but it is by no means the only one. Under certain circumstances, people tend to place more importance on serving principles of equality (everyone should receive the same) or need (people should receive according to their needs) than on equity. The justice motive theory states that in situations where a close friend is involved, our decisions and reactions will be geared toward satisfying the needs of that person. Whereas in more distant relationships, equality is very often regarded as the standard for distributive justice. Equality is typically espoused in settings where group members are close to one another and/or it is difficult, costly or contentious to try and pinpoint precisely who did what and with what effect (Baron/Kreps 1999). We tend to rely on the equity norm of distributive justice when we perceive another person solely via a given role and performance varies significantly across individuals in that role.

From the company's point of view, the prevailing theory contends that different principles of justice serve different purposes. Equality validates people's feelings of membership in the organization. Equity can foster the motivation to produce, and need ensures that the basic needs of the organization's members are fulfilled. Whether or not there is a trade-off between the use of equality and equity is an ongoing discussion. There does not have to be a trade-off if equality also promotes productivity. Chapter 1 examined situations in which this may be true: in the provision and care of firm-specific pool resources, in multi-tasking (team) and fuzzy tasking, in the generation of implicit knowledge, and when productivity is boosted by creativity. Using Hewlett Packard as our example, later in this chapter we will illustrate how companies can promote cohesion and social harmony by applying procedural fairness, while meeting task objectives via distributive principles based on equity.

1.2 Procedural Justice

Studies in *procedural justice* look at questions relating to the fairness, adequacy and social acceptance of *outcome determination,* i.e. of the *procedures and rules followed when making decisions and that culminate in certain results.* In evaluating procedural justice, a number of *formal aspects* should be considered.

Formal Criteria for Ensuring Procedural Justice

The main prerequisites of procedural justice are set out in Box 7-2. *Interpersonal aspects* of the way procedures are applied can also play a role. This has to do with how a company's procedural rules are translated into practice by line managers. Important principles here are honesty, courtesy, swift and thorough feedback, equal treatment and credibility.

Box 7-2

Formal Criteria of Procedural Justice in the Treatment of Employees – A Fairness Checklist

Consistency: everyone should have the same opportunities over a given period.

Lack of prejudice: procedures should not be used to satisfy personal interests.

Accuracy: accuracy should be ensured by making use of a range of different sources in the search for information.

Opportunities for correction: there should be opportunities for revising decisions.

Being representative: all legitimate interests should as far as possible be taken into account.

Participation is a very important aspect of procedural justice. A great deal of research has been dedicated to the evaluation of the effect participation has on employee satisfaction. Although traditional psychology often suggests that participation is beneficial (see Chapter 8), there are some instances where it may also have a negative impact.

Procedural Justice and Participation

To understand the impact participation has on employee satisfaction, we must first distinguish between two forms of participation: "choice" and "voice." "Choice" represents a more direct form of influence. Cafeteria-style benefit plans for example allow employees to select a combination of fringe benefits and wage package, thereby influencing their outcomes. Flexitime programs are another instance where employees are given the freedom to determine their working schedules, i.e. to influence their inputs. Justice research has shown that offering people a choice almost always results in greater satisfaction and acceptance of decisions. Chapter 8 presents a study that examines this phenomenon.

"Voice" represents a more indirect form of influence. It is a means for employees to articulate their interests – to make their voice heard. By exercising their voice, employees are attempting to bring about reform. Very often the opportunity to express oneself or to communicate leads to greater satisfaction even if the results are unpleasant, i.e. even if the outcome is regarded as inequitable. Justice research has shown over and over again that subjects found guilty after they had voiced their opinion were more accepting of the verdict than were subjects who had no voice. This effect has been called the "fair process effect." It has been replicated in the participation study in Chapter 8. However, occasionally, the opposite effect, called the "frustration effect," has been observed. In these rare cases, employees who had an opportunity to communicate were less satisfied with a negative result than employees who had no opportunity to communicate. In practice this negative satisfaction effect has often been observed with employee suggestion systems. Employee suggestion systems are a very straightforward means of allowing employees to use their voice. In the best-case scenario, they are a source of revenue for businesses, profitable for employees and a good way to enhance motivation. If the frustration effect surfaces, however, the suggestion system may backfire. Thus it is important to know what conditions cause the frustration effect. Generally speaking this effect can be observed only in situations where communication (or voice) is not integrated into a broader fairness context, i.e. where fairness tends to be more lip service than real policy. For example, in order for an employee suggestion system to function properly, it must be administered fairly. The suggestion committee should be composed of representatives from various departments of an organization (to guarantee lack of prejudice and broad representation). It should also be based on clearly established rules to ensure consistency (Folger/Greenberg 1985).

Thus we have seen that procedural justice is only effective if taken seriously by management and if all elements are given due consideration. Hewlett Packard's wage system is the perfect example of an integrated approach to fairness.

Procedural Justice at Hewlett Packard

The U.S. computer product manufacturer Hewlett Packard provides a well-known example of the application of the criteria of outcome-related and procedural fairness. The company's management principles, the legendary "HP Way," stipulate that employees are to be treated with consideration and respect. This principle also underlies a carefully thought-out wage system.

An employee's individual pay comprises two elements:

- An employee's job description determines the possible range of pay, defined by both the market value and the internal value of an activity.

- An employee's actual pay within the relevant wage group is determined by two things: a performance appraisal conducted jointly with the employee's line manager, and a comparison of an employee's performance with that of other employees in similar positions. The comparison is carried out by a "ranking committee."

The aim of comparing employees in different departments is to ensure *distributive justice. Procedural justice* is sought through the application of a list of rules which fulfill the checklist criteria set out in Box 7-2.

- **Consistency** is achieved by applying the wage system throughout the company worldwide.

- The criterion of **lack of prejudice** is satisfied by assigning the task of comparing performance to a ranking committee, rather than to the employee's direct supervisor.

- If the employee is not happy with the assessment, he or she can make a complaint to a further committee. Results are also communicated and explained personally to employees by their line manager. There are, therefore, sufficient **opportunities for correction.**

- Finally, performance is evaluated on the basis of an employee's goals, which are worked out by employees and their line managers jointly. A large degree of employee participation in the process ensures that the decisions finally arrived at are considered to be **representative.**

2. Fairness, Attitudes and Behavior

Numerous empirical studies have proven that fairness counts (see Alexander and Ruderman 1987; Folger and Konovsky 1989; Greenberg 1990). Fairness alters employees' attitudes toward their company and toward other employees. It also alters observable behavior.

2.1 Fairness Alters Employee Attitudes

A lot of work has been done on the effect of fairness on *income and job satisfaction.* Researchers started looking at this issue in the 1970s, and have concluded again and again that both *distributive* and *procedural justice* play a positive role here. In one study, it was found that 52% of income satisfaction was the result of distributive justice, and another 14% was attributable to the observance of procedural justice (McFarlin and Sweeney 1992). Thus, income satisfaction among employees is influenced primarily by aspects of (distributive) fairness.

Empirical studies have concluded that *procedural justice* increases both the amount of trust employees place in their line manager and *commitment to the company.* Procedural justice is also a prerequisite for establishing authority. Employees are more willing to follow directives voluntarily and they feel more obliged to follow rules if procedural justice is guaranteed. This means fairness is crucial for securing individual support of a company's pool resources, as described in Chapters 1 and 2.

Box 7-3

Procedural Justice and Common Pool Resources

As described in Chapter 1, it is impossible to force employees to support a company's pool resources. A company is dependent on the voluntary efforts of the majority of its employees to maintain its good reputation and nurture relationships with suppliers and customers. The company may establish rules of conduct, but whether employees follow these rules depends primarily on the ability of the company's leaders to ensure voluntary compliance.

In a study during the California water shortage in 1991, Tom Tyler and Peter Degoey (1995) established the circumstances under which the residents of San Francisco were prepared to engage in voluntary conservation efforts recommended by a locally appointed water authority. They proved that the legitimacy of the authority was almost solely influenced by the procedural fairness of that authority. Furthermore it was discovered that procedural justice also influenced the residents' willingness to transfer control of the outcome to the authority.

These findings are relevant in several ways to organizations. They demonstrate that rules of conduct have a greater impact if the administering authority observes procedural fairness. They also offer an example of how common pool resources may be managed in a flat hierarchy and show that, to a certain extent, people are willing to sacrifice their own freedom for "the common good."

2.2 Fairness Alters Employee Behavior

The effects of *distributive justice* on changes in behavior have been researched extensively. Taken as a whole, the various studies (e.g. Konrad and Pfeffer 1990) have found that a lack of distributive justice elicits the following reactions: underpayment (relative to persons with whom an employee compares him- or herself) motivates the employee concerned to reduce his or her *performance,* while *overpayment* leads to an increase in performance, but only *in the short term.* This result is consistent with the crowding-out effect explained in Chapter 1.

The effects of *procedural justice* on performance are less well researched. However, there are studies which have shown a positive correlation. Here we will focus on two particularly relevant areas where procedural justice has been shown to be important: the creation and transfer of knowledge (Section 2.2.1) and organizational citizenship behavior (Section 2.2.2).

2.2.1. Procedural Justice and Transfer of Knowledge

The findings of Kim and Mauborgne (1998) outlined in Box 7-4 show that procedural fairness is crucial to knowledge transfer. The results thus support the findings described in detail in Chapter 2 on the relationship between intrinsic motivation and the generation of the resource "knowledge."

Box 7-4

Procedural Justice and Transfer of Knowledge
Kim and Mauborgne (1998) investigated the question of how to ensure that the staff and managers in a company share their knowledge voluntarily and over and above the level they are required to.

Their study identified procedural fairness as the key prerequisite for knowledge transfer. According to their findings, employees find procedures fair when

1. they are included in decision-making;

2. any decisions made are explained; and

3. the rules of the process are clearly defined.

Source: Kim, W. C./Mauborgne, R. (1998): Procedural Justice, Strategic Decision Making, and the Knowledge Economy, in: Strategic Management Journal 19, pp. 323-338.

The following example illustrates the importance of these conditions. One day Kim and Mauborgne were called in to assist a company whose development team was failing to deliver useful results. Everything had been tried: the team had been put together on a multifunctional basis, modern project management tools were being used, and a well-devised wage system was in place. Nonetheless, mistrust reigned, no one felt responsible and ideas were jealously guarded. What had gone wrong? In an early project phase, a prototype designed by the marketing and production representatives had been ignored by the development engineers, who were greater in number. The engineers' proposal was then developed. Although from the point of view of marketing and production it was clear that the engineers' proposal would fail if implemented, the marketing and production team preferred to let the engineers fall on their faces. Insufficient involvement of various members of staff, and the failure to explain why their suggestions had been rejected, had done lasting damage to cooperation within the team.

2.2.2. Procedural Justice and Organizational Citizenship Behavior

The effects of procedural fairness have also been thoroughly examined in recent research on organizational citizenship behavior (OCB). This research looks at members of an organization as citizens of an enterprise who, like citizens of a country, observe the rules of their community, show solidarity toward their colleagues and contribute to the common pool of resources of a company (the company's public goods). The significance of firm-specific pool resources was examined in detail in Chapter 2.

Organizational citizenship behavior describes the behavior of employees who go beyond the duties stipulated in their employment contract or job description. They provide voluntary inputs, so-called extra-role behavior, which are not demanded by line managers, and the lack of which cannot be punished. Organizational citizenship behavior can refer to a company as a whole, or to individual employees within their narrower environment. In practical terms, it might involve the following aspects of behavior (some examples):

Company-related OCB

- making innovative suggestions
- voluntarily assuming tasks (including unpleasant ones)
- being willing to do overtime to ensure that important deadlines are met
- speaking positively of the company outside work

Staff-related OCB

- offering to help colleagues who have fallen behind with their work
- assisting new members of staff to settle in
- contributing to a pleasant atmosphere at work

In its effect on performance, OCB is particularly interesting for two reasons. Firstly employment contracts are often very complex and usually long-term in nature, which means they are always incomplete. Employees thus always have room for maneuvering which is covered neither by the tasks set out in their job description, nor by directions from their line manager. At some time or other, everyone has experienced how inefficient cooperation becomes when staff decide to work "by the book". OCB can be understood as the basic willingness of employees to use their room for maneuvering for the benefit of their colleagues or their organization as a whole. This is all the more important, the more difficult it is to standardize work processes, and the more interdependent the areas of activity of different employees are, for instance in the case of complex tasks which need to be tackled in teams. OCB thus serves as a lubricant ensuring the smooth operation of organizational processes. It is one of the most important facilitators of a company's common pool of resources (see Chapter 2).

The second reason OCB is particularly interesting stems from the fact that it can be rewarded only very inadequately through individual performance incentives. The company and employee-related aspects of OCB described are difficult to measure, as they revolve around typical "multiple-task" problems (see Chapter 1). Trying to cover these aspects in formal performance appraisals, and providing a corresponding reward for them, would be more or less impossible. The problem is particularly difficult for tasks in which the generation and transfer of knowledge play an important role, because no one can be forced to share his or her (implicit) knowledge (see Chapter 2). OCB is thus based heavily on intrinsic motivation.

Procedural Justice, Organizational Citizenship Behavior and Productivity

Empirical studies have had little success in establishing a clear relationship between procedural justice and individual employee performance. However, there are many empirical findings that have established a strong link between procedural justice and organizational citizenship behavior. Since OCB is an important aspect of employee behavior and, as such, is necessary for the smooth functioning of an organization, how is this possible?

The reason for this might be that performance, as it is measured in formal performance appraisals, is heavily influenced by other factors such as performance-based monetary incentives, so that the residual effect of procedural justice is negligible at best. As noted earlier, OCB is very difficult to measure and therefore is not properly reflected in formal performance appraisals.

If one views the behavioral responses of employees toward procedural fairness as kind acts intended to reward the kindness and respect experienced by the employee him- or herself, it is reasonable to assume that individuals will choose a form of reciprocation allowing them a high degree of control over the amount of reciprocation, regardless of demands or potential sanctions. Since employees do have a great deal of control over the amount of OCB they exhibit, OCB is the ideal way of showing their appreciation for fair treatment. We should therefore expect to see a much higher correlation between procedural fairness and OCB (or extra-role behavior) than between procedural fairness and individual performance (or in-role behavior), which has in fact been verified by many empirical studies.

Unfortunately, few studies have been carried out to investigate the direct connection between OCB and overall productivity. The reasons for this are threefold. Firstly, individual measures of success are by definition unsuitable in this context. OCB is very difficult to measure, and its positive effects do not necessarily show up at the individual level, rather they tend to manifest primarily at the group level. Secondly, the examination of group performance is problematic where it is based on judgment by line managers, whose sensitivity towards the different aspects of OCB varies greatly. However, several studies have been conducted (although mostly on the basis of judgments by line managers) which do show a positive correlation between OCB and group or departmental performance (see the summary of findings in Bretz/Hertel/Moser 1998).

The third problem is that sometimes it is difficult to promote both in-role and extra-role (or organizational citizenship) behavior at the same time. Here we would like to discuss the problem of worker controls and their impact on justice perceptions and OCB.

Worker controls, or monitoring, has two potential effects on OCB that conflict with each other. On the one hand, worker controls can destroy intrinsic motivation and OCB. On the other hand, monitoring employees' behavior is necessary to ensure fair appraisal of their performance, and fairness has been proven to have a positive effect on OCB. We would like to look at these conflicting effects in more detail below.

As shown in Box 7-2, one important criterion for judging the fairness of a process is that decisions must be based on accurate, unbiased information. One way to gather information about employee performance is monitoring by the supervisor. In this way monitoring or work controls may be viewed as a prerequisite for procedural justice, which has been proven to be important in the promotion of OCB. On the other hand, since OCB, by definition, does not directly contribute to task accomplishment, employees who are being monitored may tend to focus on emphasized in-role behaviors. Niehoff and Moorman (1993) found evidence of this two-fold effect in their empirical study about the correlation between methods of monitoring and OCB. These findings are consistent with the crowding-out effect explained in Chapter 1. Since OCB is primarily based on intrinsic motivation, monitoring employees too closely may cause a shift in their perceived locus of control from an internal to an external one, thus destroying their motivation to display organizational citizenship behavior.

How can this trap be avoided? Once again, as in the case of participation and "voice," as shown in Section 1.2, it is important that monitoring be embedded in a broader context of fairness. If employees' concerns about fairness in outcomes and procedures are taken seriously, the result is the creation of trust between managers and employees. In a trusting relationship, employees are much less likely to interpret monitoring as an unwelcome form of control, and are more likely to understand that monitoring is necessary for maintaining the integrity of the evaluation system. Another finding of OCB research underscores the importance of trusting relationships between supervisor and employee. It seems that OCB is less influenced by a general perception of fairness in the processes at work within the company as a whole. It is more important that employees receive fair treatment from their direct supervisor. In other words, it is not enough to set out fair principles in guidelines or management handbooks; what matters is that these principles are put into practice by individual managers.

3. Concluding Remarks

We have shown that both distributive and procedural justice have significant effects on employee attitudes and behavior. The analysis of the empirical findings clearly shows that justice considerations are particularly important in situations where relevant outcomes cannot be measured (or only at prohibitive cost) and thus cannot be motivated by extrinsic rewards. Since a work environment where justice considerations are taken seriously enhances employees' intrinsic motivation, justice – procedural justice, in particular – plays an important role in the generation of common pool resources, the production and transfer of (implicit) knowledge and employees' display of organizational citizenship behavior.

At this point, a word of caution is appropriate. It is not enough just to apply fair principles. They also need to be communicated! Only when employees understand the reasoning behind decisions and can express an opinion on these decisions can fairness exercise a positive influence on their willingness to engage in behaviors beneficial to the organization.

The most important conclusion we can draw from this is that by ensuring fairness, a considerable effect can be achieved at relatively little expense, as explained by Tom Tyler, one of the leading researchers in the area of procedural fairness:

"...investment in fair procedures might well be among the least costly methods for improving organizational attitudes, cohesion, and compliance. This is a strong recommendation for the application of procedural justice concepts." (Lind and Tyler 1988, p. 201)

4. Further Reading

For an overview of research on justice, see:

Lind, E. A./Tyler, T. R. (1988): The Social Psychology of Procedural Justice, New York.

Liebig, S. (1997): Soziale Gerechtigkeitsforschung und Gerechtigkeit in Unternehmen, Munich/Mering.

Baron, J. N./Kreps, D. M. (1999): Strategic Human Resources. Framework for General Managers, New York.

Tyler, T. R. / Blader, S. L. (2000): Cooperation in Groups: Procedural Justice, Social Identity, and Behavioral Engagement, Psychology Press, Philadelphia.

For practical applications of fairness in human resources management, see:

Folger, R. (1998): Organizational Justice and Human Resource Management, Thousand Oaks/London/New Dehli.

Greenberg, J. (1996): The Quest for Justice on the Job, Thousand Oaks/London/New Dehli.

Folger, R./Greenberg, J. (1985): Procedural Justice: An Interpretive Analysis of Personnel Systems, in: Research in Personnel and Human Resources Management, vol 3, pp 141-183.

For a discussion of the importance of fairness in knowledge management, see:

Kim, W. C./Mauborgne, R. (1998): Procedural Justice, Strategic Decision Making, and the Knowledge Economy, in: Strategic Management Journal 19, pp 323-338.

Empirical studies on the effect of fairness on employee attitudes and behavior may be found in:

Alexander, S./Ruderman, M. (1987): The Role of Procedural and Distributive Justice in Organizational Behavior, in: Social Justice Research 1, pp 177-198.

Folger, R./Konovsky, M. A. (1989): Effects of Procedural and Distributive Justice on Reactions to Pay Raise Decisions, in: Academy of Management Journal 32, pp 115-130.

Greenberg, J. (1990): Organizational Justice: Yesterday, Today, and Tomorrow, in: Journal of Management 16, pp 399-432.

Konrad, A. M./Pfeffer, J. (1990): Do You Get What You Deserve? Factors Affecting the Relationship Between Productivity and Pay, in: Administrative Science Quarterly 35, pp 258-285.

McFarlin, D. B./Sweeney, P. D. (1992): Distributive and Procedural Justice as Predictors of Satisfaction with Personal and Organizational Outcomes, in: Academy of Management Journal 35, pp 626-637.

Tyler, T./Degoey, P. (1995): Collective Restraint in Social Dilemmas: Procedural Justice and Social Identification Effects on Support for Authorities, in: Journal of Personality and Social Psychology, vol 69, pp 482-497.

Empirical findings on the connection between procedural fairness and organizational citizenship behavior are presented in:

Bretz, E./Hertel, G./Moser, K. (1998): Kooperation und Organizational Citizenship Behavior, in: Speiß, E./Nerdinger Friedemann, W. (eds): Kooperation in Unternehmen, Munich/ Mering.

Moorman, R. H. (1991): Relationship Between Organizational Justice and Organizational Citizenship Behaviors: Do Fairness Perceptions Influence Employee Citizenship?, in: Journal of Applied Psychology 76, pp 845-855.

Moorman, R. H./Blakely, G. L./Niehoff, B. P. (1998): Does Perceived Organizational Support Mediate the Relationship Between Procedural Justice and Organizational Citizenship Behavior?, in: Academy of Management Journal 41, pp 351-357.

Niehoff, B. P./Moorman, R. H. (1993): Justice as a Mediator of the Relationship Between Methods of Monitoring and Organizational Citizenship Behavior, in: Academy of Management Journal 36, pp 527-556.

For an examination of the theoretical basis of the connection between procedural fairness and organizational citizenship behavior, see:

Organ, D. W. (1990): The Motivational Basis of Organizational Citizenship Behavior, in: Research in Organizational Behavior 12, pp 43-72.

Tyler, T. R. (1989): The Psychology of Procedural Justice: A Test of the Group-Value Model, in: Journal of Personality and Social Psychology 57, pp 830-838.

Chapter Eight

MATTHIAS BENZ

Management of the Unwritten – How You Can Improve Employment Relationships Through Participation and Communication

Introduction

This chapter studies two work organization tools which can help employee motivation: participation and communication. They increase the trust and loyalty of employees towards their employer and they lead to stronger employee attachment to the company, while improving the working environment and job satisfaction of employees. Participation and communication are of particular importance in areas where employment relationships cannot be completely defined. They are, therefore, an important component of the "management of the unwritten."

1. The Problem: Why are Employment Contracts Incomplete?

Many motivation problems in companies would not arise if employment relationships were regulated by *complete employment contracts*. Such employment contracts would specify, in precise detail, the performance to be rendered by an employee under all conceivable conditions. Thus, the company would receive precisely the job performance it expected from the employee and the employee would receive a salary that was based precisely on his or her job performance.

In reality, however, the opposite holds true: employment contracts between companies and their employees are often very incomplete. Usually only the basic framework of an employment relationship is spelled out and many aspects are left uncovered. Is there a contradiction in this?

1.1 The Reason Why Companies Exist

The economic theory of the firm says: not at all. The reason for this becomes clear when one considers, in general, how work is exchanged in an economy for money (of course, the same considerations also apply to the trading of goods; here, however, we are looking only at the exchange of work performance). Economists call such acts of exchange "transactions." Some of these transactions take place within companies – in the form of an ordinary employment relationship. Other transactions, however, are conducted outside companies through markets; someone employs a tradesman, for example, and pays him for a specific job. Whether an exchange of work for money takes place on a market or within an organization depends primarily on the type of transaction. Simple transactions are most efficiently carried out through markets. It is not worth the trouble for the parties in an exchange to set up a company for a one-time job to be carried out by a tradesman, since the price and the performance promised can be clearly spelled out. However, companies are better suited for other, more complex transactions. This is particularly the case for repeated transactions or when specific investments are required which would go by the board on severance of an exchange relationship. Chapter 2 sets out in detail how non-tradable, collectively produced *pool resources* are the real reason for the existence of companies.

Collective pool resources are characterized by the fact that the contribution to their creation by individual members of an organization cannot be clearly attributed. Since it is not possible to attribute contributions to particular individuals, it is also not possible to include the corresponding activities in clear agreements with precisely specified performance and counter-performance (prices). If this were possible, there would be no reason *not* to obtain the relevant performance through the market, for example in the form of a contract for work and services or through outsourcing. In contrast, the strength of companies lies in their ability to motivate employees to perform their work, even if the work done cannot be clearly attributed. This must be borne in mind in view of the increasing desire to introduce artificial markets within companies through profit centers and internal pricing. Essential competitive advantages may be lost in doing this (see Chapter 6).

1.2 The Importance of Implicit Employment Contracts

Since employment contracts in companies are incomplete, relationships between companies and their employees are based, to a large extent, on *implicit employment contracts*. This refers to any components of an employment relationship which are not formally set out in an employment contract and which, therefore, cannot be enforced by an external party (e.g. a labor court).

In organizations, implicit employment contracts play a key role. In many areas, employees have to rely on the trustworthiness of the company since they are unable to enforce their claims before a court. Will promised wage increases really be granted? Does the company's commitment to ensuring job security have any substance? Will the training courses which were promised really be carried out, and can one place trust in the company's promotion policy? On the other hand, companies also have to be able to rely on employees not to breach implicit employment contracts and to act in the interests of the company of their own accord.

Therefore, the proper functioning and the success of a company depend to a significant extent on the quality of implicit employment contracts. "Management of the unwritten" is one of the most important tasks for a company. However, how can a company improve the quality of its implicit employment relationships? This is a crucial part of "management by motivation."

Neither organizational and control mechanisms nor pay incentives can guarantee that employees will adhere to implicit contracts (see Chapters 1 and 2 for a detailed examination of this). On the contrary, a certain degree of intrinsic work motivation is required to ensure that implicit rules are not continually broken. Therefore, in this chapter, a study will be made of two other work organization tools with which employees can be motivated. It will be shown that participation and communication significantly improve the quality of implicit employment contracts in a company.

2. The Answer: Participation and Communication as Motivators

2.1 Participation

Participation is defined here as the individual influence employees have over decisions at their place of work. This *individual* and *direct* participation must be clearly distinguished from *collective* and *indirect* forms of participation such as, for example, the codetermination required by law in Germany and enshrined in the Works Council Constitution Act of 1972 and the Codetermination Act of 1976. Direct, individual participation starts at the individual employee level, not at the level of company management. It gives individual employees direct influence over decision-making and is not based on representation through a delegate. Box 8-1 shows the various forms of employee involvement and participation.

Box 8-1

Different Forms of Employee Involvement and Participation

Individual, direct participation

- Influence over decisions that directly affect an employee's own place of work.

Collective, indirect codetermination

- Employees' representatives serving on the board of directors or work council of a company.
- For example, statutory codetermination in Germany.

Profit-sharing

- Payment of a portion of the company's profit to employees.

Employee self-management

- Employees decide on company matters democratically and with equal rights.

Individual participation means that employees are included in decisions which affect their own workplace. This means, for example, having a say in the organization of work and its objectives, in training measures, work schedules, health and safety standards or acquisitions such as software. This kind of participation may take various forms. In many companies, opportunities for participation are integrated into the normal work process without having any formal structure. In other companies, formal structures are created or a parallel process is even set up outside regular work structures. Quality circles and autonomous work groups are examples of such institutionalized "involvement programs." They are described in greater detail in Box 8-2.

Box 8-2

Examples of Employee Participation

Quality circles are made up of approximately ten employees. They meet once a month on a voluntary basis to discuss topics of their own choice relating to their area of work. The goal is to identify problems and develop recommendations for their solution. Quality circles have free rein as to the topics they choose and the method with which they deal with them. However, any decision to implement a recommendation is usually up to a higher level in the hierarchy. Nevertheless, quality circles are often entrusted with the implementation and monitoring of improvements.

In contrast to quality circles, autonomous work groups represent a form of participation anchored into regular everyday work. A small group of employees is assigned almost full responsibility for producing a product (or part of it) or a service. The autonomous work group is then responsible for deciding how it will plan and implement the task and control the quality of production.

Translation from: Antoni, C. H. (1999): Konzepte der Mitarbeiterbeteiligung: Delegation und Partizipation, in: Hoyos, C./Frey, D. (eds.): Arbeits- und Organisationspsychologie, Weinheim.

Participation, Motivation and Productivity

The importance of participation for employee motivation is stressed in research by social psychologists. Numerous studies confirm its positive effects. Participative forms of decision-making, whether informal or institutionalized, give employees a certain degree of self-determination and responsibility. They show that the company values and takes seriously the commitment and interest of employees. This can promote intrinsic work motivation. Employees will of their own accord behave with greater commitment to the interests of the company even where there is no binding rule inducing them to do so. Participation thus leads to more productive implicit employment relationships.

The effect of participation programs on the productivity of companies has been examined mainly by economists and researchers in business management in numerous studies. In an overview analysis, David I. Levine and Andrea Tyson evaluated all studies (43 in total) which appeared up to 1990. They summarize the results as follows: "There is usually a positive, often small, effect of participation on productivity, sometimes a zero or statistically insignificant effect, and almost never a negative effect." (Levine/Tyson 1990, p. 203). The effects of participation on the productivity of companies are thus less clear than those on the motivation of employees. However, it may be said that even though participation might not always work, it at least appears not to harm company productivity.

2.2 Communication

The term communication is defined here to mean institutionalized communication between management and staff. This may include various setups:

- A comprehensive *open-door policy* that enables employees to communicate any concerns they may have to their superiors at any time. Hierarchical obstacles impeding communication can be overcome through this.
- Today, many companies organize *regular meetings* at company and departmental levels.
- *Employee committees* may be established to hold regular discussions with management.
- Finally, there are also other forms of communication such as in-house newsletters and intranets.

Communication and Motivation

Why should communication be of importance for the management of motivation? In recent years, behavior-oriented economists have found clear results in this regard. People behave in a more cooperative manner if they are able to communicate with each other. This also applies in a situation where there are *no binding rules* which would oblige them to behave in a cooperative manner. An example is set out in Box 8-3.

Communication causes individuals to voluntarily behave in a more cooperative way. It is, therefore, an important prerequisite for making employment relationships that are only implicit productive. A leading American social scientist, Elinor Ostrom, summarizes this in the following manner: “Exchanging mutual commitment, increasing trust, creating and reinforcing norms, and developing a group identity appear to be the most important processes that make communication efficacious.” (Ostrom 1998, p. 7)

Box 8-3

Communication Leads to Cooperative Behavior
In a behavioral experiment at the University of Zurich, the participants were each given 13 Swiss francs. They were free to decide whether to keep the amount for themselves or give any portion of it to a second person who had not received any money. If the identity of the person to whom the donated amount was going to go was not known, the participants gave away only 26% on average (approx. 3.25 Swiss francs). However, if the participant was able to communicate with the recipient in advance, an average of 48% (approx. 6.50 Swiss francs) was given away.

Source: Bohnet, I. and B. S. Frey (1999): Social Distance and Other-Regarding Behavior in Dictator Games: Comment. American Economic Review 89: 335-339.

Furthermore, people see the results of a process as being fairer if they are able to express their opinion on a matter. They are then more prepared to accept results that are less advantageous to them. This socio-psychological finding on “procedural fairness” is also of importance to companies. Well-developed communication structures are a sign that a company values the fairness of the decision-making process. In return, greater acceptance of decisions, even those that might be unpleasant, can be expected.

Procedural fairness is also closely connected with organizational citizenship behavior (“OCB”), as is described in detail in Chapter 7. If employees are treated fairly, they tend to behave more like “company citizens,” i.e. they see it, for example, as a matter of course to stick to rules, to support their colleagues when they need help, or to work overtime when the situation so demands.

The theoretical considerations in this section suggest that participation and communication are important for the management of motivation. They can be expected to improve the quality of implicit employment relationships. Is this also borne out by empirical studies?

3. A Concrete Application: Worker Representation and Participation Survey

Theoretical considerations will be examined in the following, using an American survey, the Worker Representation and Participation Survey ("WRPS"). The WRPS is well-suited to this issue, since American labor market conditions place a lot of weight on implicit employment contracts whereas there are few explicit regulations on protection against dismissal. This was expressed in earlier times in the "hire and fire" rule: employers were able to hire people and fire them again practically at will. Flexibility and weak employment regulation are still the order of the day. For example, paid vacations or contributions to social insurance are not mandated by the state but are up to each individual company.

These conditions are not necessarily to be considered positive. However, nowadays the concept of "Americanizing" the labor market is often advanced in other parts of the world too. Deregulation and flexibilization will mean that in Europe, for example, employment relationships will have to rely increasingly on implicit rules. The American example therefore is well-suited to draw conclusions that may be important in the future for many other labor markets around the world.

The WRPS was commissioned in 1994 by the National Bureau of Economic Research, and supervised by two leading labor economists, Richard B. Freeman and Joel Rogers. A total of 2,408 employees in the United States were questioned. These were employees working for private companies or non-profit organizations with at least 25 employees, who were not owners of the company or with upper management. The WRPS is thus a representative sample of employees from numerous sectors, occupations and companies. This allows generalized interpretations to be derived from it which apply beyond the individual company.

3.1 Can the Quality of Implicit Employment Contracts Be Measured?

How can the quality of implicit employment contracts be measured empirically? An advantage of the WRPS is that it offers various measures for these "soft" and thus difficult-to-quantify factors. Thus *overall* a reliable picture can be drawn. Five components comprising various aspects were selected for the analysis. They are trust in the company, loyalty to the company, attachment to the company, working environment and job satisfaction. All of these components are characterized by the fact that they cannot simply be spelled out in a contract of employment or otherwise enforced. On the contrary, they can only be regulated in an implicit manner. A lot of trust and loyalty, a high degree of attachment to the company, a good working environment and satisfied employees are a good indication that implicit employment relationships in a company are effective.

The variables *trust, loyalty and attachment to the company* were measured in the survey on a scale of 1 (low) to 4 (high). The exact wording of the questions asked can be found in the appendix to this chapter. The variable *company attachment* means whether an employee is thinking of leaving the company or wants to stay there long term. The variables *working environment* and *job satisfaction* were only measured on a three-level scale. A low rating of 1 stands for a poor working environment or for low job satisfaction, 2 for an average working environment or moderate job satisfaction and 3 for a good working environment or high job satisfaction.

The survey is not a bad testimonial to American employers. In general, employees consider the employment relationships in their company to be good. On average, the respondents have some trust in the company (the average rating is 3.11 with the maximum being 4). The same applies to loyalty (3.36). The average rating for attachment to the company was somewhat lower (2.76). On average, the working environment was rated as average to good (2.67 with a maximum rating of 3). There was also considerable job satisfaction among the respondents. The average employee reports moderate to high job satisfaction (2.43).

Of course, there are big differences between the individual employees interviewed. The analysis attempts to explain these differences in relation to trust, loyalty, attachment to the company, working environment and job satisfaction on the basis of the different employee opportunities for participation and communication.

3.2 Operationalizing Participation and Communication

The opportunities for participation are operationalized using two variables. One variable, *participation,* comprises the informal opportunities for employees to have a share in decisions. The other variable, *involvement program,* comprises institutionalized participation programs such as quality circles and autonomous work groups.

The variable *participation* measures the *subjective perception* of the share in decision-making in the workplace directly on a scale of 4 (low) to 16 (high). Polling for this was based on the factors work organization, training, work schedules, wage increases, work objectives, equipment or software, health and safety standards and preferential employee conditions. (See the appendix for the construction of this variable and the questions asked.) The *involvement program* variable represents an *objective* measure. It has a rating of 1 if the employee takes part in an involvement program such as quality circles, total quality management or autonomous work groups (otherwise it is rated 0).

On average, the opportunities for employees to participate are not very extensive and they vary considerably. For the variable *participation* the average employee rates 10 index points, which is right in the middle between very few and a lot of opportunities for participation. The standard deviation is 3 index points. In addition, only 31.5 percent of the respondents take part in an involvement program.

The opportunities for communication are measured using the *communication* variable. It represents an index which can have values ranging from 0 to 3. If they exist, each of the following setups is given one index point: a comprehensive open-door policy, regular meetings between management and staff, and employee committees that hold regular discussions with management. The communication structures are generally just average (the average value is approx. 1.5 index points) and vary greatly between the different companies (the standard deviation is approx. 1 index point).

3.3 Empirical Analysis

Descriptive Analysis

The effects of participation and communication on the quality of implicit employment contracts are initially displayed in Table 8-1. This provides a graphic overview of the results, before more precise statistical tests are presented. The table shows how high the proportion is of respondents with a lot of / few opportunities for participation and a lot of / few communication opportunities in the two upper and the two lower classes of each of the dependent variables. For example, the lower right-hand field shows the connection between working environment and communication opportunities. The percentages are to be understood as follows: of the respondents who indicated a poor working environment, 61.4 percent have few communication opportunities, whereas 38.6 percent have a lot. It is the opposite for respondents who have a good working environment. In this case, only 42.2 percent have few communication opportunities whereas 57.8 percent have a lot.

The results in Table 8-1 show that participation and communication contribute significantly to the quality of implicit employment contracts. Let us take the variable *trust* as an example. Employees who enjoy a lot of opportunities to participate have more trust in their company. Among those who have a lot of trust in their company, the percentage of employees who have a lot of participation opportunities is 60.2 percent, whereas the percentage of employees who have few participation opportunities is only 39.8 percent. The picture for employees who do not trust their company is the exact opposite. In this case, the percentage of employees with few participation opportunities is 57.6 percent, whereas the percentage with a lot of participation opportunities is only 42.4 percent. This positive effect is confirmed by the variable *involvement program.* Employees who take part in an involvement program represent a greater percentage in the category “a lot of trust” than “little trust”. There is a similar effect in the case of the variable *communication.* If a company has well-developed communication structures, the likelihood that employees will have a lot of trust in their company is one and a half times higher (the percentage is then 60.8 percent as opposed to 39.2 percent when there are only few opportunities for communication).

These results are confirmed for all five variables used to measure the quality of implicit employment relationships. The descriptive analysis suggests that participation and communication increase company loyalty, strengthen the attachment of the employee to the company and improve both the working environment and job satisfaction.

Table 8-1: The Positive Effects of Participation and Communication - Overview

		Opportunities to Participate		Involvement Program		Opportunities for Communication	
		few	a lot	no	yes	few	a lot
Trust	low	57.6%	42.4%	80.5%	19.5%	68.1%	31.9%
	high	39.8%	60.2%	63.5%	36.5%	39.2%	60.8%
Loyalty	low	63.3%	36.7%	81.1%	18.9%	65.6%	34.4%
	high	40.2 %	59.8%	66.4%	33.6%	45.0%	55.0%
Company attachment	low	54.1%	45.9%	77.4%	22.6%	58.3%	41.7%
	high	36.3%	63.7%	62.2%	37.8%	40.5%	59.5%
Job satisfaction	low	57.8%	42.2%	75.9%	24.1%	56.5%	43.5%
	high	36.2%	63.8%	65.0%	35.0%	43.7%	56.3%
Working environment	poor	57.0%	43.0%	77.6%	22.4%	61.4%	38.6%
	good	38.3%	61.7%	64.7%	35.3%	42.2%	57.8%

Notes: The percentages indicated correspond to the portions of all respondents in the two lower categories (e.g. trust = 1 or 2) or the two upper categories (e.g. trust = 3 or 4). The distribution is different in the case of working environment and job satisfaction; a poor working environment here represents values of 1 or 2, a good working environment a value of 3. Similarly, low job satisfaction represents values of 1 or 2, high job satisfaction a value of 3. Few opportunities to participate means that the variable participation takes on a value of between 4 and 9, a lot of participation represents a value of between 10 and 16. Few opportunities to communicate means that the variable communication takes on a value of 0 or 1, a lot of communication represents a value of 2 or 3.

Statistical Analysis

Additional statistical tests need to be conducted in order to make generalized statements about the effect of participation and communication. A descriptive analysis does not take into account the fact that various factors have an influence on the quality of implicit employment relationships simultaneously. For example, it might be reasonable to assume that there are better employment relationships in small companies or that they vary depending on the job of an employee or what sector of industry a company is in. Any such additional influencing factors have to be examined in order to ensure that the empirical results are not biased. Any inference that the results have universal validity can only be made once it is shown that the positive effects of participation and communication are not interfered with by other effects.

Such a statistical test can be conducted by way of a multiple regression analysis. This procedure allows for incorporation of all relevant factors simultaneously into one estimation equation. The results are then easy to interpret. The effect determined for a single variable is true *ceteris paribus,* i.e. where the influences of all other variables are kept constant in the calculation. The effect of the individual variables can thus be isolated.

The results of the multiple regression analyses conducted for the dependent variables *trust, loyalty, attachment to company, job satisfaction and working environment* are reproduced in detail in the appendix to this chapter (Tables 8-2 and 8-3). The estimation procedure used is also outlined there in greater detail, and it is explained how the results are to be interpreted. The following is a summary of the results.

Participation Improves the Quality of Implicit Employment Contracts

The empirical study confirms that employee participation has positive effects on various aspects of employment relationships that cannot be simply stipulated in an employment contract or otherwise enforced.

Trust

Participation increases the trust that employees have towards the company they work for. For the variable *participation* a positive effect was estimated which is very significant in statistical terms and which is of considerable magnitude. Employees with the most opportunities to participate have a 20.6 percent greater likelihood of trusting the company they work for than those with only very few opportunities to participate. This is confirmed by the second variable used, *involvement program.* The effect of being part of an involvement program is both positive and significant.

Loyalty

Here as well, both participation variables demonstrate a positive effect. A lot of opportunities for participation and the introduction of involvement programs increase the likelihood, in a statistically highly significant manner and to a considerable extent, that employees will feel loyalty towards the company they work for. The effects here are + 34.9 percent for the variable *participation* and + 13.0 percent for the variable *involvement program.*

Company attachment

The more an employee is able to participate in decision-making, the more likely it is that the employee will want to stay with the company longer term. Having a lot of opportunities to participate causes an employee to be 31.0 percent more likely to be among those who are not thinking of leaving the company. However, this highly significant positive effect is not confirmed for the second variable, involvement program. The coefficient here is also positive, but statistically not significant.

Job satisfaction

Employees like their job better when they are able to exercise some influence over decision-making at their workplace. This is shown by the effect of + 32.9 percent determined for the variable participation (significant at the 99 percent level). High job satisfaction is also promoted by involvement programs. Participants in such programs have a 9.1 percent greater likelihood of being happy in their work.

Working environment

A lot of opportunities for participation will result in a better working environment. Both the variable *participation* and the variable *involvement program* show a significant positive effect. In the presence of these effects, the likelihood that employees will work in an environment of encouragement rather than discouragement increases significantly (+ 25.7% and + 8.1% respectively).

Overall, these results draw a clear picture. Participation is an important component of the "management of the unwritten". Both informal opportunities to participate and institutional participation programs are forms of work organization that can improve the quality of employment relationships.

Communication Improves the Quality of Implicit Employment Contracts

Communication structures in a company have substantial positive effects on those areas of employment relationships which can only be regulated on an implicit basis.

Trust

Well-established communication structures increase employee trust in the company to a considerable extent. The likelihood that employees trust their company is higher by 32.9 percent than in the case where there are no structures through which employees are able to communicate with management.

Loyalty

Employee loyalty increases in line with the extent of the opportunities for communication within a company. A significant positive effect of + 25.4 percent was determined for the variable communication, i.e. in companies which have a comprehensive open-door policy, regular meetings between management and staff, and management and employee committees, about 25 percent more of the employees will have a lot of loyalty to the company than in companies that do not use any of these forms of communication.

Company attachment

Well-established communication structures contribute to a high level of attachment to the company. Where there are a lot of opportunities for management and staff to communicate with one another, this has a positive and very significant influence on attachment to the company. 24.7 percent more employees intend to stay with their company long term.

Job satisfaction

The influence of communication is of a lesser magnitude here but is still positive. The change in the likelihood of being among those with a high level of job satisfaction is + 9.8 percent if there are well-developed opportunities for communication (significant at the 90 percent level).

Working environment

If a company has extensive communication structures, the likelihood that employees will work in an environment of encouragement rather than discouragement increases substantially. 17.2 percent more of the employees indicate having a good working environment, compared to a situation where management gives staff very little opportunity to communicate their concerns.

These results suggest that communication, too, is an important component of the "management of the unwritten". Implicit employment relationships can be improved by a company setting up extensive communication structures.

4. Conclusion

Which motivational tools can companies employ if the activities of employees are regulated only incompletely through employment contracts? In this chapter it was shown that participation and communication can be used as alternative motivating factors. The results presented are particularly noteworthy since they are based on a broad survey. They allow the results of case studies (see Chapters 9 and 10) to be generalized. In the statistical analysis, checks are carried out for numerous influencing factors that cannot be taken into account in case studies. Thus it can be shown that, as a general rule, participation and communication can improve the quality of implicit employment contracts.

There are various practical ways of allowing employee participation. They range from informal participation in decision-making in the workplace directly (with respect to organization and means and goals of work) to institutionalized involvement programs such as quality circles and autonomous work groups. Communication structures in a company can be enhanced by way of an open-door policy, regular meetings between management and staff and institutionalized meetings between management and employee committees.

Participation and communication-oriented employee management has a positive effect in areas of work which can only be regulated implicitly because many of the activities and outcomes cannot be stipulated by way of an employment contract or otherwise enforced. It causes employees to be committed to their work of their own accord because it increases the trust and loyalty that employees have toward the company. This leads to stronger employee attachment to the company and also improves the working environment and job satisfaction. Participation and communication are, therefore, important elements of "management by motivation".

5. Further Reading

The economic theory of the firm was developed by:

Coase, R. (1937): The Nature of the Firm, in: Economica 4, pp 386-405.

Its most important proponent is currently:

Williamson, O. E. (1985): The Economic Institutions of Capitalism. Firms, Markets, Relational Contracting, New York.

The importance of implicit employment contracts in companies is discussed by:

Rousseau, D. M. (1995): Psychological Contracts in Organizations: Understanding Written and Unwritten Agreements, Thousand Oaks/London/New Dehli.

A good overview of employee participation in the United States is to be found in:

Levine, D. I. (1995): Reinventing the Workplace. How Business and Employees Can Both Win, Washington D.C.

Levine, D. I./Tyson, L. (1990): Participation, Productivity, and the Firm's Environment, in: Blinder, A. (ed): Paying for Productivity, A Look at the Evidence, Washington, pp 183-237.

The role of participation in intrinsic motivation is shown in:

Deci, E. L./Ryan, R. M. (1985): Intrinsic Motivation and Self-Determination in Human Behavior, New York.

Schwartz, B. (1990): The Creation and Destruction of Value, in: American Psychologist 45, pp 7-15.

Procedural fairness research has been substantially influenced by:

Tyler, T. R./Lind, A. E. (1988): The Social Psychology of Procedural Justice, New York/London.

A detailed presentation of the Worker Representation and Participation Survey as well as initial evaluations by the commissioning party can be found in:

Freeman, R. B./Rogers, J. (1999): What Workers Want, Ithaca/London.

The data set can be accessed under:

Freeman, R. B./Rogers, J. (1998): Worker Representation and Participation Survey – Waves 1 and 2: Data Description and Documentation. Cambridge, MA: National Bureau of Economic Research (http://www.nber.org).

6. Appendix

6.1 Survey Questionnaire and Variables

Below, the exact wording is given of the questions used to operationalize the variables.

Trust:	In general, how much do you trust your (company/organization) to keep its promises to you and other employees? Would you say you trust your (company/organization): 4 A lot / 3 Somewhat / 2 Only a little / 1 Not at all?
Loyalty:	How much loyalty would you say you feel toward the (company/organization) you work for as a whole? – 4 a lot / 3 some / 2 only a little / 1 or no loyalty at all?
Company attachment:	Which one of the following four statements best describes how you think of your current job? Is it: 4 a long-term job you will stay in? / 3 An opportunity for advancement in this same (company/organization)? / 2 Part of a career or profession that will probably take you to different companies? / 1 A job you will probably leave that is not part of a career?
Job satisfaction:	On an average day, what best describes your feeling about going to work? Would you say you usually:

	3 Look forward to it / 2 Don't care one way or the other/mixed feelings / 1 Wish you didn't have to go
Working environment:	At your workplace, would you say employees generally encourage each other to make an extra effort on the job, discourage each other from making an extra effort, or would you say they don't care how hard other employees work? 3 Encourage / 2 Don't care / 1 Discourage
Participation:	How much direct involvement and influence do you have in *(various dimensions)*? 4 A lot of direct involvement and influence / 3 Some direct involvement and influence / 2 Only a little direct involvement and influence / 1 No direct involvement and influence? One half of the random sample was asked about their influence over decision-making in relation to the four dimensions *work organization, training, work schedules and wage increases,* and the second half about *work goals, equipment or software, health and safety standards and preferential employee conditions.* The individual dimensions were evaluated on the above scale of 1 (no direct influence) to 4 (a lot of direct influence). For each individual, the variable "participation" summarizes the four dimensions in one index. Thus, for those polled, there is a minimum of 4 index points (4 x 1: no direct influence) and a maximum of 16 index points (4 x 4: a lot of direct influence).
Involvement program:	Some companies are organizing workplace decision-making in new ways to get employees more involved – using things like self-directed work teams, total quality management, quality circles, or other employee involvement programs. Is anything like this now being done in your (company/organization)? 1 Yes / 0 No Are you personally involved in any of these programs at work? 1 Yes / 0 No

Communication: Now let's talk about company policies regarding wages, benefits, and other things affecting employees as a group. Which of the following, if any, does your (company/ organization) have to deal with issues that affect employees as a group? Is/are there:
Regular "town" meetings with employees, called by management? (1 Yes / 0 No); An open door policy for groups of employees to raise issues about policies with upper management? (1 Yes / 0 No); A committee of employees that discusses problems with management on a regular basis? (1 Yes / 0 No).

6.2 Detailed Presentation of the Results

The results of the multiple regression analyses conducted for the dependent variables *trust, loyalty, company attachment, job satisfaction* and *working environment* are set out in Tables 8-2 and 8-3. The estimation procedure used takes into account the circumstance that the dependent variables can only take on values of 1, 2 and 3 (or 4) ("ordered probit estimation"). Only the effects of the variables *participation, involvement program* and *communication* are set out in the tables. However, as argued in the text, the estimations control for a number of other influencing factors. They include: company characteristics (type of organization, company size, group size), position in the operation (supervisor, lower or middle management), personal characteristics (length of time employed, age, sex, number of jobs, hourly wage), seven control variables for an employee's level of education, nine control variables for the job carried out and fifteen control variables for the sector of business in which the company operates. Due to space restrictions, the complete analysis is not published here, but it can be obtained from the author on request.

Interpretation of the Results

In Tables 8-2 and 8-3, two values are shown for each explanatory variable. In the left-hand column are the estimated coefficient and the z-value of the coefficient, which provides information about its statistical reliability. A z-value of more than 2 means significance at the 95 percrent level, i.e. it can be assumed with 95 percent probability that the connection determined is not coincidental. With the estimation method used, an intuitive interpretation is not feasible from the coefficients given. Therefore, the marginal effects are also shown in the right column.

They show by how much the likelihood changes of being in the relevant highest category (e.g. *trust* = 4) if a variable changes from its minimum to its maximum. For example, the marginal effect of the variable *involvement program* on employee trust, at 12.6 percent, is to be interpreted in the following manner: if two persons A and B are different only to the extent that A takes part in an involvement program (*involvement program* = 1) and B does not (*involvement program* = 0), the likelihood that A will figure among employees who have a lot of trust in their company increases by 12.6 percent.

The quality of the overall estimation is expressed by x^2. Its value is statistically significant for all estimations carried out, i.e. the variables used explain, in their entirety, the variation in the dependent variable in a statistically reliable way.

Table 8-2: The Positive Effects of Participation and Communication – Results of Weighted Ordered Probit Estimations

	Trust		**Loyalty**	
	Estimate (z-value)	Change in likelihood of being in the highest category of trust	Estimate (z-value)	Change in likelihood of being in the highest category of loyalty
Participation opportunities (4=low to 16=high)	0.189** (3.02)	+ 20.6%	0.308** (4.62)	+ 34.9%
Participating in involvement program (0=no, 1=yes)	0.335** (3.39)	+ 12.6%	0.333** (3.14)	+ 13.0 %
Communication opportunities (0=none to 3=a lot)	0.309** (7.26)	+ 32.9%	0.217** (4.89)	+ 25.4%
Number of observations	825		824	
χ^2 (whole equation)	208.91**		187.87**	

** significant at the 99% level; * significant at the 95% level. The estimation equation includes the following control variables (not shown): company characteristics (type of organization, company size, group size), position in the operation (supervisor, lower or middle management), personal characteristics (length of time employed, age, sex, number of jobs, hourly wage), seven control variables for an employee s level of education, nine control variables for the job carried out and fifteen control variables for the sector of business in which the company operates.

Table 8-3: The Results of Weighted Ordered Probit Estimations (Continued)

	Company Attachment		Job Satisfaction	
	Estimate (z-value)	Change in likelihood of having high attachment to company	Estimate (z-value)	Change in likelihood of having high job satisfaction
Participation opportunities (4=low to 16=high)	0.285** (4.39)	+ 31.1%	0.312** (4.30)	+ 32.9%
Participating in involvement program (0=no, 1=yes)	0.106 (1.08)	+ 4.0%	0.258* (2.21)	+ 9.1 %
Communication opportunities (0=none to 3=a lot)	0.224** (5.21)	+ 24.7%	0.088(*) (1.81)	+ 9.8%
Number of observations	813		821	
χ^2 (whole equation)	246.86**		139.56**	

	Working Environment	
	Estimate (z-value)	Change in likelihood of indicating a good working environment
Participation opportunities (4=low to 16=high)	0.262** (3.54)	+ 25.7%
Participating in involvement program (0=no, 1=yes)	0.254* (2.08)	+ 8.1%
Communication opportunities (0=none to 3=a lot)	0.173** (3.48)	+ 17.2%
Number of observations	802	
χ^2 (whole equation)	96.33**	

** significant at the 99% level; * significant at the 95% level; (*) significant at the 90% level.

Part IV

Case Studies

Chapter Nine

JETTA FROST AND LEO BOOS

Managing Motivation in the Banking Industry: The ING Barings Case Study

Introduction

This chapter will detail how ING Barings Bank, a subsidiary of the Dutch banking and insurance group, International Netherlands Group (ING), manages motivation. ING Barings has recognized that performance-based compensation alone is not sufficient to significantly enhance employee performance and increase the length of time an employee stays with a company. For this reason, they have developed an extensive set of motivational tools covering eight areas/subjects. Fundamental to the ING concept is the combination of these different areas/subjects in such a manner as to achieve the best balance between the needs of the employees and the interests of ING Barings.

These days, investment bankers, with their above-average salaries and bonuses, are generally regarded as income maximizers. As a consequence, we would naturally expect "pay for performance" to be the method of choice in investment banking for successfully motivating employees to work harder. Particularly in the Anglo-Saxon financial centers, employees are in fact paid salaries with a high variable component. As a rule, however, this component hardly ever corresponds to the actual performance of individual employees. Instead it tends to follow the market level of salaries paid in the banking industry. Even so, these salaries alone are not sufficient to significantly raise employee performance and increase the length of time an employee stays with a company. The human resources managers of ING Barings, the investment banking subsidiary of the Dutch banking and insurance conglomerate, International Netherlands Group (ING), also recognized this fact. According to them, (individual) performance elements in employees' salaries are not enough to motivate employees. Instead, they use an extensive array of motivational tools, which includes, in addition to such classical extrinsic motivators as salary, bonus and stock options, numerous other measures containing powerful intrinsic motivators.

The first two sections of this chapter will describe the business environment of the investment banking industry, and of the company, ING Barings. The third section will describe the various motivational tools used by ING Barings.

1. Investment Banking in the Early 1990s: From Gold Digger to Grave Digger

In February 1995, the then 233-year old Barings Bank was in financial ruins. Twenty-eight year old Nick Leeson, an employee at Barings' Singapore branch, had been involved in risky trading transactions that resulted in Barings' losing almost twice its equity capital. Leeson, who had joined Barings during the investment banking goldrush of the early 1990s, succeeded in digging an unceremonious grave for the venerable, old bank. This was all the more dramatic since Barings was not just one of many private British banks, but "the world's oldest and most respected London private bank" (Drucker 1999, p. 28). Up until 1890, Barings had grown in size and wealth primarily by accepting business risks and raising finance for the government, especially in the form of war bonds. This led to the Duke of Richelieu's comment that there were six powers in Europe: England, France, Prussia, Austria, Russia and the Baring Brothers. In March 1995, the Dutch banking and insurance group, ING, came to the bank's rescue. It bought Barings for one pound Sterling, and assumed its debts of US$ 1.4 billion.

1.1 Barings Brothers: Bankers and Brokers

More than a hundred years earlier, the bank owned by the Baring family had almost gone bankrupt as well (see Fay 1996). Ned Baring, the head of the bank at the time, had underwritten shares in an Argentine hydro company that proved impossible to sell in London. There was fear that if Barings went down, the entire London City would be caught up in the bank's failure. This is why the Bank of England, as well as almost all the other banks in the City of London, came to the assistance of Barings in 1890 by providing £ 17 million (current value of around US$ 1.5 billion) to rescue Barings from its financial plight. By 1896, however, the majority of the bank's capital was back in the hands of the Baring family.

Even though the hapless stock deals of 1890 did not ruin the bank, it did change the way the bank conducted its business. Just as someone who survives a car accident no longer drives the same way as before, Barings Bank avoided risks completely after 1890, and became the paragon of a conservative London bank. This was possible while financial markets were regulated: each market player left the others alone, and new competitors had no chance of breaking into the cartel.

The end of this era was in sight by 1985 as London prepared for the advent of Big Bang. The manifold agreements between the banks, which had eliminated any effective competition, were declared illegal. Due to these reforms, London became one of the world's three major financial centers, besides New York and Tokyo. Whoever wanted to take part in international financial dealings had to set up office in London. This led to old, established British brokerage houses being bought up by foreign banks at over-inflated prices.

Barings Bank at first tried to avoid this new trend. Moreover, thanks to the fact that its shares belonged to a family trust, it was protected against any unfriendly takeovers. However, it then hired a team of research analysts and brokers specializing in East Asian stocks and, as a result, participated in the Japanese stock market boom. This team set up Barings Securities, which not only generated an enormous increase in the overall profits of the Barings Bank, but also represented a new corporate culture in the old Barings. Unlike traditional bankers, the brokers of Barings Securities were much more driven by short-term financial gains and their salaries had a high bonus component. In 1986, the head of Barings Securities earned £ 2.5 million. By contrast, Peter Baring, the head of Barings Bank, "only" made £ 300,000. However, the variable component of the income earned by employees at Barings Securities was dependent on how the Japanese stock market performed. If the stock market soared, employees were paid high premiums or bonuses. In 1991, however, stock prices started to fall. There was a risk that bonuses were going to be eliminated altogether. In this industry, however, banks who do not pay bonuses risk losing their best people to competitors who do. At the time, Barings Securities looked for a way out by proprietary trading in the markets, thereby putting their own capital at risk. The lack of supervision of these risky transactions spelled the end for Barings Brothers as an independent company.

1.2 What Banks Do

Banks are financial intermediaries. They coordinate the supply and demand for capital, thereby linking the present with the future. As a result, they serve to lubricate the economy and promote economic growth. An equilibrium between supply and demand for capital can also be achieved directly, without having to resort to banks. This takes place in the stock, bond, money and currency markets, and through trading in various derivatives such as futures, options and swaps.

1.3 Information Technology is Changing Banks

The former president of Citibank, Walter Wriston, summarized what banks do as follows: "Banking is not about money; it is about information." Faster and easier access to information, supported by modern information technology, has already changed the banking business enormously. Until the late 80s, interest rate spreads were the mainstay of a bank's income. In the last few years, the spread between interest paid and interest received has become smaller and smaller, and with it the contribution of this business area to total bank profits. The reason for this is the continued erosion of the banks' information lead, as well as improved information on the part of the saving public who are no longer prepared to deposit funds for a low rate of return. Leveraging their information, they switch to investment opportunities with higher profit margins.

A similar trend can be observed in the case of borrowers. Large corporations are turning less and less often to banks for their external financing needs, and with increasing frequency, are raising funds directly in the capital and money markets. Such "disintermediation" is a threat to traditional banking business, but at the same time, opens up new possibilities in investment banking. ING Barings is active in this very area. Investment banks provide assistance to corporations in their search for debt and equity capital in the financial markets. They underwrite stock and bond issues, and agree to take any unsold securities on to their own books. They are paid for their work in the form of commissions. In addition, they provide advice to clients in connection with mergers and acquisitions. This area of activity is particularly profitable for investment banks.

These days, investment banking and portfolio management are considered to be particularly profitable business areas for banks. Expansion of these areas has top priority for many banks. As a consequence, the demand for qualified investment banking specialists in the major financial centers such as London and New York has by far exceeded supply. Again and again, this has led to the poaching not only of individual employees, but entire teams, by competitors offering attractive compensation packages. The readiness of employees to change banks is much higher in the investment banking industry than in the traditional banking business. It can be said that investment bankers have little loyalty to their employers.

This became very apparent in the investment banking division of Deutsche Bank. As of autumn 1994, the investment banking business of Deutsche Bank was consolidated under the Deutsche Morgan Grenfell (DMG) name. As a result of the consolidation, this bank, between October 1994 and May 1996 alone, poached some 200 people ranging from investment bankers to seasoned senior managers from other banks. Some of those poached were offered twice their former salaries, guaranteed for the next two years. Banking industry observers assume that such hiring practices have raised the level of salaries in the investment banking industry in London by some 30%.

Other banks, such as UBS, Dresdner Bank, Lehman Brothers, Salomon Smith Barney or Schroders, have acted in a similar fashion, and have thus contributed their part to the rising wage spiral. In the meantime, top analysts can command annual salaries of one to two million dollars, and top traders a few million dollars more. Nevertheless, investment banking continues to be an attractive business with high profit margins. That is why it is still worthwhile to poach investment bankers. In general, when switching employers, individually or with their entire team, investment bankers will be able to take any knowledge gained with them, and readily apply it at another bank. Any switch of such teams to other banks is, therefore, relatively simple, because investment banking is about relationship banking. Teams know their clients, know what their plans are from previous meetings, and are, therefore, able to transfer this knowledge, putting it to full use at any new place of work.

2. ING Barings

ING Barings is one of 50 companies belonging to the Dutch ING Group, which is active in the banking and insurance business. Around 90,000 people work for ING worldwide in over 60 countries.

Box 9-1

ING – The Gentle Lion

Over 50 legally independent companies are united under the umbrella of ING. All of these companies are active in the area of financial and insurance services. ING is thus one of the few companies to have successfully put the one-stop financial services concept into practice. ING not only grew in size in the 90s, but also increased its net profit and market capitalization. Its geographic activities are centered in the Benelux countries and the emerging markets of Eastern Europe, Latin America and Asia.

ING attributes the successful integration of banking and insurance services mostly to its takeover strategy. Even though a lion adorns the corporate logo, the company has never pursued any unfriendly takeover policy. Its motto has rather been: "Choose a bank or insurance company that is well-managed, acquire a small shareholding, build trust and then propose acquiring the majority of the shares; then, after successfully completing the acquisition, let the acquired company continue to operate in its former market with its own products plus those of ING and the ING identity, thereby unleashing synergies from the bottom up." In conversations with ING management, it was repeatedly emphasized that this strategy is a radical departure from that of other big international banks, such as the merger of the Swiss banks, UBS and Swiss Bank Corporation, or the recently failed merger of the Deutsche Bank and Dresdner Bank. In the opinion of ING management, letting individual ING companies keep their own strong identity leads to a corporate culture characterized by trust. The ING Group became known to a wider audience in the German-speaking world through its takeover of the BHF Bank in 1999.

Box 9-1 (continued)

Growth in net profit of ING (in US$ million)

1994	1995	1996	1997	1998
1.045	1.202	1.507	2.206	2.669

Growth in market capitalization of ING (in US$ billion)

1994	1995	1996	1997	1998
10	17	22	32	49.2

Growth in ING headcount (calculated in terms of full-time jobs)

1994	1995	1996	1997	1998
46,975	52,144	55,988	64,162	82,750

Within ING, corporate and investment banking activities are for the most part covered by ING Barings. ING Barings employs over 9,000 people in 49 countries. Figure 9-1 shows the company's organizational chart. The range of services it offers contains all the financial services in this area. ING Barings has a particularly strong position in emerging markets through its presence in countries such as Columbia and Paraguay, which are rather inadequately served by other international banks. After a loss of US$ 1.25 billion in 1998, ING Barings achieved a successful turnaround in 1999, posting a net profit of just under US$ 300 million.

The company is divided into three frontline divisions and the area covering support functions:

The *Corporate and Institutional Finance* division provides assistance to companies and institutions in the area of mergers and acquisitions. It prepares companies for IPOs, but also acquires companies with a view to subsequent resale after restructuring, and assists with the financing of international trade. The *Equity Markets* division is mainly responsible for research, and thus provides important information to the Corporate and Institutional Finance division. The *Financial Markets* division trades in currencies, bonds, stocks and derivatives for its own account but primarily for clients. In addition, its employees are responsible for the asset and liability management of ING Barings and the entire ING. The *Support Functions* division includes all supporting areas, which operate independently, such as Information Technology, Finance and Controlling, Legal and Compliance, Risk Management and Human Resources.

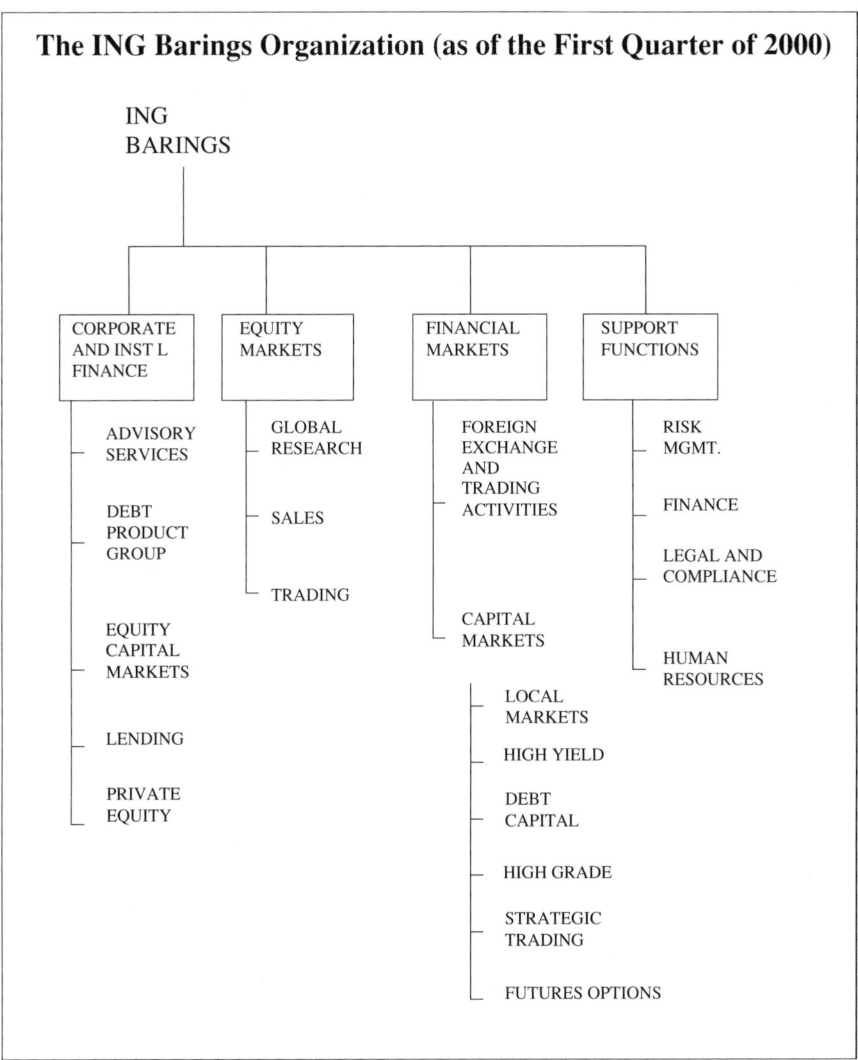
The ING Barings Organization (as of the First Quarter of 2000)
ING
BARINGS
CORPORATE
AND INST L
FINANCE
EQUITY
MARKETS
FINANCIAL
MARKETS
SUPPORT
FUNCTIONS
ADVISORY
SERVICES
DEBT
PRODUCT
GROUP
EQUITY
CAPITAL
MARKETS
LENDING
PRIVATE
EQUITY
GLOBAL
RESEARCH
SALES
TRADING
FOREIGN
EXCHANGE
AND
TRADING
ACTIVITIES
CAPITAL
MARKETS
LOCAL
MARKETS
HIGH YIELD
DEBT
CAPITAL
HIGH GRADE
STRATEGIC
TRADING
FUTURES OPTIONS
RISK
MGMT.
FINANCE
LEGAL AND
COMPLIANCE
HUMAN
RESOURCES

Figure 9-1

3. ING Barings' Motivation Management Tools

If staff turnover is used as a measure of loyalty, then employees of investment banks have little loyalty towards their employers to judge by their high rate of attrition. In investment banking, turnover rates of 20% are considered industry standard. However, it is not unheard of that individual offices sometimes lose over half their employees to competitors within a year. This constitutes an enormous loss for a bank, since a lot of effort will have to go into the subsequent rebuilding of client relationships. For this reason, ING Barings wanted to know what kind of motivational measures, apart from high salaries and attractive bonus systems, it could take to counteract this. The objective was twofold: firstly, to reduce the turnover rate, and secondly, to increase the motivation of the employees to share their knowledge with each other. This would result in knowledge remaining within the bank even if an employee switched jobs.

Based on information gained from meetings with Beat Bucher, Global Head of Human Resources for ING Barings, and Piet de Vries, Quality Manager of the ING head office of ING Barings, and an analysis of documents, we were able to identify an inventory of motivational tools which are presented below.

Fundamental to the ING concept is the combination of different motivational tools in such a manner as to achieve the best balance between the needs of the employees and the interests of ING Barings. Together with his team, the head of the Human Resources department, Beat Bucher, developed a "balance of interests" scheme, as set out in Figure 9-2. It is intended to be used to allocate the effects of the various motivational tools used by ING Barings to the corresponding needs or interests. Not every motivational tool will of course be able to equally satisfy all the interests listed. Therefore, Beat Bucher and his team have made it their aim to develop and manage an extensive repertoire of motivational tools that is capable of covering the entire range of interests.

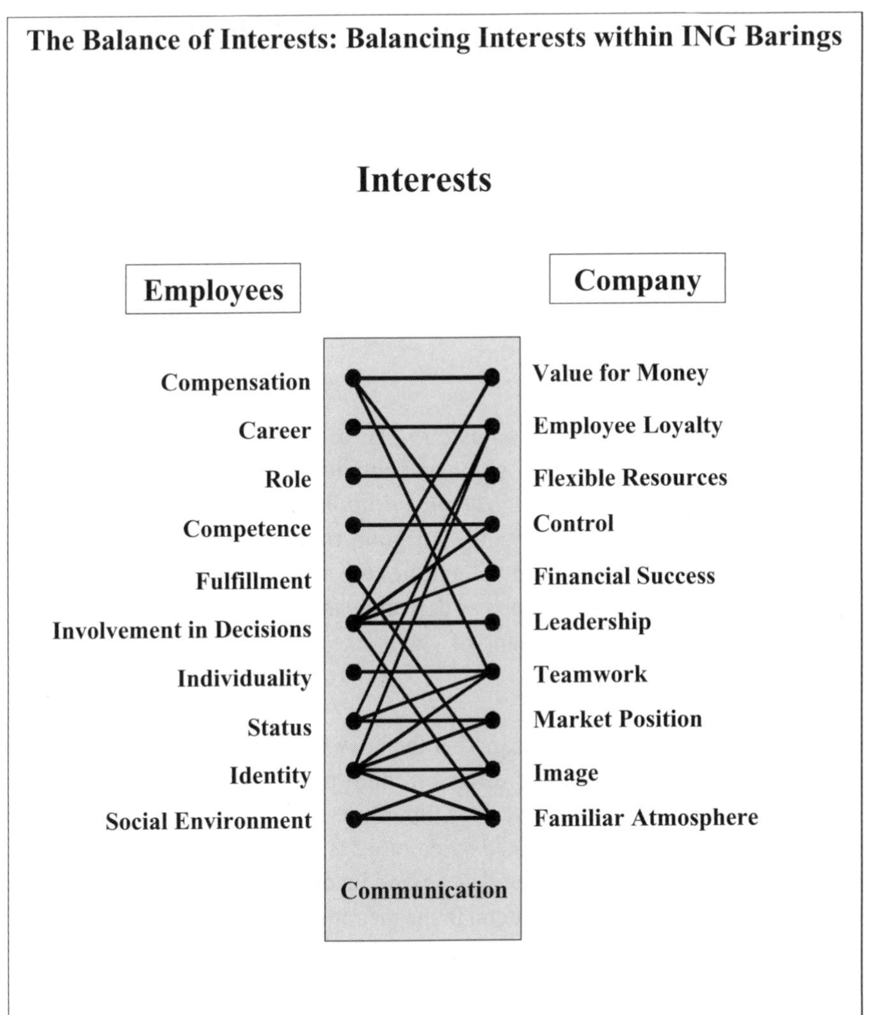

Figure 9-2

At the moment, the range of motivational tools applied by ING Barings covers eight areas/subjects: (1) the compensation structure; (2) an evaluation system of SMART objectives; (3) the structure of career development and professional training; (4) the internal communication system; (5) discussion groups and internal suggestion systems; (6) the Synergy Award; (7) the Spotlight Award; and (8) community investment programs.

3.1 First Motivational Tool: The Compensation Structure

Generally, the level of basic compensation is very similar amongst various investment banks since it is geared towards the job specifications for any given area of responsibility. This is different, however, for additional elements of a compensation package. At ING Barings, the compensation package consists of three elements: cash compensation, long-term monetary incentives and a flexible retirement scheme.

3.1.1 Cash Compensation

Cash compensation consists of a *basic salary,* a fixed income component, the level of which depends on the position and activity carried out within the bank. It also includes *performance-based compensation,* the level of which depends on individual employee performance. In good times, this performance-based compensation can easily amount to ten times the annual basic salary for traders and other frontline specialists, such as derivative analysts. Employees in support functions can double the amount of their fixed income, generally through bonuses.

However, at the moment, it appears that the "pay for performance" principle in this industry only works in one direction: high profits mean high bonuses. If profits are not as good the next year, however, the link between profits and bonuses is not going to be accepted by employees. No matter what, bonuses are going to increasingly be considered as a fixed income component, at least in the major international financial centers. In the meantime, some competitors already offer performance-related bonuses guaranteed over several years (bonuses on the basis of a "*retention scheme*"). They are thus barely linked to individual employee performance anymore. In a labor market in which demand exceeds supply, there are limits to how free management is to structure bonus levels at will. As Beat Bucher very aptly puts it: "In successful business years, employees will use company profits as the basis for bonus calculations, and in less successful years, the emphasis will be on current market levels of compensation."

3.1.2 Long-Term Monetary Incentives

ING Barings has attempted to develop long-term employee ties to the company through *deferral programs* which raise the financial barrier for employees wishing to leave the company. Thus, 30% of any performance-based bonus exceeding US$ 175,000 is converted into shares for a total period of ten years.

After two years, the employees only receive 50% of the shares, and the remaining 50% after three years, provided they still work for the company. That would give them a seven-year window in which they may sell their share package. At the moment, however, the labor market in the big financial centers is very tight. As a result, successful bankers changing jobs can expect that their new employer will take over any blocked shares for them so that despite the change of jobs, they will not have to suffer any financial penalties. In such a case, the intended length of time an employee stays with a company is not increased at all, but on the contrary, leads to an even steeper salary spiral for banking specialists.

In addition, depending on ING and ING Barings profits, stock options are given to employees at the management level and to so-called "high potentials," i.e. to particularly highly qualified specialists in the frontline business. The options have a maturity of three years.

3.1.3 Flexible Retirement Schemes

In banking circles, there is a lot of talk about the so-called "magic number." This number has to do with the combination of the age to be reached and amount of money to be saved in order to allow a person to stop working. This is why the flexible pension scheme structure at ING Barings is a considerable advantage. Many bank employees earn very high salaries even in their junior years. Their goal is to save up enough money by the time they reach 40 or 50, so that they can afford to retire or start a second career. For this reason, ING Barings in London selected a retirement scheme that allows employees, through additional voluntary contributions, to leave the company with a full pension before reaching the official age of retirement. This frees up attractive positions for the promotion of junior bankers, while promoting the ING Barings goal of fostering employee commitment to achieving corporate goals during their employment with the company. They are not going to try to sit out their jobs for decades doing as much as is needed and no more just to secure a claim on the pension fund, and thus blocking any structural change.

Overall, it can be said that ING Barings has hardly any room left for the structuring of compensation and bonuses for its specialists. The granting of monetary incentives is closely linked to current market levels of salaries in the investment banking industry. In particular, if bonuses are increasingly viewed as a fixed component of compensation, it becomes questionable whether ING Barings will indeed be able to motivate its employees to provide a higher level of performance using this kind of motivational tool.

3.2 Second Motivational Tool: The SMART Objectives

Individual employee contributions at ING Barings are evaluated by means of the so-called SMART objectives, as shown in Box 9-2. They are the basis for the amount of any performance-related bonus. However, as emphasized by Beat Bucher, Head of the Human Resources department, ING Barings management would like to prevent bonus payments being determined by the application of a "certain formula which results in a maximum bonus". Thus, the SMART objectives should primarily serve as feedback to employees with respect to their performance, and only secondarily as the yardstick for their performance-based compensation.

Objectives should be determined jointly by supervisors and individual employees, and thereafter, agreed upon. The employees are provided with certain subjects/areas for which they are required to independently formulate goals. These are then aligned with each other. One such goal may be, for example, that a trader generate a trading volume of US$ 20 million in his or her area, that a branch manager strive to achieve a staff turnover rate of 15% at the most, or that a supervisor ensure that those under him or her receive a total of 60 days of professional training seminars. At the end of the year, the degree of actual attainment of the goals is assessed in a meeting with the employee concerned.

Box 9-2

The SMART Objectives

The S, M, A, R and T criteria are interdependent, and stand for:

S = *specific,* i.e. individual target objectives to be achieved by each employee;
M = *measurable,* i.e. the expected performance must be measurable on the basis of concrete, operational criteria, e.g. sales, number of transactions, number of suggestions for improvements to reduce costs;
A = *achievable,* i.e. the level of performance agreed on with an employee must also be achievable within a given period of time in accordance with the framework of a standard industry job description;
R = *relevant,* i.e. the objectives must be achievable by individual employees in relation to their specific function, and must not be determined by external, non-controllable factors;
T = *time-bound,* i.e. the timeframe within which any identified objectives should be achieved.

Objectives that are difficult to quantify are assessed within the framework of a *360-degree job evaluation,* or a *270-degree evaluation* for top management. The aim of these evaluations is to identify additional elements relating to collaboration and quality of work that are not easily quantifiable. 360-degrees means that the person to be evaluated, his or her supervisors, his or her peers, his or her subordinates, as well as external and internal clients chosen jointly by the person being evaluated and his or her supervisor, are included in the performance evaluation. For this purpose, a written questionnaire is used containing a standardized section and an open-question section. After assessment of the various evaluations, a gap analysis is conducted with the aim of discovering any differences between the self-evaluation and the evaluations of other parties. This procedure is designed to facilitate joint agreement between the person to be evaluated and his or her supervisor on measures for changes and personal objectives. As a rule, 360-degree evaluations are conducted once a year, and for management functions even twice a year, if required by market and structural changes.

In the final analysis, the SMART objectives evaluation system has many elements in common with the requirements of Management by Objectives ("MbO"). MbO aims to achieve an objective results-oriented employee performance evaluation system. If coupled with external (monetary) incentives, it will have an extrinsic motivational effect (control aspect). However, as a prerequisite, any performance requirements must be clearly defined, and any achievements attributed and controlled. If this is not the case, ING Barings exposes itself to the "multi-tasking" problem that was mentioned in Chapter 1. If its employees receive performance-related salaries on the basis of goals evaluated using SMART objectives, and if these goals are not always easily measurable, then extrinsically motivated employees will concentrate on achieving the easily measurable goals, and will neglect the other activities, which are difficult to measure, such as the voluntary exchange of information. This may be the reason why Beat Bucher advises against using the SMART objectives like a set formula; they should allow supervisors room for their own performance evaluations. In this case, however, ING Barings management must ensure that in any performance evaluation process, the criteria of fairness and transparency in relation to employees is observed (see Chapter 7 for a discussion of the fairness principle). By using the tool of 360- and 270-degree evaluations, ING Barings appears to be going in the right direction. The performance of ING Barings employees is evaluated by various groups, and the results discussed in depth. Beat Bucher emphasizes, in particular, the importance of the feedback function via the discussion at the end of an evaluation. This provides employees with information on their performance. The information aspect of extrinsic motivation becomes operational. It means that the employees will be better able to assess and evaluate their own performance on the basis of the feedback received. Moreover, if ING

Barings is successful in creating working conditions in which its employees are prepared to assist in the process of setting goals, while setting goals for themselves, intrinsic motivation could be furthered.

3.3 Third Motivational Tool: Professional Development and Training

A wide range of options for professional development and training is regarded as an important motivational tool within ING Barings. The main focus is to increase the amount of time employees remain with the company and to position the company as an attractive employer for potential junior bankers.

Career planning is largely the responsibility of the employees themselves. ING Barings calls it a two-way process. They support their employees in developing their professional skills, not by means of a general trainee program, but rather by means of individually agreed measures, such as attending specialized courses or the opportunity to work abroad at another ING Barings subsidiary. In return, however, they expect employees to formulate those goals that they wish to achieve, and what support they would like to have in this regard from ING Barings.

Two years ago, the ING Business School was established in Marquette Castle in the Netherlands. Its main focus is to enhance the professional qualifications of ING management employees, by assuming a network function for the exchange of information, as well as facilitating educational discussion panels for ING employees spread all over the world. In order to take part in such programs, input from supervisors is required.

The ING Barings promotion system is also part of the career planning process. The company has a rank system consisting of five levels: Senior Management Directors (approx. 25), Managing Directors (approx. 300), Directors (approx. 700), Vice-Presidents (approx. 1,300) and Associates (approx. 2,000). However, promotion to a higher rank does not necessarily entail any financial advantage. At ING Barings, the compensation structure is determined on the basis of the demands of the position, which means that salaries are only adjusted upwards if the new position entails additional functions. Nevertheless, at ING Barings, promotion to a higher position is considered to be an important motivational factor. It has, above all, an extrinsic motivational effect. However, if an employee regards the promotion as a confirmation and appreciation of his or her performance, this can heighten his or her self-esteem and increase intrinsic motivation.

ING Barings views *team projects* as an important stepping-stone in the professional development of its employees. In such team projects, junior employees get an opportunity to handle, "on the job", demanding and complex tasks, and to gain experience in the various business areas. As a result, junior employees like to emphasize that ING Barings was ready to give them the chance at an early stage in their career to take on responsibility and be able to influence decision-making processes, in international teams, without having to work their way up the company ladder. Complex, demanding project teamwork with a high degree of decision-making flexibility fosters intrinsic motivation because it bolsters the experience of competency and self-determination.

3.4 Fourth Motivational Tool: The Internal Communication System

In the "balance of interests" (Figure 9-2), ING Barings regards internal communication as the basis for successful management of motivation. For example, the company's management realized the necessity of regularly informing employees, right down to the lowest level on the corporate ladder, about how business was going. After the takeover of ING Barings by the ING Group, the entire top management spent several months on the road in branches all over the world discussing with employees the new strategic direction the company was taking.

In order to sustain this dialogue, an extensive *"Daily Newsweb"* was established. When employees boot up their computers in the morning, the first thing they see on their screens is the latest ING Barings news, including the headlines of the day, the latest external and internal press releases, successful transactions and deals with a commentary from the CEO, information on initiatives taken to change the organizational structure, as well as an update on any vacant key positions and which new specialists the company was successful in hiring. Senior management and members of the Operations Committee are also required to publish their agenda two weeks in advance on the News web so that employees may know where and when they can be reached. The purpose of this is to encourage employees to contact their supervisors quickly and directly in case any questions or problems arise.

Once a month, a so-called *management information meeting* is held at a fixed time. This takes place in the form of a worldwide videoconference in which some 1,850 members of management from over 50 countries take part. Those who are unable to participate due to time differences receive a video recording the next day. A summary is also published on the Newsweb. During the videoconference, the CEO reports on the current business situation and answers any questions that relate to this. In addition, each conference deals with one or two special topics for which appropriate experts are invited to make a statement. Such special topics might, for example, include the introduction of a new bonus policy or a discussion about a new management idea.

It was observed that employees of ING Barings appear to appreciate these two measures aimed at supporting an open and transparent information policy. In particular, it was observed that an increasing number of suggestions, questions and ideas were directed to management from the floor. At the same time the corporate board wants to make sure that senior management does not use any advance information to build up positions of power, but instead, to foster a dialogue with employees working under them and include those employees in the decision-making process. This is also in line with the results of empirical research, which show that communication increases the intrinsic motivation of employees to cooperate (see Bohnet 1996).

3.5 Fifth Motivational Tool: Discussion Groups and Internal Suggestion Systems

A suggestion system enabled by way of intranet and discussion groups is designed to provide the employees of ING Barings with the opportunity to develop suggestions relating to various topics which lie outside their work sphere in the line organization. In this way, they take part in shaping improvements within the company on an ongoing basis.

Through the so-called *cost challenge,* which is the name of the intranet suggestion system, individuals or groups can provide suggestions as to how the company could reduce its costs. Ideas for cost minimization may be submitted on the web page, “Return to Profit”. The Cost Management Committee then submits these suggestions to the parties responsible for review and eventual implementation. Those who make suggestions will not receive any kind of reward. In this manner management wants to prevent a situation where good ideas are only developed if there is a reward. At ING Barings, the development of suggestions and ideas is and should remain a form of professional self-expression of an employee.

Discussion groups are time-limited and serve as a secondary structure to complement actual line positions, similar to quality circles. Any participation in these groups is voluntary. Employees are invited to participate by the Human Resources department, an employee's supervisor, or the CEO personally. They are selected from different divisions of the company to ensure a variety of perspectives and to prevent "operational blindness". In our discussions with ING Barings managers, it was always emphasized that these invitations are almost always accepted. This is attributed to the fact that ING Barings employees have a great interest in being able to express their opinions. Critical to the success of discussion groups is, however, that management not only be available as a discussion partner, but also that any recommendations developed in discussion groups be quickly implemented. This gives employees a high level of trust in discussion groups. Discussion groups are also useful for providing creative thinkers a forum to air their unconventional ideas.

Together with management, the Human Resources department normally sets the topics to be discussed. Reading articles on the topic and preparing arguments in advance are a good way to stimulate discussion.

Top management of one of the company's large banking subsidiaries, for instance, once initiated a discussion group because it wanted to take action to improve the bad work environment and lack of cooperation between employees. Within two weeks, eight discussion groups were under way. The head of the Human Resources department of ING Barings acted as facilitator. The suggestions of the group members were recorded during each meeting and passed on to the Management Committee through the CEO. The committee was assigned to evaluate the suggestions and implement them in a meaningful manner as quickly as possible. Just four weeks after the first meeting of the discussion groups, individual coaching for the top managers at the branch was introduced as a result of the meetings.

In the end, it is through the discussion groups at ING Barings that knowledge sharing is promoted to generate firm-specific pool resources. In the example described, the concern was to promote teamwork and to foster a corporate culture based on trust. Within these groups, members have to be motivated intrinsically to share their knowledge and to deviate from self-interested behavior because it is nearly impossible to single out individual contributions to these firm-specific pool resources. Thus, any contribution to the common pool of knowledge resources (which may only be tacit) by the members of the group can only be motivated intrinsically. This is the case at ING Barings, provided the employees are able to voluntarily participate in these groups and are prepared to reflect about changing goals. It requires that their performance be compensated not only on the basis of quantitative objectives; otherwise, pool resources that are difficult to measure will not be generated.

3.6 Sixth Motivational Tool: The Synergy Award

ING Barings is one of the legally independent subsidiaries of the ING Group. All companies represented in the Group are active in the area of banking and insurance. That means, on the one hand, that different companies such as the Postbank in the Netherlands or ING Direct in Canada, may be confronted with very similar issues. On the other hand, it also happens frequently that different ING subsidiaries in a given country, for example in Poland, will conduct their business independently of each other. Even though this corresponds to the principle of decentralized units with a high level of autonomy in decision-making, which was discussed in Chapter 8 as being the ideal type of profit center organization, ING management is concerned that too high a level of autonomy in the business units would result in too little cooperation and collaboration between them.

In 1996, the ING Board of Directors decided, for this reason, to set up the ING Synergy Award, to be awarded once a year. The objective of this award is to create a platform for promoting cooperation between the different business units. The award was established to emphasize the importance of synergy between business units and as a means of improving the total performance of the management center.

In principle, any project team within ING may submit its project to the award competition if it meets the following three participation requirements:

- First, the project must have a focus on integrated financial services.
- Second, at least two different business units of ING must be involved.
- Third, the project must show substantial tangible results for the ING Group.

Evaluation of projects submitted is based on the so-called ING Synergy Model, the fundamental concepts behind which are summarized in Box 9-3.

Box 9-3

The ING Synergy Model

The ING synergy model follows the principle that each project submitted to the competition must produce tangible results for the ING Group. These results are achieved in two different ways: either by making optimal use of its local subsidiaries or by applying ideas from other group members to local situations.

As indicated below, the model is divided into the two criteria groups, results and opportunities, which in turn include four criteria.

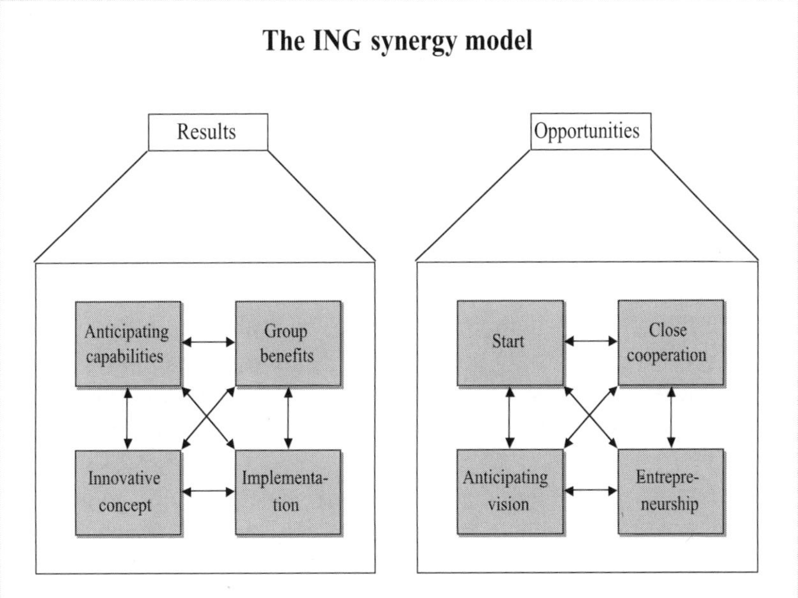

The ING synergy model

Box 9-3 (continued)

Project teams should indicate how their project contributes to ING Group benefits. The four criteria for "Results" are the following:

Anticipating capabilities: Here the project teams should give the auditors an overall view of how their business units anticipate market developments, for example through concrete measures that enable client expectations to be better assessed, factors that allow the acquisition of a more in-depth knowledge of market conditions, or experiences from which other teams could take advantage of in the future.

Innovative concepts: Synergy projects are meant to create innovative ideas that are then developed into new concepts, such as how client needs can be better satisfied, or how new product-market combinations could be achieved. This may, for example, result in new and more efficiently designed processes. Another measure for the novelty value of concepts is whether they succeed in winning public attention.

Implementation: Synergy projects should not only incorporate concrete, measurable results, but at the same time create the organizational conditions for their implementation, for instance by evaluating and expanding existing production capacity, providing timely information to and involving the employees concerned, adapting goals to new developments and, in the event any problems arise, requesting the support of top management.

Group benefits: It is the primary goal of any synergy project to generate and demonstrate an additional advantage for ING. In order to achieve this, anticipated capabilities, innovative concepts and implementation must be aligned and well orchestrated. Furthermore, any submission will be reviewed in order to determine if there was any active exchange of knowledge, skills and experiences during the project, and whether the project has improved the image of ING or the job satisfaction of its employees. In this area, project teams should give the judges a good impression of how they successfully dealt with local opportunities.

The four criteria for "Opportunities" are the following:

Start: Right at the beginning of a project, it must be clarified whether all business units involved are indeed in a position to contribute to the success by determining, for example, which of the different units are responsible for what kind of input, and to what degree top management is prepared to become involved.

Anticipating vision: Any successful criteria formulated in a synergy project should also be helpful for other ING business units in achieving success. It is the goal of any synergy project to simultaneously reflect about ways to transfer knowledge gains to other business units.

Entrepreneurship: Projects should be characterized by a certain degree of entrepreneurship. Project members are responsible for procuring the necessary resources from ING. In addition, they must be able to provide creative solutions to unexpected project developments that might arise down the road.

Close cooperation: Any teamwork between the business units involved must be characterized by a readiness to learn from each other across cultural differences within the group and to share knowledge and network relationships with other team members. This may result, for example, in setting up multi-disciplinary project teams, or in top management accepting mentoring duties.

Once a year, a winning team is chosen. Each team member receives a miniature version of the Synergy Award trophy for his or her desk. There are no monetary prizes. However, in the last few years, it has become customary to offer the winning team a special surprise as an expression of appreciation for the team's efforts.

When, for example, a project team from the Dutch Postbank and the Canadian Bank Direct won the award, the judges of the competition were able to convince the University of Montreal to allow this competition to become the subject of an MBA case study.

This year, the prize will be awarded on the occasion of the international ING management conference. The winners will be announced in the ING in-house newspaper. All projects in the competition and the team members will be introduced in ING-owned publications to provide a basis for further discussions and suggestions.

During the last competition period, 24 projects were on the shortlist for the Synergy Award. The first criterion for qualification was the relation of the project to the criteria of the Synergy Model as described in Box 9-3. Five-person audit teams then assessed submitted projects that met the minimum requirements. These teams were mainly composed of junior ING employees, approximately 300 in all. Within the company, it is considered an honor to be allowed to be part of these teams. A panel of judges consisting of top management, including the CEO of ING, made the final decision for the award of the prize. Box 9-4 contains a brief presentation of two 1998/99 winning projects.

Box 9-4

The Synergy Award: The 1998/99 Winning Projects

The aim of the *Euro Navigator Project* was to combine financial products, consulting services and other services for corporate clients in such a manner that they have direct electronic access, across Europe, to national payment systems. This was meant to facilitate international payment transactions and strengthen the position of ING as a European financial services provider. A new unit, ING International Cash Management, was established for this project. The project team was composed of ING Barings employees, as well as employees from four other ING companies. They all dedicated themselves to this project on a full-time basis and in the meantime have become cash management consultants assisting other companies with the introduction of this system.

Poland has become the second most important market for ING after the Benelux countries. It was therefore the aim of the *ING Poland Platform Project* to coordinate the strategies and business activities of the eight ING companies in Poland, including ING Barings, in order to avoid duplication of processes, and to make better use of country-specific experiences. In the end, the organization of the platform model was incorporated into the structure of the Group, i.e. every month, representatives of the eight companies meet under the rotating leadership of the General Manager of one of the companies in order to align business activities with each other. For example, employees of various ING Barings units provided support for Slaski Bank's corporate client section in the execution of complex transactions and thus ensured that the bank was able to successfully perform its mandates.

The Synergy Award is an award given by ING executive management as a symbol of recognition. The main objective is not the group prize, but rather recognition and feedback for the achievement. In this case, it is the informative aspect of the reward that produces the effect, reinforcing the internal conviction that control can be exerted, i.e. the team attributes the result achieved to its own efforts. Intrinsic motivation of team members is thus fostered. We were told that it is often the submission of their projects to the competition that causes teams to reflect on their project work with a critical eye. There were, for instance, ongoing heated discussions amongst team members as to whether the application of the synergy criteria would mean a qualitative improvement of their work environment. Many teams reported that it was during the process of filling out the application forms for the competition that they realized how to better formulate many of their project ideas. In such cases, the Synergy Award may be able to help tackle unfamiliar tasks or tasks which are perceived as being difficult.

Furthermore, such discussions will promote communication and the exchange and diffusion of information and ideas within a team. Similar to the discussion groups described in Section 3.5, this is a prerequisite for the transfer of implicit knowledge and for making a contribution to the generation of firm-specific pool resources. As far as cooperation between inter-departmental teams is concerned, it can be concluded that it is next to impossible to determine the individual contribution of any team member from the results achieved.

For motivation management at ING, this has the following implication: ING management must ensure that the supervisors of individual team members do not try to elicit a team member's contribution to a project goal through individual monetary incentives. The direct link between teamwork and employee compensation in the balance of interests, as set out in Figure 9-2, suggests that this risk exists. From this, the conclusion could be drawn that the willingness of an employee to become active in a team could be promoted through monetary incentives (extrinsic motivation). In the first two chapters, extensive arguments were given as to why this is not feasible: individual team members could be tempted to "free-ride" and profit from the work of others without having made any contribution themselves. There could be a risk of "multi-tasking" and "fuzzy tasking" (see Chapter 1 for the definition of these two problems).

In teams that work well, the contributions of team members normally go beyond factors that can be measured and controlled. It is thus important for ING to create conditions that also promote the intrinsic motivation of its employees. The project groups described in this section can contribute to this, provided they offer the following working conditions: integrated tasks that include personal responsibility, joint decision-making and problem-solving, common standards and a strong team spirit.

3.7 Seventh Motivational Tool: The Spotlight Award

The concept behind the Spotlight Award entails a similar goal. This award is granted at ING Barings once a month. It, too, is meant to reward teamwork between a number of business units, particularly those that are geographically distant from each other. In contrast to the long-term collaboration in projects rewarded through the Synergy Award, the focus of the Spotlight Award is on short-term projects, so-called "transactions". A transaction can be the activity connected with an IPO for a corporate client or the execution of a takeover, such as a Mexican cement firm wishing to acquire a plant in Indonesia. This requires a lot of work from the local subsidiaries, as well as professional support by one of the subsidiaries in a major financial center to ensure successful completion of the transaction.

Managers at ING Barings are encouraged to nominate once a month a number of successful transactions completed within their area of responsibility. From these, the Management Committee chooses one in which the collaboration between the virtual teams across the various units was particularly successful. It is important to company management that the Spotlight Award should constitute recognition that has a high symbolic value. The winning team does not receive any monetary or other award. Instead, the client for whom the winning team carried out the transaction may donate £ 5,000 to a public institution of their choice.

3.8 Eighth Motivational Tool: Community Investment Programs

The community investment programs are carried out in cooperation with the "East London Partnership" and coordinate the voluntary social work of ING Barings employees who donate their time. The headquarters of ING Barings is in the City of London, in direct proximity to the East End, one of the poorest residential areas in Great Britain. Everyday, ING Barings employees thus witness the contrast between the world of profitable investment banking in the City and the world of the underprivileged in their immediate neighborhood. "Many ING Barings employees consider themselves to be living on the sunny side of life, to be earning above-average salaries, and for this reason, want to do something for those who are not as fortunate, and for their own peace of mind," says Beat Bucher, Head of the Human Resources department. He also has experienced that employees who take part in the community investment programs are more motivated and have a better work ethic.

At the time, some 100 Barings employees, including the CEO, make their professional experience available by helping in the financial management of an orphanage, in working out a business plan for a foundation for the homeless, or in raising money for a theater. Last year, for example, ING Barings sponsored an art auction for the renovation of a local theater in Hackney, the poorest neighborhood of London. ING Barings paid for the food and beverages, provided a room for the auction, helped in printing the invitations, used its business connections to advertise the auction, and invited its employees to participate. The auction took in over £ 52,000. In addition to these activities, Barings employees also give tutoring lessons in schools to enable children to graduate successfully, and they also provide support to school administrators.

Beat Bucher's observations may be interpreted to mean that the community investment programs help provide many ING Barings employees with a special feeling of accomplishment. To have been engaged collectively and voluntarily in charitable works brings out a sense of duty that is motivated intrinsically and which is carried over by those involved to their job at ING Barings. Again, it is important to ensure that employees become active in the program of their own volition and do not feel obliged to take part for reasons of image or even compensation. This would severely curtail their voluntary effort, with the risk of displacing those efforts (crowding-out effect, as discussed in Chapter 1) and lowering the employees' intrinsic motivation.

4. Motivation Management and the Battle for Talent

Currently, the investment banking industry pays high salaries and bonuses. This applies to ING Barings Bank as well. If the bank, as an employer, did not keep up with the level of salaries and bonuses offered by its direct competitors within the industry, it would have considerable difficulty in being able to attract qualified personnel. Still, ING Barings management has had to realize that it is not enough to pay the standard high industry salaries and bonuses in order to protect themselves against losing large numbers of their employees. The bank, in 1998, suffered a turnover rate of between 25 to 50% in the two most important branches in London and New York.

Based on this experience, ING Barings management began to reflect about ways to motivate current and new employees to stay with the company. In collaboration with the Human Resources team, an inventory of motivational tools was developed. The most important of these tools were presented in Section 3 of this chapter. The wide range of tools is truly impressive: from flexible retirement schemes to involvement in community investment programs, ING Barings is trying to reconcile the needs of its employees with the interests of the company using a broad repertoire of motivational tools. ING Barings' primary goals are a) to reduce the turnover rate and strengthen employee loyalty and b) to boost employee motivation to share their knowledge with each other.

What can be concluded from this for motivation management? The case of ING Barings shows that measures to promote extrinsic motivation and conditions that foster intrinsic motivation must go hand-in-hand. They cannot be applied as standalone measures to the exclusion of other alternatives. Extrinsic and intrinsic motivation are interdependent and, as a rule, occur simultaneously. This is why ING Barings, with its range of motivational tools, wants to promote both types of motivation.

At ING Barings, providing extrinsic incentives is still a prominent factor. That is why the compensation package, with its different elements, and fine-tuned career development are placed right at the top of the balance of interests (see Figure 9-2). However, it remains open whether this is indeed sufficient to trigger the desired performance-enhancing effect in employees. Pay for performance only works if the remuneration can be closely linked to individual employee performance. As mentioned, however, high salaries and high bonuses are dictated by prevailing market conditions. These incentives thus lose their attractiveness if job applicants or employees view them as givens. It appears that banks in the investment banking industry seem to be increasingly less able to independently influence these tools of extrinsic motivation.

For this reason, it will undoubtedly become more important in the future for ING Barings to create working conditions that promote intrinsic motivation in its employees. With its inventory of tools, ING Barings has already developed a very interesting and solid foundation including an internal communication system, discussion groups and project work within the framework of the Synergy Award. These measures primarily encourage cooperation and the exchange of knowledge between employees.

The management of motivation should not restrict itself to motivating employees intrinsically by providing interesting work while simultaneously motivating them extrinsically through the promise of a bonus. Chapter 1 set out the reasons why extrinsic and intrinsic motivation do not act cumulatively, but under certain conditions, are mutually detractive. The crowding-out effect may occur, meaning that an extrinsic incentive may undermine intrinsic motivation, or supplant it. Thus, ING Barings will have to carefully examine to what extent, for example, the effects of the Synergy Award could be hampered by compensation based on individual employee performance. Who would be willing to divulge his or her knowledge, if colleagues could simply copy such ideas and profit from them at his or her expense? Who would be willing to voluntarily take part in discussion groups if, by so doing, there were less time to pursue quantitative goals (SMART objectives)? There is a great risk of running into the multi-tasking and fuzzy-tasking problems. The fact that extrinsic motivation can reduce job satisfaction and drastically diminish willingness to share knowledge with colleagues must become an important topic of conversation at ING Barings as well as in the investment industry. There is still a lot of work to be done to achieve a balance between the optimization of the relationship between extrinsic and intrinsic motivation.

The following should be kept in mind: *managing motivation* entails an adequate weighting of motivational measures in order to appropriately motivate the employees to fulfill corporate goals. *Intrinsic motivation* is necessary in order to facilitate the exchange of tacit knowledge and to ensure contributions to the creation of firm-specific pool resources, as well as to facilitate participation in the development of solutions for complex, non-quantifiable objectives. *Extrinsic motivation* helps to stimulate employee willingness and ability to perform. At ING Barings, a promotion or the winning of the "Spotlight Award" is a confirmation and expression of appreciation of good performance.

In the end, however, the inventory of motivational tools employed by ING Barings clearly demonstrates that the bank does not want to be drawn into the battle for highly qualified personnel through its compensation packages alone. Present and new employees who are more interested in the monetary aspect of the workplace, and have the necessary qualifications, are turning toward quite different challenges. Those who are looking for risk, adventure and big money have recently been more attracted by the New Economy than by investment banking, according to current statistics (The Economist, March 25, 2000, p. 88). These days, Internet and start-up companies typify the "gold digger" mentality, similar to the investment banking industry back in the early 1990s. An individual bank relying solely on monetary incentives would have no chance of winning the battle. Furthermore, the experience of the old Barings, where gold diggers too easily turned into grave diggers, argues against the exclusive use of compensation packages as a motivational tool. Probably, ING Barings, with its refined motivational tools and its presence in emerging markets, will be able to succeed in offering jobs that are equally as interesting as but have a great deal less risk attached to them than alternatives at the "dotcom" companies.

It seems very likely that ING Barings will succeed in managing motivation and in reaching its goal of reconciling the needs of the employees with the interests of the company through its wide range of measures.

5. Further Reading

The changing fortunes of Barings Bank has been narrated in detail by:

Fay, S. (1996): The Collapse of Barings, New York/London.

Another perspective is provided by:

Drucker, P. (1999): Innovate or Die, in: The Economist, September 25, 1999, pp 27-34.

Manual ING Group Synergy Award 2000.

Empirical research on cooperation and communication was undertaken by:

Bohnet, I. (1996): Kooperation und Kommunikation. Eine Analyse individueller Entscheidungen, Tubingen.

Chapter Ten

RALPH TRITTMANN, DIRK STELZER,
ANDREAS HIERHOLZER AND WERNER MELLIS

Managing Motivation in Software Development – A Case Study at SAP AG

Introduction

Human input is the key production factor in the field of software development. In turn, employee motivation plays a considerable role in the productivity of a software company.

Using SAP AG as a case study, the relevance of employee motivation with regard to the successful realization of projects for improving software development processes will be discussed. An analysis of what motivates employees at SAP will be carried out, showing that a strongly intrinsic sense of motivation pervades throughout the company. This investigation will conclude that successful improvement projects are planned in a way which is conducive to intrinsic forms of motivation.

1. Motivation and Software Development

Software is becoming an increasingly important factor in the growth of companies and economies. An average car has approximately 80,000 lines of software code while a good-quality television set contains up to 150,000. Heinrich von Pierer, the CEO of Siemens, estimates that his company makes around half its sales with products which owe their competitive edge to the software inside them. Over the course of the last few years, the share of gross national product accounted for by the software industry has grown steadily. At the same time the forecasts for future growth are substantially higher than the average for other sectors, while current developments, in e-commerce for example, suggest that software will play an even more important role in the years to come.

Human input is the key production factor in the area of software development. In turn, employee motivation plays a considerable role in the productivity of a software company. Software development is an extremely dynamic industry, due in part to technical progress as well as the rapidly changing requirements of customers. In view of this, companies operating in this field must focus on permanent product innovation and continual improvement of development processes. Only with highly motivated employees is this possible. It is evident therefore that at software companies employee motivation is at a premium. Astonishingly though, only a few empirical studies examining work motivation in the software development industry in greater detail have been conducted until now.

During the course of 1997 and 1998 we carried out a study of projects aimed at improving software development processes at one of the world's largest suppliers of business application software, SAP, a German company based in Walldorf near Heidelberg. Empirical studies at other companies have proved that making changes in software development processes can be complex, time-consuming and difficult. However, our initial experiences at SAP tended to contradict this theory completely. Making improvements seemed neither a difficult nor unusual process within the company. SAP employees would initiate and implement improvements whenever they recognized inefficiencies in any given process or opportunities for improvement. These improvements to development processes at SAP seemed to stem from numerous incremental changes that spanned the whole company.

On the following pages we aim to take a closer look at the relationship within SAP between employee motivation and the successful realization of projects for improving software development processes. The term "software development" covers all the development and management activities involved in producing a software product, including the associated peripheral services. Changes in software development therefore comprise all changes in both development and management processes.

In general, we can distinguish two different models for improving software development processes.

The first one is called the "bureaucratic improvement model". This term applies when projects for improving software development processes are governed by a defined and documented set of rules and when adherence to these rules is monitored. Explicit motivational tools are employed in this model with a view to promoting goal-oriented behavior among employees. This model is described in its ideal form in the ISO 9000 Standards or the Capability Maturity Model.

The second model is called the "organic improvement model". Its main philosophy is that there are no explicit rules governing the improvement of software development processes. Improvement projects are initiated by individual employees without them being explicitly instructed to do so or being offered special remuneration. Projects develop organically according to the way each one is organized, meaning that they can be continually adapted to individual circumstances. Objectives as well as resources used may alter over the course of time and the people involved may also change. The majority of improvement projects we observed at SAP belong in the category of the organic improvement model.

Bureaucratic improvement projects are structured according to fixed rules. Whether a project is successful depends both on the suitability of the rules and the extent to which these rules are applied by employees. Organic improvement projects do not have any such guidelines, as they are shaped essentially by employees themselves.

This chapter will argue that the success of "organic improvement projects" depends first and foremost upon whether the design of a project harmonizes with the nature of employee motivation in a company. We aim to illustrate this theory by way of the results of our study at SAP. Employee motivation within the bureaucratic improvement model is indeed of considerable importance, yet this element plays a significantly greater role in the organic model due to the absence of any explicit rules.

In the following section, we will describe the motivation factors which contribute towards job satisfaction at SAP. We will refer here to the sum total of these factors as "the nature of employee motivation". Using the results of our study, we will then outline the projects employed for improving software development processes and distinguish between those projects which were "successful" and those which were "less successful". In Section 4 we will show that successful improvement projects harmonize with the nature of employee motivation, whereas projects which are less successful do not. In Section 5 we will offer our conclusions.

2. The Nature of Employee Motivation at SAP

2.1 Method of Study

The aim of this examination was to gain a better understanding of processes aimed at improving software development at SAP. Given the current level of knowledge in this field, we decided to take an exploratory approach. The case study approach was chosen because it is well-suited for conducting explorative research.

Due to the extraordinary business success it has enjoyed, SAP seemed to offer a particularly interesting environment in which to carry out the study. Founded in 1972, SAP has grown to become the world market leader in business application software, with annual sales growth averaging 44 percent. Walldorf, where the company management is based, is the main development center for its flagship product, SAP R/3. The development of R/3 is divided into various areas which in turn are split into several departments. The sheer size of SAP meant that it was necessary to restrict our analysis to the "Logistics" development area, which at the time of the case study employed some 800 staff. SAP uses an ISO 9001-certified quality management system which covers SAP development processes worldwide as well as the service and support systems offered by SAP Germany.

Box 10-1

Facts about SAP

- Founded in 1972
- Headquarters: Walldorf near Heidelberg, Germany
- World market leader in business application software
- Most important product: SAP R/3 - integrated business application software (over 20,000 installations worldwide)
- Sales for the 1999 financial year: US$ 5.11 billion
- Average annual sales growth: 44 percent
- Number of employees at year-end 1999: approximately 21,700 worldwide

Our survey of motivation factors was carried out as part of a comprehensive interview-based analysis. (Please note that the terms "motives" and "motivation factors" are used here as synonyms.) Once we had explained the aims of the survey, we interviewed 13 SAP employees asking them what they viewed as important in their jobs. As an aid to answering this question, we provided them with several response categories such as recognition, pay, freedom to make one's own decisions and opportunities for promotion. The people interviewed were five software developers and two employees from each of the four management spheres of SAP (Development Manager, Product Manager, Program Director and Quality Manager). This ensured we had a cross-section of the various spheres of responsibility within the development area Logistics.

In order to increase the reliability of their statements, interviewees were confronted with the responses of colleagues who had been interviewed already. Remuneration was the only topic to produce any conflicting points of view.

The individual responses were grouped with the help of an affinity diagram and interpreted as motives, or motivation factors. The headings of these groups were then used as titles for each motivation factor. These factors will now be discussed.

2.2 Motivation Factors

The motivation factors identified cannot be perfectly isolated from each other. Partially, they refer to similar aspects. To ensure easy understanding of this framework of motives, individual motivation factors are grouped into one of the categories shown below. We distinguish between work-related factors, factors relating to the working environment and feedback-related factors. Box 10-2 provides a summary of all these factors.

Box 10-2

Motivation Factors Identified

Work-Related
- Stimulating work
- Individual initiative
- Personal responsibility
- Rationality principle
- Willingness to make or accept changes

Working Environment
- Individual freedom
- Team-oriented environment
- Professionally knowledgeable co-workers
- Friendly and collegial working atmosphere

Feedback
- Professional recognition
- Career progression
- Excellent reputation of SAP
- Remuneration

Work-Related Factors

All the interviewees mentioned *stimulating work,* i. e. varied and intellectually challenging tasks, as being an element essential to their jobs. Related to this is the importance of *individual initiative.* The interviewees interpreted this as the opportunity to search out challenges independently and so be able to choose one's own field of activity. In their opinion, the assumption of *personal responsibility* is a desire to bring their own knowledge and skills into play in their respective fields of work, and so enjoy a certain freedom in the way problems are solved. The presence of a so-called *rationality principle* is also viewed as important. The interviewees expect an explicit rationale behind actions and not the mere communication of measures. They want to know the reasoning behind particular rules and identify a tangible purpose to their everyday work. Linked to this is the *willingness to make or accept changes,* meaning the desire to query existing parameters and alter them, if necessary.

Factors Relating to Working Environment

SAP interviewees identified the need for *individual freedom* by noting the importance of flexible working hours and doing away with formal rules. The desire to work in a *team-oriented environment* was another motivation factor, while the theme of professional and social environment at work was another significant element. *Professionally knowledgeable co-workers* are an expression of this, as well as the need to work in a *friendly and collegial atmosphere.*

Feedback-Related Factors

The need for *professional recognition* was expressed as an additional motivation factor. The clearest form of acknowledgment is when a colleague is recognized as a leading authority in a particular specialist area. Related to this is the ability of employees to identify with the results of their own work. In this connection it seemed to be important for them to see that the product of their efforts could be used by customers or their colleagues. Promotion in the classic sense of "moving up the ladder" was of lesser importance for them. Indeed, the idea instead of *career progression* was preferable for them, i. e. assuming responsibility in new fields of work, thus widening one's range of functions. The *excellent reputation of SAP* with the public at large was identified as an additional motivation factor. The only aspect which produced conflicting responses was *remuneration.* While the majority of interviewees regarded salary as being of less importance, other colleagues considered it a valuable form of job recognition.

2.3 Categorization of Motivation Factors

As was explained in Chapter 1, there are two basic types of motivation. *Extrinsic* incentives serve to satisfy needs indirectly, especially through monetary compensation. *Intrinsic* incentives also satisfy needs, but in a more direct way. Someone who is intrinsically motivated does a job for its own sake.

When attempting to group all the motivation factors into these two opposing categories, it is immediately obvious that the nature of respondents' motives is fundamentally intrinsic. The motivation factors mentioned refer mainly to the work itself, and the importance of job recognition and promotion is also regarded essentially from the specialist, i. e. work-related point of view. The only extrinsic motivation factor mentioned was remuneration. However, as can be seen from the relevant data, the responses given concerning this motive were extremely varied. The belief championed by modern business theory that man's primary goal is maximization of income ("homo oeconomicus") thus does not appear to apply to SAP.

The nature of employee motivation at SAP, as revealed by the motives of individual employees, is basically unrelated to the extent to which employees feel these motives to be satisfied by the SAP environment. However, it is noticeable how much the structural and management principles of SAP do harmonize with the profile of employee motivation that emerged from our interviews. The company's flat hierarchy with only three layers of command, the presence of hardly any formal parameters, plus the substantial amount of individual freedom enjoyed by SAP employees would seem to be well suited to satisfying the motives expressed.

3. Improvements in Software Development at SAP AG

3.1 Method of Study

Most projects for improving software development at SAP concentrate on making small, incremental changes. These are rarely, if ever, documented. A preliminary study was required to identify them, calling upon 29 employees selected at random. They were asked to outline any such projects they had taken part in during the previous 12 months, providing information about the number of persons involved, the outcome of each project and the way in which changes were implemented. From these interviews we were able to identify 21 improvement projects, the overwhelming majority of which were classed as a success by the interviewees. Six successful projects and six less successful projects were selected from this total of 21 in order to identify the factors that made improvement projects a success. This preliminary study also helped us identify some fundamental features consistent in all improvement projects at SAP. These, as well as other contributing factors documented in previous studies relating to improvements in software processes, formed the basis of a standardized interview guideline.

The 12 improvement projects selected were then analyzed in greater detail in 36 interviews with SAP employees based on the guideline. The interviewees were divided into two groups: (a) those who took an active role in the preparation and launch of an improvement project, and (b) those who were merely passively affected by the change implemented. For each project analyzed at least one employee from both these categories was interviewed. To ensure the most complete documentation possible, we recorded all answers given during the interviews. We supplemented this material by the analysis of internal documents, in order to gain an even more detailed insight into SAP's unique software development processes.

The projects we examined were conducted in various areas and were directed at different objects. For instance, we looked at an improvement effort which spanned all development areas at SAP aimed at improving the testing process. At the same time we also analyzed a new deputization concept which was confined to just one department. In this case, measures were developed and implemented to ensure that essential tasks carried out by the department in question could be performed by at least two members of staff.

There is a conflict between research and practical experience as to what the most suitable and efficient indicators are for measuring the success of a project. Due to the special nature of improvement projects at SAP we decided to use a subjective definition of the word "success" when evaluating them. We classed a project as successful if those employees actively involved plus those merely passively affected both regarded the eventual outcome as successful. We rated a project as less successful if one or both the following criteria were fulfilled:

- Active participants and employees passively affected viewed the results as less successful.
- The project was abandoned before any tangible result could be achieved.

When analyzing the interview protocols, responses which were similar in content given by interviewees participating in successful projects were grouped into factors. The same procedure was carried out for interview protocols covering less successful projects. We describe a factor as a "success factor" if it fulfils two criteria:

1. It enables a clear distinction to be made between successful and less successful improvement projects, or in other words: when a factor is included in the list of successful projects it cannot be included in the list of less successful ones. Because the presence or absence of a factor does not necessarily imply a causal link, a second criterion was used.

2. There is a plausible connection between the presence of a factor and the success of an improvement effort. The plausibility of this connection was determined in twelve further interviews with SAP employees. In this way, we were able to identify 24 factors contributing to the success of improvement projects at SAP.

3.2 General Characteristics of the Improvement Projects Studied

Through our selective analysis of improvement projects we identified some general features characteristic of improvement projects at SAP. These features were common to all projects examined, both successful and less successful ones.

Numerous Improvement Projects Without Extrinsic Incentives

All 29 SAP employees interviewed during the preliminary study had been involved in at least one project within the previous twelve months. These projects seem in fact to be uncommonly frequent at SAP. This is all the more remarkable as there is no framework of incentives supporting these projects. What is more, successful implementation is not necessarily rewarded by special remuneration or other forms of recognition.

Decentralized Improvement Projects

At SAP there is no special organizational unit responsible for the planning, management and coordination of improvement projects. Neither is there any institutionalized body connected with these projects. Instead, the majority of projects we looked at were carried out in a decentralized way. Employees would identify problems or opportunities for improvement, independent of their position within the internal organizational structure, and then initiate changes accordingly.

No Formal Planning of Improvement Projects

In general, improvement projects within SAP are not linked to any formal planning structure. Indeed, their implementation seems as informal as their conception. It was typical that none of the projects examined was subjected to a cost-efficiency analysis beforehand and implementation milestones were defined in only one of the projects.

No Explicit Criteria for Decisions Relating to Implementation

No specific criteria were conceived in any of the cases studied for deciding whether to implement changes or not. As a rule, decisions were made on the basis of arguments put forward by those involved, yet without any criteria ever being clearly defined.

No Specific Measurement of Success

None of the improvement projects we studied were subject to any specific form of success measurement. Evaluation was based mainly on subjective views and was supported in part by feedback from individual employees or clients. However, systematic analysis of this feedback to gauge levels of satisfaction was carried out in one case.

Great Amount of Individual Freedom for Employees

SAP employees enjoy a remarkable amount of individual freedom at work. We discovered that this is expressed through the significant amount of license given to initiate and organize projects. What is more, employees even have the right to offer their critical appraisal of any guidelines issued by the management board. If they reject management-board rulings this has no negative implications from their point of view.

Little or No Attempt to Review and Disseminate Findings

At SAP there seems to be a negligible interest in collating and disseminating observations derived from the improvement efforts, hence none of the interviewees mentioned any project review ever being carried out. In only one instance were the results of a project widely publicized, this being via the internal magazine, “SAP inside”.

The general characteristics identified for improvement projects at SAP are summarized in Box 10-3.

Box 10-3

General Characteristics of Improvement Projects

- Numerous projects without extrinsic incentives
- Decentralized
- No formal project planning
- No explicit criteria for decisions relating to implementation
- No specific measurement of success
- Great amount of individual freedom for employees
- Little or no attempt to review and disseminate findings

The projects we analyzed for improving software development processes at SAP can be grouped clearly under the organic improvement model. With no explicit rules for initiating or carrying out improvements, projects are set in motion when employees seize the initiative themselves and manage to obtain the help of a sufficient number of colleagues. No explicit requirements or incentives exist for the implementation of improvement projects. In spite of this – or rather perhaps because of this – our study identified numerous projects aimed at improving software development at SAP.

3.3 Factors Contributing to the Success of Improvement Projects

In the case study, 24 factors were defined as factors influencing the success of improvement projects at SAP. There is not enough scope in this chapter to describe all these factors individually. In view of this we have decided to examine just seven factors which represent the clearest distinction between those projects which were successful and those which were less successful. As Table 10-1 shows, these factors in general are spread evenly across all the successful projects. However, the factors can only be found in very few of the less successful projects.

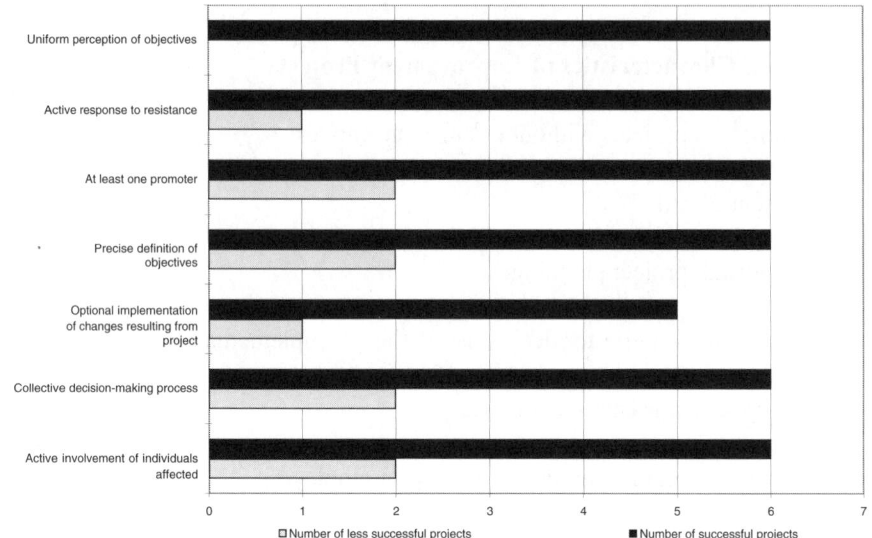

Uniform Perception of Objectives

"Uniform perception of objectives" describes the extent to which employees involved in improvement projects perceive the project's objectives consistently. In response to the question asking which objectives the project was designed to achieve, all interviewees involved in successful projects mentioned the same goals. When commenting on the less successful results, however, the selection of objectives offered was heterogeneous. Most notable of all were the marked differences in the perception of change objectives between employees who were actively involved in an improvement project and those who were merely passively affected.

Active Response to Resistance

An "active response to resistance" describes the efforts to minimize potential resistance from employees affected by the planned changes. There was evidence in all the successful projects of a conscious attempt to take a proactive approach towards dissenting voices. In this way potential resistance was anticipated and taken into account when implementing changes. Additionally, changes continued to be introduced step-by-step and any criticism arising during the course of this process was then used to make modifications. A similar approach was taken in just one of the less successful projects.

At Least One Promoter

An employee who sets in motion, organizes and manages an improvement project is regarded as the "promoter" of the project. The attitude of this person is one of total commitment during the whole process. All the successful projects were masterminded by at least one such figure. Interviewees involved in projects left uncompleted viewed the lack of such a person as the reason for the premature end of these improvement projects.

Precise Definition of Objectives

When determining the objectives of an improvement effort either precise definitions are made, or merely rough outlines given. Precise objectives were common to all the successful projects examined in this case study. In contrast, most of the less successful projects had vague objectives – a "general improvement in quality" being described for instance by the interviewees as the principle aim of one of these projects.

Optional Implementation of Changes Resulting from Project

In this respect we ascertained – with just one exception – that in the case of all the successful projects it was merely an optional choice whether the resulting changes were adopted. However, in nearly all the less successful projects SAP employees were explicitly instructed to implement the changes.

Collective Decision-Making Process

All the successful improvement projects we examined were characterized by a collective decision-making process with regard to implementation. This would involve a detailed discussion about procedure, followed by a resolution based on consensus. In comparison, decision-making for the less successful projects tended to be of an authoritarian nature, or else the project was aborted before an explicit decision regarding implementation could be made.

Active Involvement of Individuals Affected

"Involvement of individuals affected" is a success factor defined by the degree to which the individual affected by the results is involved in bringing these about. The participants of successful improvement projects made great efforts to involve colleagues who would be affected by the results. Using this approach, people who would eventually be affected by particularly extensive projects would be selected to play an active development role.

4. Relationship Between Motivation Factors and Factors Contributing to the Success of Improvement Projects

The success of "organic improvement projects" depends first and foremost upon whether a project harmonizes with the nature of employee motivation. In the previous section the improvements we examined were classed as organic projects. Assuming our theory is correct, successful improvement projects harmonize with the nature of employee motivation at SAP, but less successful ones do not. This means that the factors which contribute to the success of improvement projects are complemented by a congruent set of motivation factors.

Uniform Perception of Objectives

When employees are all aware of the objectives of individual improvement projects this is reflected in the *team-oriented environment and rationality principle* motivation factors. Individual employees want to be aware of the objectives and purpose of their activities. This wish can be satisfied through team-oriented problem-solving, provided that all those working on a project share the same awareness of what they are aiming for.

Active Response to Resistance

A proactive approach to resistance is closely related to the *rationality principle.* This term describes the need for actions to be explained and argued cogently. An improvement project which chooses to override any criticism that arises fails to satisfy such criteria. Bearing in mind that SAP employees like to challenge existing rules and change them where necessary *(willingness to make or accept changes),* an active response to resistance is required instead of merely dictating measures without consultation.

At Least One Promoter

Promoters are necessary to provide the impetus for successful improvement projects. A possible reason for the premium placed on such a person is the unwillingness of SAP employees to accept and apply new guidelines without first examining their implications. This situation is above all a reflection of the *rationality principle.* According to this principle, a project needs someone who can offer continuous dialogue in order to rationalize measures being taken.

Precise Definition of Objectives

The influence that a precise definition of objectives has on the ultimate success of a project is closely related to the *rationality principle.* SAP employees want to know the objectives behind the measures and expect to be given reasons why a project is to be carried out. The clearer and more detailed these aims are, the easier these should be to rationalize.

Optional Implementation of Project Results

At SAP, it would seem that for improvement projects to be successful it is important that any new measures or changes introduced should merely be optional for those potentially affected. *Individual initiative* and *personal responsibility* play a role in this respect. Individual initiative means that the interviewees wish to be proactive in structuring their own program of activities. Personal responsibility is reflected through their need for a certain degree of freedom when solving problems.

Collective Decision-Making Process

The role of a collective decision-making process in successful implementation of an improvement project is relevant to the need to handle jobs through teamwork *(team-oriented environment).* It is therefore logical to suggest that rather more authoritarian forms of decision-making are rarely conducive to a *friendly and collegial working atmosphere.*

Active Involvement of Individuals Affected

The active involvement of those individuals affected by improvement projects runs in parallel with the wish of SAP employees to incorporate their own ideas and utilize their own skills when solving problems *(personal responsibility).* This is acknowledged through the active participation of these individuals in the projects concerned. Active involvement can also be viewed in relation to a *willingness to make or accept changes.* Without such levels of involvement it is unrealistic to expect any new rules to be accepted and applied as a matter of course.

The relationship we have just described between motivation factors and success factors is summarized in Box 10-4.

A close relationship exists between the success factors we have identified and the nature of employee motivation at SAP. While this supports our theory regarding the success of organic improvement projects, we should add that of

Box 10-4

Relationship Between Success Factors and Motivation Factors

Success factors harmonize with motivation factors:

Success factors	*Motivation factors*
Uniform perception of objectives	Team-oriented environment Rationality principle
Active response to resistance	Rationality principle Willingness to make or accept changes
At least one promoter	Rationality principle
Optional implementation of changes resulting from project	Individual initiative Personal responsibility
Collective decision-making process	Team-oriented environment Friendly and collegial working atmosphere
Active involvement of individuals affected	Personal responsibility Willingness to make changes

Some of the motivation factors here point emphatically to the success of the organic improvement model applied at SAP. This is reflected particularly through the need for individual freedom at work, i. e. the rejection of formal parameters. Bureaucratic improvement projects held together by concrete guidelines invariably stand in the way of this desire.

5. Conclusion

Using data from a wide-ranging case study, we have discussed the relevance of employee motivation for the successful realization of projects to improve software development processes at SAP. The improvement projects examined as part of this study are described here as "organic". We divided these projects into two groups: those which were successful and those which were less successful. Comparison between these two categories shows that successful projects harmonize ideally with the nature of employee motivation at SAP. In contrast, less successful projects clash with these motivation factors. One can conclude from this that efforts to improve software development processes at SAP are only likely to be successful if they take employee motivation into account. It is evident therefore that recognition and acknowledgement of the nature of employee motivation is essential to the success of improvement projects.

Modern economic theory usually adopts the "homo oeconomicus" approach, meaning the assumption that man's main preoccupation is that of maximizing income. In spite of this, we could find hardly any evidence of extrinsic incentives in our study of employee motivation at SAP, as employee motives are of a fundamentally intrinsic nature. In view of this, it would make little sense to introduce a system of extrinsic incentives to help in the implementation of improvement projects. If in fact such a scheme were to be put into practice, the organic improvement model, which is characterized by the absence of any remunerative incentives, would be abandoned. However, the overwhelming majority of organic improvement projects at SAP were classed as a success. The implicit motivational tools at the disposal of the organic improvement model (participation and autonomy) harmonize with the intrinsic nature of employee motivation at SAP. If indeed extrinsic incentives were introduced it would probably lead to the situation described in Chapter 1, i. e. intrinsic forms of motivation would be suppressed by remunerative rewards.

SAP is currently undergoing a complete reorganization in connection with the launch of its software products on the Internet. Under the heading of "mySAP.com" (http://www.mySAP.com), not only will the range of products offered by SAP change, but the whole structure of development and management activities too. It remains to be seen whether these changes will affect both the nature of employee motivation and improvement strategy at SAP, and if so, to what extent.

6. Further Reading

Sources related to the software industry:

Anderson, C. (1996): A world gone soft: a survey of the software industry, in: IEEE Engineering Management Review 24 (4), pp 21-36.

Arthur, W. B. (1996): Increasing returns and the new world of business, in: Harvard Business Review 74 (4), pp 100-109.

Advice and recommendations for improving software development processes:

ISO 9004-1 (1994). Quality management and quality system elements. Part 1: Guidelines, Geneva.

Paulk, M. C./Weber, C. V./Curtis, B./Crissis, M. B. (1995): The capability maturity model: guidelines for improving the software process. Reading, MA.

The following empirical studies discuss the management of software development:

Brodbeck, F. C./Frese, M. (eds) (1994): Produktivität und Qualität in Software-Projekten. Psychologische Analyse und Optimierung von Arbeitsprozessen in der Software-Entwicklung, Munich/Vienna.

Cusumano, M. A./Selby, R. W. (1995): Microsoft secrets: how the world's most powerful software company creates technology, shapes markets, and manages people, New York.

Carmel, E. (1995): Cycle time in packaged software firms, in: Journal of Product Innovation Management 1, pp 110-123.

Stelzer, D. (1998): Möglichkeiten und Grenzen des prozessorientierten Software-Qualitätsmanagements, Cologne (postdoctoral thesis).

Stelzer, D./Mellis, W./Herzwurm, G. (1998): Technology diffusion in software development processes: the contribution of organizational learning to software process improvement, in: Larsen, T./McGuire, E. (eds): Information systems, innovation and diffusion: issues and directions, Hershey, PA, pp 297-344.

The role of employee motivation in software development is examined in the following works:

Bach, J. (1995): Enough about process: what we need are heroes, in: IEEE Software 12 (2), pp 96-98.
DeMarco, T./Lister, T. (1991): Wien wartet auf Dich! Der Faktor Mensch im DV-Management, Munich/Vienna.
Rasch, R. H./ Tosi, H. L. (1992): Factors affecting software developers' performance: an integrated approach, in: MIS Quarterly 16 (3), pp 395-413.
Weinberg, G. M. (1971): The psychology of computer programming, New York.
Yourdon, E. (1995): Peopleware, in: Application Development Strategies 7 (8), pp 1-16.

Notes on case research:

Benbasat, I./Goldstein, D. K./Mead, M. (1987): The case research strategy in studies of information systems, in: MIS Quarterly 11 (3), pp 369-386.

The empirical observations presented in this chapter are considered in more detail in the following works:

Trittmann, R./Stelzer, D./Hierholzer, A./Mellis, W. (1999): Changing software development: a case study at SAP AG, in: Pries-Heje, J./ Ciborra, C./ Kautz, K./ Valor, J./ Christiaanse, E./ Avison, D./ Heje, C. (eds): Proceedings of the 7th European Conference on Information Systems, Copenhagen, pp 692-703.
Trittmann, R./Hierholzer, A./Stelzer, D./Mellis, W. (1999): Veränderungen der Softwareentwicklung: Ergebnisse einer Fallstudie in der SAP AG im Vergleich zu den Empfehlungen der ISO 9000. Paper presented at the "Organisation" workshop, Verband der Hochschullehrer für Betriebswirtschaft e. V. on 26/27.02.1999 in Zurich.

Part V

Conclusion

Chapter Eleven

MARGIT OSTERLOH AND BRUNO S. FREY

Managing Motivation to Achieve a Sustainable Competitive Advantage

For some time now, performance-related pay has been the hallmark of progressive management credos. Companies, government offices and even universities have come under pressure to increase efficiency by basing a larger part of employee compensation on success-oriented performance criteria. In particular, the granting of bonuses or stock options is viewed by many as an integral part of performance-based compensation.

This book challenges the tenets upon which this practice is based. Performance-based compensation has numerous grave disadvantages, and these disadvantages become greater the more complex and knowledge-intensive the tasks to be performed become.

1. The Problems of Performance-Based Compensation

1.1 Measurement Problem

Performance-based compensation is ideal when it comes to simple tasks (e.g. pricework). Installing windows in cars is an example of a task perfectly suited to this type of incentive. Performance-based compensation really does boost employee performance when applied to this type of task. But how does one measure the performance of a software engineer, a doctor, university professor or consultant? Even in the case of independent consultants, the service performed is generally paid for on the basis of the hours worked or on a fixed fee, i.e. on the basis of input rather than output criteria. With this kind of work, often the positive or negative results of the activity are only visible after a longer period of time, and usually it is very unclear as to how much an employee has contributed to its success or failure. And in order to pay employees for their performance, alternative criteria that are easily measured such as hours worked, sales made, the number of publications produced or the number of employees managed must be utilized.

But this creates two problems. Firstly, employees will ignore objectives that are difficult or impossible to measure (quality, originality, customer satisfaction, etc.) in favor of objectives that are easy to measure (multi-tasking). Secondly, they will not be motivated to think about whether the alternative criteria used are suited to achieving company objectives or whether they make any contribution whatsoever to corporate goals (fuzzy tasking).

Thus performance-related pay systems require the results of an activity to be measurable or that quantifiable alternative criteria with no dysfunctional effects can be established. These conditions are all the more difficult to fulfill the greater the knowledge factor contributing to the total added value of an activity and the more specialized the knowledge workers. Generally speaking, these activities often presuppose the existence of internalized (i.e. intrinsically pursued) professional standards.

1.2 Team Problem

The team problem arises when several employees perform a complementary task which cannot be attributed to individual employees. The firm-specific pool resources created by this activity are the firm's lifeblood – if this were not so, then it would be easy to outsource such tasks. All employees benefit from the firm's pool resources even if they have not contributed to them. As it is difficult to establish who contributed to these public goods, there is a danger that employees will free-ride at the expense of others. For these people, teamwork means letting the others in the team do the work. Social pressure can help minimize this type of behavior within the team, but with activities that are difficult to monitor, it becomes almost impossible to record contributions made by individual team members. This is often the case with extra-role behavior, or with assistance and support functions requiring an effort above and beyond the normal call of duty. It is particularly difficult to prove that proper responsibility has been taken for highly qualified specialist activities which call for a great deal of implicit experience. Extrinsically motivated employees closely guard this knowledge as it enables them to create a monopolistic advantage. But it is exactly this influx of implicit individual knowledge that forms the basis for firm-specific knowledge which is difficult to imitate and which is currently considered to be the most important source of sustainable competitive advantage.

1.3 Selection Problem

High performance incentives may attract those people who lack intrinsic motivation, i.e. who are not interested in the task itself or in the objectives of the company. This is actually beneficial if the task at hand is easy to measure and can be attributed to individual employees. Problems will only arise if the activity is not conducive to a clear output measurement or if it requires teamwork where the individual contributions are difficult to measure. In such cases, extrinsically motivated employees have an incentive to promote alternative criteria that are easy to measure, but which often have dysfunctional consequences. The selection problem proves to be a bigger drawback, the more important the role of knowledge-intensive teamwork is.

1.4 Manipulation Problem

All monetary performance incentives carry the inherent danger that employees will try to influence the compensation to their own advantage at the expense of the company. On the one hand, the criteria used to determine performance-related pay can be manipulated. On the other hand, employees can attempt to influence the amount of compensation. Such deception is also possible with stock options, which are considered an integral part of performance-based compensation. Thus the management of a company may tend to pay smaller dividends in order to boost the share price. Even top echelons of management are therefore not always averse to manipulation tactics. Empirical research shows that there is only a slight correlation between manager compensation and company performance. By contrast, factors such as the presence of managers in key decision-making bodies have a considerable effect on the level of managers' salaries.

1.5 Crowding Out Problem

Most people work not only to earn a good income, but also because they enjoy what they do and are orientated to norms which enhance their sense of identity. In other words, not only are they extrinsically motivated, they are also intrinsically motivated. The crowding out problem arises because there is a trade-off between these two different types of motivation. As soon as payment is used as an incentive, intrinsic motivation is reduced. Therefore, performance-related pay has a negative effect on performance where a high level of intrinsic motivation is required to perform a task. This negative effect is heightened as the problems of measurement, teams, selection and manipulation worsen, as is typical in the case of highly qualified and specialist teamwork. If sustainable competitive advantage is to be secured and maintained, it is crucial to have a large proportion of this kind of work generating added value.

These problems do not argue against either the fair remuneration of employees based on market salaries or the supportive evaluation of performance, as a form of informative feedback. However, we contest the notion that performance-based compensation is the ideal way to boost employee motivation. The more complex and knowledge-intensive an activity is, the less this holds true. What is needed is a diverse range of motivation management tools tailored to the complexity of the problem.

2. Basic Principles of Management by Motivation

2.1 Tailoring the Incentive System to the Type of Activity

Salaries and other incentives should be adapted to the personality type that appears to be suited to the task at hand. As empirical research shows, performance-based salaries attract those employees who are primarily interested in their income. With tasks that are easy to evaluate and calculate, such compensation produces good results. However, for activities requiring knowledge-intensive teamwork, creativity, loyal fulfillment of obligations or the observance of formal rules, motivational instruments that are not based on monetary compensation should primarily be employed.

2.2 Variety of Motivational Instruments

The more complex the activity, the more varied the motivational tools must be. For knowledge-intensive teamwork, the degree of autonomy, the opportunity for participation and communication are of great importance in addition to a fair salary. Equally important is supportive and informative feedback from a manager and colleagues, which strengthens both the existing psychological contract between them and cognitive self-control.

2.3 Workflow

Organizational structures influence autonomy and the employee's opportunity to participate and communicate. While they often presuppose a certain motivational structure, they at the same time create it. Taylor's organizational structure is based solely on extrinsic motivation. The crowding out effect results in this type of motivation ultimately becoming predominant. Conversely, participatory group structures are primarily targeted at intrinsically motivated employees, thus enabling them to create suitable conditions. As the type of intrinsic motivation which promotes the company's goals is not easy to control, companies are forced to resort to motivational tools that work via extrinsic effects. Sometimes extrinsic incentives provide motivation for employees to take on difficult tasks which later prove to be enjoyable. However, it should be clear by now that the number of tasks that can be driven solely by extrinsic motivation is declining. As a result, companies are increasingly turning to organizational structures which provide for partial autonomy in a team, but which also ensure coordination and the control of outputs, such as the profit center organization, for example. Here too, however, it is obvious that complex tasks require complex processes. In particular, knowledge-intensive teamwork necessitates substantial modifications to the apparently simple profit center concept.

2.4 Fairness

It is imperative that fairness standards be applied when defining working hours and compensation schedules. Not only is it important that employees recognize that the results are fair, the company must also adhere to procedures that are perceived to be fair. Unfair treatment permanently destroys intrinsic motivation.

3. Managing Motivation to Achieve a Sustainable Competitive Advantage

Motivation management creates corporate resources that are difficult to replicate. These resources aid the company in developing a sustainable competitive advantage. Both extrinsic and intrinsic motivation are necessary for this development.

In a knowledge-based society, the focus will increasingly be on those tasks that require employees to enjoy and identify with their work. Managing intrinsic motivation is much more demanding than managing extrinsic motivation. By its very nature, intrinsic motivation is always voluntary.

However, companies can create favorable conditions that will foster its development. Our book shows how to do just this.

Authors

Matthias Benz

Matthias Benz earned an M.A. in History and Economics in 2000 from the University of Zurich in Switzerland. He is currently research assistant to Bruno Frey at the Institute of Empirical Research in Economics, University of Zurich. His main research interests include the economic theory of motivation, personnel economics, and political economy.

Iris Bohnet

Iris Bohnet is Assistant Professor of Public Policy, Kennedy School of Government, Harvard University. She completed her M.A. in 1992 and received a Ph.D. in Economics in 1997. From 1992 to 1997 she was research assistant to Bruno Frey at the Institute of Empirical Research in Economics, University of Zurich. In 1997/98 she worked at the University of Berkeley, California, as a research associate. Her research examines the role of incentives, trust and cooperation in contractual relationships.

Leo Boos

After completing his college degree, Leo Boos trained as a professional nurse. From 1993 to 1998 he studied Economics at the University of Zurich (M.A.). Since 1998 he has been assistant to Margit Osterloh at the Institute for Research in Business Administration, University of Zurich.

Bruno S. Frey

Bruno S. Frey was Professor of Economics at the University of Constance in Germany from 1970 to 1977. Since 1977 he has been Professor of Economics at the University of Zurich in Switzerland. Recipient of honorary doctorates in Economics at both the University of St. Gallen (Switzerland) and the University of Göteborg (Sweden), he has written over 350 articles for professional journals as well as fourteen books, several of which have been translated into nine different languages.

Jetta Frost

Jetta Frost is Assistant Professor at the Institute for Research in Business Administration, University of Zurich. She received a Ph.D. in Economics in 1997 from the University of Zurich. Her main areas of research cover process management and the role of motivation in a knowledge-based theory of the firm.

Andreas Hierholzer

Andreas Hierholzer received a Ph.D. in Economics and Computer Science in 1996 from the University of Cologne (Germany). Since 1996 he has been working at SAP AG in Walldorf, Germany, and currently holds the post of Development Manager of the Customer Relationship Component for the SAP Insurance Solution. He has published a number of articles in professional journals.

Marcel Kucher

Marcel Kucher completed his Ph.D. in Economics in 2000 at the University of Zurich. From 1995 to 2000 he was research assistant to Bruno Frey at the Institute of Empirical Research in Economics, University of Zurich. Currently working for McKinsey & Company, his research focuses on the economics of power, history and the financial markets.

Werner Mellis

Werner Mellis was systems engineer and project manager at Nixdorf Computers from 1984 to 1989, and he headed up various research departments at Daimler Benz from 1989 to 1992. Since 1993 he has been Professor of Economics and Computer Science at the University of Cologne. His principal area of research is the management of software development, and he has written numerous articles for professional journals as well as several books.

Felix Oberholzer-Gee

Felix Oberholzer-Gee is the Class of 1965 Wharton Term Assistant Professor of Business and Public Policy at the Wharton School, University of Pennsylvania. He received his Ph.D. in Economics from the University of Zurich in 1996. His research interests include labor economics and political economy.

Margit Osterloh

Margit Osterloh is Professor of Business Administration and Executive Director of the Institute for Research in Business Administration at the University of Zurich. She is a specialist on the subjects of organizational science and the management of innovation and technology. Her research focuses on the role of women in organizations, the impact of new technology in the working place, and business ethics. She has published over 80 articles in professional journals and is author of four books.

Sandra Rota

Sandra Rota completed her M.A. in Economics in 1999 at the University of Zurich, and since then has worked as a research assistant to Margit Osterloh at the Institute for Research in Business Administration, University of Zurich.

Dirk Stelzer

Dirk Stelzer is Professor of Information Management at Ilmenau Technical University in Germany. He received a Ph.D. in Business Information Systems from the University of Cologne. Author of more than 30 articles in professional journals as well as three books, he currently specializes in information management for digital goods.

Alois Stutzer

Alois Stutzer earned an M.A. in Economics in 1997 from the University of Zurich. He has since been working as a research assistant at the Institute for Empirical Research in Economics, University of Zurich. He is author of several articles and a book on happiness and economics.

Ralph Trittmann

Since 1998, Ralph Trittmann (M.A.) has been a research assistant in Economics and Computer Science at the University of Cologne. He is the author of a number of articles that have been published in professional journals.

Antoinette Weibel

Antoinette Weibel received an M.A. in Economics from the University of Zurich in 1996. She has since been working as a research assistant to Margit Osterloh at the Institute for Research in Business Administration, University of Zurich. Currently, she is writing her Ph.D. dissertation on the role of trust in business networks.

References

Abowd JM, Kaplan DS (1999) Executive Compensation: Six Questions That Need Answering. Journal of Economic Perspectives 13 (4): 145–168

Alexander S, Ruderman M (1987) The Role of Procedural and Distributive Justice in Organizational Behavior. Social Justice Research 1: 177–198

Amabile T (1996) Creativity in Context: Update to the Social Psychology of Creativity. Boulder, Colorado

Amabile T (1998) How to Kill Creativity. Harvard Business Review: 77–87

Anderson C (1996) A World Gone Soft: A Survey of the Software Industry. IEEE Engineering Management Review 24 (4): 21–36

Antoni CH (1999) Konzepte der Mitarbeiterbeteiligung Delegation und Partizipation. In: Hoyos C, Frey D (eds) Arbeits- und Organisationspsychologie. Weinheim

Argyris C (1964) Integrating the Individual and the Organization. New York

Arthur WB (1996) Increasing Returns and the New World of Business. Harvard Business Review 74 (4): 100–109

Austin RD, Hoffer Gittell J (1999) Anomalies of High Performance. Reframing Economic and Organizational Theories of Performance Measurement. Harvard Business School, Harvard University

Bach J (1995) Enough about Process. What We Need Are Heroes. IEEE Software 12 (2): 96–98

Backes-Gellner U, Geil L (1997) Managervergütung und Unternehmenserfolg – Stand der theoretischen und empirischen Forschung. WISU, vol 5, pp 468–475

Barkema HG (1995) Do Executives Work Harder When They Are Monitored? Kyklos 48: 19–42

Barnard CI (1938) The Functions of the Executive. Cambridge, Massachusetts

Bartlett CA, Ghoshal S (1995) Rebuilding Behavioral Context. Turn Process Reengineering Into People Rejuvenation. Sloan Management Review 37 (1): 11–23

Baurmann M (1996) Der Markt der Tugend. Tubingen

Bazerman MH (1994) Judgment in Managerial Decision Making. New York

Becker G (1976) The Economic Approach to Human Behavior. Chicago

Benbasat I, Goldstein DK, Mead M (1987) The Case Research Strategy in Studies of Information Systems. MIS Quarterly 11 (3): 369–386

Bertrand M, Mullainathan S (2000). Do CEO's Set Their Own Pay? The Ones Without Principals Do, NBER Working Paper No. 7604

Bierhoff HW, Herner MJ (1999) Arbeitsengagement aus freien Stücken. Zur Rolle der Führung. In: Schreyögg G, Sydow J (eds) Managementforschung 9, Berlin, pp 55–87

Bohnet I (1996) Kooperation und Kommunikation. Eine Analyse individueller Entscheidungen. Tubingen

Bretz E, Hertel G, Moser K (1998) Cooperation und Organizational Citizenship Behavior. In: Speiß E, Nerdinger Friedemann W (eds) Kooperation in Unternehmen. Munich Mering

Brodbeck FC, Frese M (eds) (1994) Produktivität und Qualität in Software-Projekten. Psychologische Analyse und Optimierung von Arbeitsprozessen in der Software-Entwicklung. Munich Vienna

Bumann A (1991) Das Vorschlagswesen als Instrument innovativer Unternehmensführung. Ein integrativer Gestaltungsansatz am Beispiel der Schweizerischen PTT-Betriebe. Freiburg

Büsch K-H, Thom N (1982) Kooperations- und Konfliktfelder von Unternehmensleitung und Betriebsrat beim Vorschlagswesen. Betriebliches Vorschlagswesen 4: 163–181

Calder BJ, Staw BM (1975) The Self-Perception of Intrinsic and Extrinsic Motivation. Journal of Personality and Social Psychology 31: 599–605

Carmel E (1995) Cycle Time in Packaged Software Firms. Journal of Product Innovation Management 1: 110–123

Coase R (1937) The Nature of the Firm. Economica 4: 386–405

Coenenberg AG (1992) Kostenrechnung und Kostenanalyse. Landsberg Lech

Core JE, Holthausen RW, Larcker DF (1999) Corporate Governance, Chief Executive Officer Compensation, and Firm Performance. Journal of Financial Economics 51: 371–406

Csikszentmihalyi M (1975) Beyond Boredom and Anxiety. San Francisco

Cummings A, Oldham GR (1997) Enhancing Creativity. Managing Work Contexts for the High Potential Employee. California Management Review 40: 22–38

Cusumano MA, Selby RW (1995) Microsoft Secrets. How the World's Most Powerful Software Company Creates Technology, Shapes Markets, and Manages People. New York

Deci EL, Flaste R (1995) Why We Do What We Do. The Dynamics of Personal Autonomy. New York

Deci EL, Koestner R, Ryan RM (1999) A Meta-Analytic Review of Experiments Examining the Effects of Extrinsic Rewards on Intrinsic Motivation. Psychological Bulletin 125 (3): 627–668

Deci EL, Ryan RM (1985) Intrinsic Motivation and Self-Determination in Human Behavior, New York

Deckop JR (1988) Determinants of Chief Executive Officer Compensation. Industrial and Labor Relations Review 41 (2): 215–226

DeMarco T, Lister T (1991) Wien wartet auf Dich! Der Faktor Mensch im DV-Management. Munich Vienna

Drucker P (1999) Innovate or Die. The Economist, September 25, 1999: 27–34

Eccles RG (1985) The Transfer Pricing Problem. A Theory for Practice. Lexington, Massachusetts

Etienne M (1997) Grenzen und Chancen des Vorgesetztenmodells im Betrieblichen Vorschlagswesen. Eine Fallstudie. Berne

Ewert R, Wagenhofer A (1995) Interne Unternehmensrechnung, 2nd edn. Berlin

Fay S (1996) The Collapse of Barings. New York London

Fehr E, Gächter S (1998) Reciprocity and Economics. The Economic Implications of "Homo Reciprocans." European Economic Review 42: 845–859

Fehr E, Gächter S (2000) Fairness and Retaliation. The Economics of Reciprocity. Journal of Economic Perspectives, to be published

Finkelstein S, Boyd B (1998) How Much Does the CEO Matter? The Role of Managerial Discretion in the Setting of CEO Compensation. Academy of Management Journal 41 (2): 179–199

FitzRoy FR, Kraft K (eds) (1987) Mitarbeiterbeteiligung und Mitbestimmung im Unternehmen. Berlin

Folger R (1998) Organizational Justice and Human Resource Management. Thousand Oaks London New Dehli

Folger R, Konovsky MA (1989) Effects of Procedural and Distributive Justice on Reactions to Pay Raise Decisions. Academy of Management Journal 32: 115–130

Freeman RB, Rogers J (1998) Worker Representation and Participation Survey – Waves 1 and 2. Data Description and Documentation. National Bureau of Economic Research, Cambridge, Massachusetts (http://www.nber.org)

Freeman RB, Rogers J (1999) What Workers Want. Ithaca London

Frese E (1995) Profit Center Motivation durch internen Marktdruck. In: Reichwald R, Wildemann H (eds) Kreative Unternehmen. Spitzenleistungen durch Produkt- und Prozessinnovationen.

Frese E (1998) Grundlagen der Organisation. Konzept, Prinzipien, Strukturen, 7th edn. Wiesbaden

Frey BS (1990) Ökonomie ist Sozialwissenschaft. Die Anwendung der Ökonomie auf neue Gebiete. Munich

Frey, BS (1997a) Not Just for the Money. An Economic Theory of Personal Motivation. Cheltenham Northampton

Frey BS (1997a) Markt und Motivation. Wie ökonomische Anreize die (Arbeits-) Moral verdrängen. Munich

Frey BS (1997b) A Constitution for Knaves Crowds Out Civic Virtues. Economic Journal 107: 1043–1053

Frey BS, Oberholzer-Gee F (1997) The Cost of Price Incentives. An Empirical Analysis of Motivation Crowding-Out. American Economic Review 87: 746–755

Frey BS (1999) Economics as a Science of Human Behavior, extended 2nd edn. Boston

Frey D, Fischer R, Winzer O (1996) Mitdenken lohnt sich – für alle! Ideenmanagement durch Vorschlagswesen in Wirtschaft und Verwaltung. München

Bayerisches Staatsministerium für Arbeit und Sozialordnung, Familie, Frauen und Gesundheit (publ)

Gibbons R (1998) Incentives in Organizations. Journal of Economic Perspectives 12: 115–132

Grant RM (1996) Toward a Knowledge-Based Theory of the Firm. Strategic Management Journal 17: 109–122

Grant RM (1998) Contemporary Strategic Analysis. Oxford

Greenberg J (1990) Organizational Justice Yesterday, Today, and Tomorrow. Journal of Management 16: 399–432

Greenberg J (1996) The Quest for Justice on the Job. Thousand Oaks London New Dehli

Hall BJ, Liebman JB (1998) Are CEOs Really Paid Like Bureaucrats. Quarterly Journal of Economics 111 (3): 653–691

Hamel G, Prahalad CK (1996) Competing for the Future. Boston

Hansen MT, Nohria N, Tierney T (1999) What's Your Strategy for Managing Knowledge. Harvard Business Review (March–April 1999): 106–116

Harvard Business School Cases #9-394-009, 9-394-010, 9-394-011 (1993) Sears Auto Centers

Heckhausen H (1989) Motivation und Handeln, 2nd edn. Berlin

Herzberg F, Mausner B, Snyderman BB (1959) The Motivation to Work. New York

Hirschmann AO (1987) Leidenschaften und Interesse. Politische Begründungen des Kapitalismus vor seinem Sieg. Frankfurt

Holmstrom B, Milgrom P (1991) Multitask Principal-Agent Analyses. Incentive Contracts, Asset Ownership and Job Design. Journal of Law, Economics and Organization 7: 24–52

Huber R (2000) Lohn allein macht nicht glücklich. Die Weltwoche, No 8, February 24: 86

ISO 9004-1 (1994) Quality Management and Quality System Elements. Part 1 Guidelines. Geneva

Jensen MC, Murphy KJ (1990) Performance Pay and Top-Management Incentives. Journal of Political Economy 98 (2): 225–264

Kaplan RS, Atkinson AA (1989) Advanced Management Accounting, 2nd edn. Englewood Cliffs, New Jersey

Kieser A (1999) Management und Taylorismus. In: Kieser, A (ed) Organisationstheorien, 3rd edn. Stuttgart Berlin

Kim WC, Mauborgne R (1998) Procedural Justice, Strategic Decision Making, and the Knowledge Economy. Strategic Management Journal 19: 323–338

Kliemt H (1993) Ökonomische Analyse der Moral. In: Ramb B-T, Tietzel M (eds) Ökonomische Verhaltenstheorie. Munich, pp 281–310

Kohn A (1993) Punished by Reward. The Trouble With Gold Stars, Incentive Plans, A´s, Praise, and Other Bribes. Boston

Kohn A (1994) Why Incentive Plans Cannot Work. Harvard Business Review 5, 1993: 54–63

Konrad AM, Pfeffer J (1990) Do You Get What You Deserve? Factors Affecting the Relationship Between Productivity and Pay. Administrative Science Quarterly 35: pp 258–285

Kreuter A (1997) Verrechnungspreise in Profit Center Organisationen. Munich Mering

Kruglanski AW (1975) The Endogenous-Exogenous Partition in Attribution Theory. Psychological Review 82: pp 387–406

Lambert R, Lanen W, Larcker D (1989) Executive Stock Option Plans and Corporate Dividend Policy. Journal of Financial and Quantitative Analysis 24(4): pp 409–425

Lazear EP (1998) Personnel Economics for Managers. New York

Lazear EP (1999) Personnel Economics. Past Lessons and Future Directions. Journal of Labor Economics 17: 199–236

Levine DI (1995) Reinventing the Workplace. How Business and Employees Can Both Win. Washington D.C.

Levine DI, Tyson, L (1990) Participation, Productivity, and the Firm's Environment. In: Blinder A (ed) Paying for Productivity. A Look at the Evidence. Washington, pp 183–237

Liebig S (1997) Soziale Gerechtigkeitsforschung und Gerechtigkeit in Unternehmen. Munich Mering

Likert R (1961) New Patterns of Management. New York

Likert R (1967) The Human Organization. Its Management and Value. New York

Lind EA, Tyler TR (1988) The Social Psychology of Procedural Justice. New York

Loewenstein G (1999) Because It Is There. The Challenge of Mountaineering... for Utility Theory. Kyklos 52: 315–343

Losse K-H, Thom N (1977) Das Betriebliche Vorschlagswesen als Innovationsinstrument. Eine empirisch-explorative Überprüfung seiner Effizienzdeterminanten. Frankfurt

Luhmann N (1973) Zweckbegriff und Systemrationalität. Frankfurt

March J, Simon H (1976) Organisation und Individuum. Menschliches Verhalten in Organisationen. Wiesbaden

Maslow A (1954) Motivation and Personality. New York

McFarlin DB, Sweeney PD (1992) Distributive and Procedural Justice as Predictors of Satisfaction with Personal and Organizational Outcomes. Academy of Management Journal 35: 626–637

McGregor D (1960) The Human Side of Enterprise. New York

Montesquieu ChL (1749) De l'esprit des lois. Paris

Moorman RH (1991) Relationship Between Organizational Justice and Organizational Citizenship Behaviors. Do Fairness Perceptions Influence Employee

Citizenship? Journal of Applied Psychology 76: 845–855

Moorman RH, Blakely GL, Niehoff BP (1998) Does Perceived Organizational Support Mediate the Relationship Between Procedural Justice and Organizational Citizenship Behavior? Academy of Management Journal 41: 351–357

Murphy KJ (1985) Corporate Performance and Managerial Remuneration. An Empirical Analysis. Journal of Accounting and Economics 7 (1–3): 11–42

Murphy KJ (1999) Executive Compensation. In: Ashenfelter O, Card D (eds) Handbook of Labor Economics, vol 3. Amsterdam, pp 2485–2563

Nonaka I, Takeuchi H (1995) The Knowledge-Creating Company. New York Oxford

Oelz O (1999) Mit Eispickel und Stethoskop. Zurich

Organ DW (1990) The Motivational Basis of Organizational Citizenship Behavior. In: Staw BM, Cummings LL (eds) Research in Organizational Behavior 12, pp 43–72

Osterloh M (1999) Wertorientierte Unternehmensführung und Management-Anreizsysteme. In: Kumar BN, Osterloh M, Schreyögg G (eds) Unternehmensethik und die Transformation des Wettbewerbs. Shareholder-Value – Globalisierung – Hyperwettbewerb. Stuttgart, pp 183–204

Osterloh M, Frey BS, Frost J (1999) Was kann das Unternehmen besser als der Markt? Zeitschrift für Betriebswirtschaft 69: 1245–1262

Osterloh M, Frost J (1998) Prozessmanagement als Kernkompetenz. Wie Sie Business Reengineering strategisch nutzen können, 2nd edn. Wiesbaden

Osterloh M, Löhr A (1994) Ökonomik oder Ethik als Grundlage der sozialen Ordnung? Wirtschaftswissenschaftliches Studium: p 406

Osterloh M, Wübker S (1999) Wettbewerbsfähiger durch Prozess- und Wissensmanagement. Mit Chancengleichheit auf Erfolgskurs. Wiesbaden

Ostrom E (1998) A Behavioral Approach to the Rational Choice Theory of Collective Action. American Political Science Review 92: 1–22

Paulk MC, Weber CV, Curtis B, Crissis MB (1995) The Capability Maturity Model. Guidelines for Improving the Software Process. Reading, Massachusetts

Pearce JL (1987) Why Merit Pay Doesn't Work. Implications From Organizational Theory. In: Balkin DB, Gomez-Mejia LR (eds) New Perspectives on Compensation, pp 169–178

Piore MJ, Sabel CF (1990) The Second Industrial Divide. Possibilities for Prosperity, reprint edn. New York

Polanyi M (1974) Personal Knowledge. Chicago

Polanyi M (1985) Implizites Wissen. Frankfurt

Porter ME (1998) Competitive Strategy. New York

Post H, Thom N (1980) Verbesserung und Ausbau des Betrieblichen Vorschlagswesens. Erkenntnisse einer Befragungsaktion. Betriebliches Vorschlagswesen 3: 114–136

Prahalad CK, Hamel G (1990) The Core Competence of the Corporation. Harvard Business Review (May–June 1990): pp 79–91

Prendergast C (1999) The Provision of Incentives in Firms. Journal of Economic Literature 37: pp 7–63

Rappaport A (1998) Creating Shareholder Value. A Guide for Managers and Investors, 2nd edn. New York

Rasch RH, Tosi HL (1992) Factors Affecting Software Developers' Performance. An Integrated Approach. MIS Quarterly 16 (3): 395–413

Rousseau DM (1995) Psychological Contracts in Organizations. Understanding Written and Unwritten Agreements. Thousand Oaks London New Dehli

Rousseau DM, McLean Parks J (1993) The Contracts of Individuals and Organizations. Research in Organizational Behavior 15: 1–43

Schein E (1965) Organization Psychology. Englewood Cliffs, New Jersey

Schreyögg G (1999) Organisation. Grundlagen moderner Organisationsgestaltung, 2nd edn. Wiesbaden

Schwartz B (1990) The Creation and Destruction of Value. American Psychologist 45: 7–15

Shapira Z (1976) Expectancy Determinants of Intrinsically Motivated Behavior. Journal of Personality and Social Psychology 34: 1235–1244

Spender J-C (1996) Making Knowledge the Basis of a Dynamic Theory of the Firm. Strategic Management Journal 17: 45–62

Sprenger RK (1993) Das Vorschlagswesen abschaffen. Personalwirtschaft 20 (8): 20–25

Sprenger RK (2000a) Mythos Motivation (Jubiläumsausgabe). Wege aus einer Sackgasse. Frankfurt

Sprenger RK (2000b) Das Prinzip Selbstverantwortung (Jubiläumsausgabe). Wege zur Motivation. Frankfurt

Stelzer D (1998) Möglichkeiten und Grenzen des prozessorientierten Software-Qualitätsmanagements. Post-doctoral thesis, University of Cologne

Stelzer D, Mellis W, Herzwurm G (1998) Technology Diffusion in Software Development Processes. The Contribution of Organizational Learning to Software Process Improvement. In: Larsen T, McGuire E (eds) Information Systems Innovation and Diffusion Issues and Directions. Hershey, Pennsylvainia, pp 297–344

Taylor FW (1911) The Principles of Scientific Management. New York

The Economist (1999) A Survey of Pay. The Best ... and the Rest. May 8

The Economist (1999) The Trouble With Share Options. August 7

Towers Perrin (2000) Euro Rewards 2000. Reward Challenges and Changes. Survey Results. Towers Perrin

Trittmann R, Hierholzer A, Stelzer D, Mellis W (1999) Veränderungen der Softwareentwicklung. Ergebnisse einer Fallstudie in der SAP AG im Vergleich zu den Empfehlungen der ISO 9000. Paper presented at the "Organisation" workshop, Verband der Hochschullehrer für Betriebswirtschaft e. V. on 26/ 27.02.1999 in Zurich

Trittmann R, Stelzer D, Hierholzer A, Mellis W (1999) Changing Software Development. A Case Study at SAP AG. In: Pries-Heje J, Ciborra C, Kautz K, Valor J, Christiaanse E, Avison D, Heje C (eds) Proceedings of the 7th European Conference on Information Systems, Copenhagen, pp 692–703

Tyler TR (1989) The Psychology of Procedural Justice. A Test of the Group-Value Model. Journal of Personality and Social Psychology 57: 830–838

Tyler TR, Lind AE (1988) The Social Psychology of Procedural Justice. New York London

Volkart R (1998) Shareholder Value & Corporate Valuation. Finanzielle Wert-orientierungen im Wandel. Zurich

Weinberg GM (1971) The Psychology of Computer Programming. New York

Wenger E (1999) Stock Options. Wirtschaftswissenschaftliches Studium, Issue 1: 35–58

Williamson OE (1985) The Economic Institutions of Capitalism. Firms, Markets, Relational Contracting. New York

Winter S (1996) Prinzipien der Gestaltung von Managementanreizsystemen. Wiesbaden

Yourdon E (1995) Peopleware. Application Development Strategies 7 (8): 1–16

Index

(Company and brand names are indicated in *italics*.)

Q

R

S

T

U

V

W

X

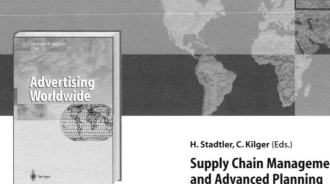